Machine Translation

Yorick Wilks

Machine Translation

Its Scope and Limits

Yorick Wilks
Department of Computer Science
The University of Sheffield
Regent Court, 211 Portobello Street
Sheffield, S1 4DP, UK
Y.Wilks@dcs.shef.ac.uk

ISBN: 978-1-4419-4447-4 e-ISBN: 978-0-387-72774-5

Printed on acid-free paper

springer.com

Foreword

This book is a set of essays covering aspects of machine translation (MT) past, present and future. Some have been published before, some are new but, taken together, they are meant to present a coherent account of the state of MT, its evolution up to the present, and its scope for the future. At certain points, "Afterwords" have been added to comment on the, possibly changed, relevance of a chapter at the time of publication.

The argument for reprinting here some older thoughts on MT is an attempt to show some continuity of one researcher's thoughts, so far as possible, in the welter of argument and dispute that has gone on over decades on how MT is to be done. The book is certainly not intended as a comprehensive history of the field, and these already exist. Nor is any one MT system described or advocated here. The author has been involved in the production of three quite different systems: a toy semantics-based system at Stanford in 1971, whose code was placed in the Computer Museum in Boston as the first meaning-driven MT system. Later, in 1985, I was involved in New Mexico in ULTRA, a multi-language system with strong semantic and pragmatic features, intended to show that the architecture of the (failed) EUROTRA system could perform better at 1% of what that cost. No comprehensive description of EUROTRA is given here, and the history of that project remains to be written. Lastly, in 1990, I was one of three PIs in the DARPA-funded system PANGLOSS, a knowledge-based system set up in competition with IBM's CANDIDE system, that became the inspiration for much of the data-driven changes that have overtaken language processing since 1990. None of these systems is being presented here as a solution to MT, for nothing yet is, but only as a test-bed of ideas and performance.

Machine translation is not, as some believe, solved, nor is it impossible, as others still claim. It is a lively and important technology, whose importance in a multi-lingual and information-driven world can only increase, intellectually and commercially. Intellectually, it remains, as it always has been, the ultimate testbed of all linguistic and language processing theories.

In writing this book, I am indebted to too many colleagues and students to mention, though I must acknowledge joint work with David Farwell (chapters 10 and 14), and Sergei Nirenburg, Jaime Carbonnel and Ed Hovy (chapter 8). I also need to thank Lucy Moffatt for much help in its preparation, and Roberta, for everything, as always.

Sheffield, 2008 Yorick Wilks

History Page

Some chapters have appeared in other forms elsewhere:

Chapter 2: Wilks, Y. (1984) Artificial Intelligence and Machine Translation. In S. and W. Sedelow (eds.) Current Trends in the Language Sciences. Amsterdam: North Holland.

Chapter 3: Wilks, Y. (1973) An Artificial Intelligence Approach to Machine Translation. In R. Schank and K. Colby (eds.) Computer models of Thought and Language. San Francisco: Freeman.

Chapter 4: Wilks, Y. (1992) SYSTRAN: it obviously works, but how much can it be improved? In J. Newton (ed.) Computers and Translation. London: Routledge.

Chapter 7: Wilks, Y. (1994) Developments in machine translation research in the US. In the Aslib Proceedings, Vol. 46 (The Association of Information Management).

Contents

Chapter 1
Introduction

Machine Translation: the State of Play in 2008

After only forty years of research and development in MT, I feel about its condition a little as Mao Tse-Tung is said to have felt about the significance of the French Revolution: that it was too early to tell. The broad facts are known to anyone who reads the newspapers, and might seem to be inconsistent: MT works, in the sense that every day MT systems, for example at the Federal Translation Division in Dayton, Ohio and the European Commission in Luxembourg, produce fully automatic translations on a large scale that many people use with apparent benefit. Moreover, many thousands of MT systems have been sold in Japan alone, and millions of people a day world-wide accept the [Translate this page] option on web browsers and see immediate gain and benefit from what it gives back. On the other hand, the absence of any intellectual breakthroughs to produce indisputably high-quality fully-automatic MT is equally clear, a fact which has led some to say it is impossible, a claim inconsistent with our first observations.

The simple statements above could have been made ten, or even twenty, years ago, and what has changed since then is twofold: first, the irruption into MT of a range of techniques from speech research, pioneered by a team at IBM Laboratories in the USA, that claimed the way out of the deadlock was the use of empirical, in particular statistical, methods which took as data very large text corpora. They argued that, with their aid, high quality MT would be possible without recourse to linguistics, artificial intelligence, or even foreign language speakers. It was not a new claim, for King had made it in a brief futuristic paper in the 1950s, (King, 1956) but a team under Jelinek at IBM reapplied speech algorithms (in particular Hidden Markov Models) so as to carry such a program out (Brown et al., 1989). The second response, one championed by Martin Kay, (Kay, 1997) was to argue that no theory, linguistic or otherwise, would deliver high-quality MT in the foreseeable future, and so the escape from the very same deadlock was to move to machine-assisted human translation (MAHT), an insight which spawned a score of systems, ones that would assist you to create a translation on a PC but with no large claims being made, or required, about automatic MT. Both positions agreed that linguistic theory was not going to deliver a solution for MT, nor was artificial intelligence (AI).

AI researchers had argued since the mid-seventies that knowledge-based systems were the key to MT, as to everything else in intelligent computation, but the problem was that they had failed to deliver knowledge bases of sufficient size to test this, thus leaving the AI case to rest only on plausible examples, such as "The soldiers fired at the women and I saw several fall" (Wilks, 1975a), where one feels that the "several" is the women not because of any linguistic selection rules or statistical regularities but because of our knowledge of how the world works. The big long-planned knowledge banks did not appear: Lenat (Lenat and Guha, 1990) is still building CyC, a large formal knowledge base, as is Nirenburg (Nirenburg et al., 1996) with MIKROCOSMOS and its successors, which are ontologies of conceptual facts, but these have not yet been brought into close contact with large scale problems, and that fact has made some observers take the statistical claims more seriously, out of weariness and desperation, and after waiting decades for AI to deliver.

Linguistics was in a far worse position than AI to survive the renewed statistical onslaught (see Chapter 7 below): Chomsky's only response (Chomsky, 1957) to early statistical claims in linguistics – such as those of (King, 1956) – was that "I saw a triangular whale" was hugely improbable, as a sentence, but nevertheless syntactically well-formed. For reasons almost no one can now remember, arguments like that were successful in repressing empirical and statistical methods for thirty years, which explains in part why IBM's claims about statistical were a little like the fall of an intellectual Berlin Wall.

AI researchers, who had long been hostile towards the ability of linguistics to solve real problems in language processing, the present author included, should perhaps have been more positive about the IBM claims when they were presented: I, for example, had long espoused symbolic theories of language which rested on quantifiable notions about the coherence or preference of linguistic items for each other, so perhaps I should have explored the possibility that the statistical movement was just offering a data-gathering method for what one had claimed all along?

IBM (which is just shorthand here for Jelinek's team that produced the CANDIDE SYSTEM (Brown et al., 1992), and their followers, did far better initially than many had expected: they could correctly translate 50+% of unseen sentences from a corpus, part of which was used for training, and to many onlookers that was a striking achievement. But they could not regularly beat SYSTRAN, the oldest and tiredest piece of MT software in the world, the one that still produces the daily translations at Dayton and Luxembourg (see Chapter 4 below). Even now, apparent victories of statistical systems over SYSTRAN in competition sometimes violate human intuitions and seem to rest of peculiarities inherent in BLEU, the new canonical MT evaluation system (see Callison-Burch et al., 2006, and discussion of this in Chapter 16 below).

The IBM researchers then backed away and argued that, even if they did need linguistic/AI information of a classic type to improve MT performance (e.g. lexicons, grammar rule sets, morphologies etc.), these too could be produced by empirical data gathering methods and not intuition. In that they were surely right, and that fact constitutes the main argument for the future of hybrid systems for MT, ones that optimize by fusing the best of symbolic and statistical methods and data. But IBM's revolution is also the origin of the way in which fallout from the IBM project has transformed the whole of computational linguistics by effectively segmenting it into a range of progressively more difficult and demanding tasks: from part-of-speech tagging to syntactic parsing, then on to the semantics of assigning word-senses and pragmatics, not all of which are of immediate and obvious relevance to MT itself.

A moment's pause is in order to consider the SYSTRAN system (Toma, 1977), still almost certainly the world's best MT performer on unseen text, somewhat despised by linguists and AI researchers alike for its simple-minded methods, at least until they needed it as a champion against the IBM statisticians in the early 1990s (see Chapter 4 below). The truth of course is that by dint of 30 years hard labour the SYSTRAN teams had produced, by hand, a version of the large coded knowledge base that was needed for the symbolic AI approach to MT to work!

Yet why did the statistical approach to MT do as well as it did so quickly, and then rapidly topped out at 50% of sentences correctly translated? This figure remains something of a mystery, both as to why such methods translate at all, and we shall turn to that in a moment, but also why that particular figure? The best explanation of the phenomenon I have seen is revealing, and also cheering for the future of hybrid systems, which is to say systems involving both statistical and non-statistical MT traditions. It has long been known from comparing evaluation methods that fidelity of translation (i.e. correctness) is closely correlated with the intelligibility of the output text. One could put this as: statistical models created a plausible model of generation intelligibility, based on an n-gram models of word sequences and, in doing so, dragged along a substantial amount of MT fidelity along with the intelligibility by virtue of the correlation. The problem with this explanation (which I owe to conversations with Ted Dunning) is that it does nothing to explain why the two factors are correlated. That remains a mystery of statistical MT, just as does the fact that the success rate of IBM's statistical system is almost exactly the redundancy rate of word and character symbols in Western languages, about 50%, and in his sketchy paper referred to earlier, King (1956) suggested this figure as one that showed that statistical MT was in principle possible, a highly unlikely claim. Like the fact that the moon and the sun are roughly the same size seen from the Earth, this seems to be a fact one can only goggle at and accept.

The moral here is clear: MT, like prophesy and necromancy, is (up to a point) easy not hard. One can do some MT (the emphasis is on "some" here) using any theory whatever, no matter how lunatic, including word-for-word substitution. In MT we should never therefore be seduced by the claims of theory, only by large-scale results.

We now have two competing research paradigms in MT, the symbolic and the statistical, each armed with a set of rock solid examples and arguments but neither able to beat – in open competition – the old commercial legacy system SYSTRAN unaided, systems inherited from the 1970's. Indeed, the MT systems made available by Google are a version of the SYSTRAN system for most languages, but new, statistically-based, systems for Chinese and Arabic. The mass of active MT work in Japan in recent years (see Chapter 9 below) has also, I believe, added to this picture a set of useful and general heuristic hints on how to do MT: work with lexicon structures not syntax, pre-process difficult structures in advance in MT input, do not think of MT as an absolute self-contained task but as a component technology that links into, and subdivides into, a range of related office tasks: information extraction, word processing, teaching systems etc. The last seems perhaps too simple and too fashionable: it may be correct but ignores the historic position of MT, as the oldest linguistic and AI task, one with the best developed and substantial evaluation methodology, so that any NLP or linguistic theory can still be reliably tested within it. The consequence of the above observations – taken together – is probably that hybrid cooperative methods are the only way forward in MT, even though the statistical and symbolic components may still for now be pursued separately, as grammars are extracted empirically from texts and texts are automatically sense-tagged. At the same time, work progresses in parallel on the development of ontologies and knowledge bases, by hand, as well as by their automatic extraction from texts (e.g. Buitelaar et al., 2005). All these efforts will meet up again in some near future, for neither can do without the other and all attempts to prove the self-sufficiency or autonomy of each part separately have failed and will probably continue to do so. This is an issue we return to in the final chapter of this book.

So, let me conclude this introduction with five aspects of the current situation in MT that are worth commenting on separately:

1. The shock wave of the "IBM statistical MT movement" described above (and in Chapter 7 below) seems to have passed, and the results are indecisive as regards a fully statistical MT project. That grand project, undertaken between about 1987 and 1994, to perform MT using only large bilingual corpora without standard linguistic techniques (grammars, lexicons etc.) did not produce a system that could beat SYSTRAN in the US Government's DARPA evaluations (White and O'Connell, 1996), given the same level of pre-exposure to the domain, although in later (NIST) evaluations SYSTRAN was beaten at some tasks. And yet, much has been changed by that project, and we cannot go back to the previous status quo, even though parts of the MT universe seem to continue unchanged: e.g. large SYSTRAN installations continue at one extreme, both commercially and on the web, while, at the other extreme, small PC-based low-quality MT systems continue to sell in Radio Shack.

2. What was given substantial new life by the IBM project was a much wider empirical, data-driven or statistical linguistics: a methodology in decline since Chomsky's original attacks on it, and which came back into MT work through its successful application to speech recognition, by the same IBM team, among others.

However, although individual linguistic tasks continue to be optimized by such methods (e.g. part-of-speech tagging and syntactic parsing) and new ones are attempted and improved (e.g. word sense tagging (e.g. Stevenson and Wilks, 2001) and speech-act-tagging of dialogue (e.g. Webb et al., 2005), it is not clear how much is directly inherited from the IBM enterprise, which did not even use part-of-speech tagging as a core module in its CANDIDE system.

However, the core modules of the IBM CANDIDE system (particularly bilingual sentence and word-alignment, and n-gram based sentence generation) have not been as easy to combine with rule-based methods to build hybrid MT systems as was assumed five years ago. Moreover, example-based translation, which has gone from being a promising idea somewhat different from IBM's methodology to a successful technology we shall discuss below, originated quite independently in Japan (Nagao, 1990) and does also require some form of alignment computation over previous translations. Much of the published work in empirical linguistics has been on a range of techniques for inducing linguistic grammars, a notion not related at all to the original IBM enterprise, except in the very general methodological sense of MT via a statistical model derived from corpora. Somers has argued (see Chapter 16 below, and Somers and Fernandez Diaz, 2004) that the clear need for linguistically-motivated syntactic research to produce large-scale and viable forms of Example-based and statistical MT show that statistical-symbolic hybrid systems are inevitable. A natural outcome from the undoubted advances in empirical speech and text work in recent years would be a striking demonstrable advance in speech-to-speech MT, from within either of the highly funded projects in that area, ATR (Sumita and Imamura, 2002) or Verbmobil; (Wahlster, 2000) and its successors, but it is by no means that that has happened in the case of either project.

3. Quite independently of all this, two other MT developments continue which do not draw much on empirical linguistics. The first is the continuing integration of low-level MT techniques with conventional word processing technology to provide a range of aids, tools, lexicons etc. for both professional and occasional translators. This now constitutes a real market, assisting translators to perform more effectively.

The remarks of Kay referred to earlier predated the more recent empirical upsurge and reflected, I believe, his deep pessimism about the ability of any form of theoretical linguistics, or theoretically motivated computational linguistics, to deliver high-quality MT. The same beliefs are also behind later work like (Arnold et al., 1994) from a group long committed to a highly abstract approach to MT that produced few if any results in the EUROTRA project; that book itself is effectively an introduction to MT as an advanced form of document processing.

4. A second continuing development, set somewhat apart from the empirical movement, is the continuing emphasis on large-scale hand-crafted resources for MT – such as large hand-made dictionaries and thesauri – which implicitly rejects the assumption of the empirical movement that such resources can be largely acquired automatically by e.g. extraction of semantic structures from machine readable dictionaries (e.g. Wilks et al., 1996) or grammars produced from tree banks or by machine learning methods (e.g. Krotov et al., 1998). This effort has continued in a number of EC projects [e.g. PAROLE/SIMPLE and EuroWordNet – (Vossen, P. (ed.) 1998] as well as the MIKROKOSMOS knowledge base for MT within the Temple and Expedition projects in Maryland (Nirenburg, op.cit.).

In the latter one can see something of the same diversion that was just noted in the Machine-Aided Human Translation (MAHT) world, which has also been conspicuous in parts of the Information Extraction community: the use of very simple heuristic methods for a the task while retaining the later option to use full-scale theoretical methods (in this case knowledge-based MT).

5. A final feature of note is a partial dissolution of MT as a clearly defined subject, rather like some say has happened to traditional subjects like geography: its boundaries go fuzzy and it is no longer clear what separates it off from neighboring disciplines. MT can now seem to be just one of a range of techniques for Information Access, along with Information Retrieval, Information Extraction, Data Mining and Question Answering. This process, like so many others, has been accelerated by the World Wide Web, and the upsurge in commercial MT it has brought (e.g. with web browser use of SYSTRAN'S Babelfish system noted earlier); this will be matched with systems that will increasingly seek to translate-then-extract-facts or, more likely, extract-then-translate. Within all this effort, it becomes harder to see exactly who is doing MT and who is not, under such descriptions as "multi-lingual information extraction".

Machine Translation now has some of the aspects attributed to the problem of flight and flying in the Nineteenth Century: there are many exemplars of the phenomenon around (more than a hundred companies world-wide sell MT products) but substantial disagreement as to how it is done, or should best be done. Many feel there must be some analogue of an aerofoil waiting to be discovered, rather than proceeding, as one could describable current MT products, as the sustained flapping of wings.

Martin Kay argued, in a well-known paper already mentioned above (reprinted, 1997) that MT was not going to work in the foreseeable future, that machine-aided translation (MAHT) was the best we could hope for, and that we should concentrate on it. He has not been proved right, largely because he failed to anticipate the large market (e.g. within the European Commission) for output of the indifferent quality (i.e. about 60% of sentences correctly translated from SYSTRAN, for example) output that full MT systems continue to produce and which is used for rough draft translations. But he did guess that the spread of PCs, to human translators along with everyone else, has meant that there is a new market for providing translation aids, in terms of access to machine dictionaries and blending the (human) skills of translating with word processing, or what is now MAT or MAHT, and which I take to include the use of poor quality MT systems whose output is subsequently postedited by humans.

Sometimes (e.g. Arnold et al., 1994) work from the perspective of highly theoretical MT is, surprisingly, directed at translators, so as to introduce them to the various notions of MT and MAT/MAHT. Pushing the flight analogy too far, one could say that such work is, in a strict sense, for the birds, those who can actually fly (i.e. by analogy, the translators themselves), and tells them what help they may expect from a little MT jockey hitching a ride on their backs and who may one day want to learn the skill himself.

The theme of that book was how to see translating by machine as a form of document processing and to introduce the practitioner to the use of tools such as on-line lexicons. One would expect its authors to agree profoundly with the position attributed to Martin Kay earlier: they are theorists and MT theory has not paid off, so the only rational way forward is theory-free MAT. But this may not be correct: it may simply be that certain kinds of theories and techniques have not worked well so far. This defeatist position also ignores the extraordinary resilience of full MT both as a discipline and commercial enterprise, and to this we shall now turn. One aspect of MT cannot be turned by time, present or future: scale. Statistical MT has kept large scale MT central, as the symbolic SYSTRAN system did before it: there can never again be a place for ingenious toy MT systems, from which many productive ideas in MT have come in the past. Pat Suppes at Stanford said of an MT system forty years ago "Come back when you can do a book". That remark was probably premature at the time but is now orthodoxy.

Part I
MT Past

Chapter 2
Five Generations of MT

Introduction (2007)

There is an ancient Chinese curse that dooms recipients to live in an interesting age, and by those standards MT workers are at present having a bad time. The reason things are interesting at the moment is that there is a number of conflicting claims in the air about how to do MT, and whether it can, or indeed has already, been done. Such a situation is unstable, and we may confidently expect some kind of outcome – always cheering for the empiricist – in the near future. This chapter was initially published as (Wilks, 1979) as an exploration of the relationship of MT to Artificial Intelligence (AI) in general, and should be seen as providing a snapshot of that intellectual period.

What happened initially was threefold. First, the "brute force" methods for MT, that were thought to have been brought to an end by the ALPAC (1966) Report have surfaced again, like some Coelacanth from the deep, long believed extinct. Such systems were sold for many years under such trade names as LOGOS, XYZYX, SMART, Weidner and SYSTRAN; and the last, and best known, has been used for thirty years by the EU in Paris (Van Slype, 1976) and Luxembourg.

Secondly, some large-scale, more theoretically based, MT projects continued, usually based in Universities, and have been tested in use, though sometimes on a scale smaller than that originally envisaged. METEO, for example, in Montreal (Chandioux, 1976), which was to have translated official documents from English to French, is still in use for the translation of the more limited world of weather reports.

Thirdly, workers in natural language in the field known as Artificial Intelligence (AI) began to make distinct claims about the need for their approach if there is ever to be general and high quality MT (Wilks, 1973a; Charniak, 1973; Schank, 1975a). Small pilot systems illustrating their claims were programmed, but their role in MT discussion was mainly of a theoretical nature.

However, these are not merely three complementary approaches, for they seem to be making different claims, and, unless we take the easy way out and simply define some level of MT appropriate to each of the enterprises, it seems they cannot all be right, and that we may hope for some resolution before too long.

These three correspond very roughly, to what are called the "generations" of MT, but to that I think we can add one or two more. The fourth is certainly the revival of empirical statistical methods in MT, which began around 1989 and lost momentum in the 90s when the early systems, like Jelinek's (see Chapter 1) failed to beat SYSTRAN decisively. However, empirical methods then colonised the whole of NLP, area by area, and now in the new millennium have returned to tackle MT itself (see Chapter 16 below). A possible fifth is that of hybrid methods, where researchers are seeking combinations of empirical methods with intelligent revivals of, earlier conceptual AI approaches (again, see Chapter 16 below).

It is interesting to notice that the reactions of Bar-Hillel and AI workers like Minsky were in part the same: Minsky (1968) argued that MT clearly required the formalization of human knowledge for a system that could be said to understand, or as Bar-Hillel reviewed the situation in 1971 (Lehmann and Stachowitz, 1971, p. 72):

> "It is now almost generally agreed upon that high-quality MT is possible only when the text to be translated has been understood, in an appropriate sense, by the translating mechanism".

In this chapter I want to explore some of the early connections between machine translation (MT) and artificial intelligence (AI). We all feel we understand the first phrase, and the second will be explained as we go along: for the moment, I ask the reader to accept some such working definition as: the use of computational methods for the simulation of distinctively human intellectual behaviour, by means of complex knowledge structures and their manipulation.

In what follows I shall first sketch some AI systems, and my argument will be that AI is relevant to, and important for the future of, MT, but that one can hope that a limited AI will be what will help in the foreseeable future, rather than those AI systems which appear to claim that they can express "all the knowledge in the universe" whatever that may mean.

A good place to start is Bar-Hillel's argument (1962) that MT impossible: for it has striking resemblances in terms of its premises (though not its conclusions) to some AI views.

Knowledge and MT

Bar-Hillel argued, even at the height of the early and finally disastrous MT period, that machine translation was not only practically but theoretically impossible, where "impossible" meant just that, and not merely difficult. "Expert human translators use their background knowledge, mostly subconsciously, in order to resolve syntactical and semantical ambiguities which machines will either have to leave unresolved, or resolve by some 'mechanical' rule which will ever so often result in a wrong translation. The perhaps simplest illustration of a syntactical ambiguity which is unresolvable by a machine except by arbitrary or ad hoc rules is provided by a sentence, say '... slow neutrons and protons...' whereas, in general, though by no means always, the human reader will have no difficulty in resolving the ambiguity through utilisation of his background knowledge, no counterpart of which could possibly stand at the disposal of computers" (1962).

The immediate historical context of Bar-Hillel's argument was the performance of early syntax analysers, which, according to legend, were capable of producing upwards of 10 grammatical parsings of sentences like "Time flies like an arrow". With respect to standard dictionary information, any of the first three words in the sentence could be taken as a possible verb. To see "time" as the verb, think of the sentence as command with the accent on the first word; to see "like" as the verb, think of the sentence as expressing the tastes of a certain kind of fly, and so on.

The standard reaction to such syntactic results was to argue only showed the need for linguistic semantics, so as to reduce the "readings" in such cases to the appropriate one. Bar-Hillel's response was to argue that it was not a matter of semantic additions at all, but of the, for him, unformalisable world of human knowledge.

The contrast can be seen by looking at our everyday understanding of so simple a sentence as "He paddled down the river in a canoe". The standard machine parser, working only with grammatical information, will not be able to decide whether the clause "in a canoe" attaches to "paddled" or "river". The first reading, the correct one of course, tells you how he went down the river. The second implies that we went down a river that happened to be inside a canoe – the same structure that would be appropriate for "He paddled down the river in an unexplored province of Brazil". The purely syntactic parser has no way of distinguishing these two possible "readings" of the sentence and, furthermore, there is a difference of opinion as to how the information that would resolve the problem should be described. Those who take a more "linguistic semantics" view would say that it is part of the meaning of "canoe" that those objects go in rivers and not vice versa; whereas those of an AI persuasion would be more likely to say that it is merely a fact about our world that canoes are in rivers. At bottom, there is probably no clear philosophical distinction between these views, but they do lead to different practical results when attempts are made to formalise and program such information.

Bar-Hillel went further and produced an example (the best-known in the history of MT) proving, as he thought, the impossibility of MT. In brief, Bar-Hillel's example was the following children's story:

Little John was looking for his toy box.
Finally he found it.
The box was in the pen.
John was very happy.

Bar-Hillel's focus is on the third senteiipnce, "the box was in the pen", whose last word we naturally interpret in context as meaning playpen and not writing pen. Bar-Hillel argued persuasively that to resolve this correctly requires knowledge of the real world, in some clear sense: at least in the sense that the difficulty cannot be overcome in terms of some simpleminded "overlap of concepts", by arguing that the concepts of "baby" and "playpen" can be seen, by lexical decomposition of some sort, to be related in a way the concepts of "baby" and "writing pen" are not. Bar-Hillel argued that that would not do, because the story would have been understood the same way if the third sentence had been The inkstand was in the pen, where the semantic "overlap of concepts" would now be between inkstand and writing pen which would yield the wrong answer on the same principles.

Bar-Hillel thought that the absolute impossibility of high-quality machine translation had been demonstrated, whereas Minsky believed that the task had now been defined, and the job of Al was to get on with it.

The contrast is clear between the views of Bar-Hillel and Minsky on one hand, and the views of linguists on the other: Chomsky's generative theories are also, in a clear sense, a reaction to the failure of the early machine translation work, in that they state the case, with great force, for a solid theory of the syntax of natural languages as a precondition for any advance with machines and language. Katz and Fodor's (1963) semantics, conjoined to a Chomsky grammar, represent, as it were, the linguistic analogue to those in machine parsing who thought that purely semantic information would be enough to resolve the multiple analyses of the notorious "Time flies like an arrow".

The essence of the Katz-Fodor method was algorithms based on the repetition of "semantic markers". We can see the limitations of that method for MT by looking at a complex (and realistic) noun phrase like the following:

> "Analyse d'une méthode dynamique specifique d'établissement de balance materiel d'une installation de retraitement de combustion nucleaire par simulation".

Roughly : Simulation analysis of a dynamic specific to the establishment of a balance of material in an installation for the treatment of nuclear combustion. In English the ambiguity of dependence of ≪ Simulation ≫ does not exist.

The problem in French concerns the dependence of "par simulation", which is at least a two-way ambiguity (of dependence on the heads "analyse" and "établissement", where the former is correct), but one could argue that it might conceivably depend (semantically speaking, that is) on either "retraitement" and "combustion" as well, since they are both processes that could be simulated, just like the earlier two. One might argue as follows: Semantics means attaching markers and looking for their repetition, so we might attach a marker, say, PROCESS to "analyse", "établissement", "simulation" (and perhaps "combustion" and "retraitement", as well).

The trouble with this course of action should be obvious: we would have attached the same plausible semantic marker to all the possibilities, and so there can be no discrimination (of the correct dependence, in this case, on "analyse"). The reader should appreciate the force of this example for if the, essentially semantic, dependence of "par simulation" on "analyse" cannot be determined by rules (stronger, as we shall see, than mere repetition of semantic markers) then a unique syntactic structure for the phrase cannot be obtained either.

What are AI Systems?

The attempt by AI research to respond to Bar-Hillel's challenge is of a different sort. It is an attempt not only to admit from the beginning the need for "knowledge structures" in an understanding system, but also to formulate theories and systems containing processes for the manipulation of that knowledge. "Processes" here is not to be taken to mean merely programming a computer to carry out a task, for many interesting AI systems have either not been programmed at all or made to do only partial demonstrations. The word "process" means that a theory of understanding should be stated in a symbol-processing manner, one in which most linguistic theories are not. This is a contentious position, because generative grammar has also been in some sense a description of a process since the earliest descriptions of transformational theory. The AI case is that it never quite comes up to scratch in processing terms.

But what is an AI theory of language, and how might it help machine translation?

AI has been concerned, for some forty years now, with the problems of human intelligence seen from a particular point of view: what would it be like to program a computer to perform intelligent tasks that we do without even thinking about them; such as seeing and understanding what we see, understanding language, and inferring from what we understand? Some choose to investigate machine performance of tasks, like chess playing, that even humans find difficult, but the "unconscious tasks" remain the heart of AI.

As applied to the field of natural language understanding this has meant constructing elementary programs to carry out written commands, translate into another language, make inferences, answer questions, or simply carry on a dialogue – all of which are presented as written responses at a teletype or video screen.

As can be seen, machine translation is by no means a typical AI language program, but no difference of principle arises between the different sorts of task, especially if we accept a slogan like Steiner's that, in some sense, all acts of understanding are acts of translation (1975).

What almost all AI language programs have in common – though they differ widely over other assumptions – is strong emphasis on the role of knowledge in understanding, and on the presentation a theory as a possible process. In some programs – like the well-known one constructed by Winograd (1972) – this last assumption leads to writing the syntactic analysis part of the program in a special "grammar programming language" PROGRAMMAR, rather than as the normal battery of grammar rules like S $\rightarrow$ NP + VP. This rule appears in all grammars and simply means that a noun phrase (NP) followed by a verb phrase (VP) is a well-formed sentence (S). In Winograd's system that grammar rule exists only as tiny program in PROGRAMMAR.

Winograd's program accepted dialogue and commands about a miniature world consisting only of a few blocks and a box, which it could appear to move about on the video screen. He wanted to show the role of knowledge of this microworld of blocks as a tool for resolving syntactic ambiguities in input to the system. So, for example, when it saw the sentence "Put the pyramid on the block in the box", it would immediately resolve the surface syntactic ambiguity of the command: that is, does it refer to a particular pyramid (on a block) to be picked up, or to a particular place to put it (on the block in the box), according to whether there actually was a block under a pyramid, or already in the box, in the small blocks scene that it understood.

Winograd's program could be called pure AI, in that it was motivated by classic problems of AI: plans (how to pick up the blocks) and theorem proving (how to show which is under the pyramid at a given moment), rather than being motivated by problems left over from the 1966 failure of machine translation, such as word-sense ambiguity, and correctly referring pronouns in discourse. Another group of AI language programs, such as the work Charniak (1973), Schank (1975a) and myself (1973, 1975) was directed more at those left-over questions: at meaning representation, and the use of inference rules: not about microworlds of blocks, but about the more general world in which we live.

Consider a simple sentence like "The soldiers fired at the women and I saw several fall", where we may be sure that any native speaker of English will understand that sentence (out of any further context, which may change matters, so let us leave it to one side) in such a way that "several" refers to the women and not to the soldiers. That cannot be done on any simple semantic (or syntactic) grounds since both soldiers and women are capable of falling. Mere proximity, in that "women" is closer to "several" in the sentence than the alternative, is known to be an unreliable guide in general. Correct reference of the pronoun "several" – and this might be vital in translation into a language where "soldiers" and "women" had different genders, for example – must almost certainly be done using some general inference rule like "If animate things have an object projected at them, they may well drop downwards". If the reader finds that implausible, he should ask himself just how he refers the pronoun correctly in that sentence.

The type of knowledge expressed in that rule is what one might call, following McCarthy partial: it is an inference that is not always true. It is a kind of knowledge that has no place in the very limited Winograd blocks world, but is central to the understanding capacities of the Charniak, Schank and Wilks systems. The three systems differ strongly in other respects: for example, the Schank and Wilks systems emphasise knowledge that can be expressed in very general terms, like the inference rule above, and develop notations of semantic primitives (actions like CAUSE, and CHANGE; entities like THING, and MAN for human being) in order to express this. In Charniak's systems, on the other hand, the knowledge is quite specific to a certain topic, like present giving.

Machine translation has traditionally been much preoccupied with the problem of finding the topic in a text: in the "Time flies like an arrow" example, with it's three classic readings, we would have the correct reading immediately if we could find out, from wider context, that the sentence is about, say, time, and not about flies or liking. The semantic system of Charniak tried to detect the topic by specific cues, while the Schank and Wilks systems did so by general rules ranging over semantic representations expressed in primitives. In the Winograd system, on the other hand, topic can never be a problem because it is always the blocks world.

There is no doubt that AI systems can be brought to bear upon the problems of machine translation: the system described in Chapter 3 actually translated English into French and resolved word-sense and pronoun ambiguities that could only be resolved with the aid of the sort of partial knowledge used in the soldiers and woman example. There is enough capacity in such systems to express knowledge about protons and neutrons so as to have no difficulty with Bar-Hillel's phrase "slow neutrons and protons". If he were to protest that it was ad hoc for the system to code only one of those entities, say, as being potentially slow, then one could reply by asking how he could know that humans do not understand this sentence with precisely such a specific coding of knowledge.

But much may depend on one's choice of examples: it is not clear that the difficulty has been eased by these AI systems for old favourites like Time Flying. The partial knowledge systems I described might well know that things that flew were normally birds or planes, rather than time, and so they would have no reason to pick out the reading where time does the flying on such preference grounds. Given that flies can indeed be timed, such systems might well decide that the "imperative reading" was the one most suited to their general knowledge about the world with which they had been programmed. This is a melancholy conclusion, because it suggests that our competence with such examples can only be credited to an ability to read them off a list of prestored clichés, together with the interpretation "we feel as if time moves quickly". This would be a sad conclusion for all theoretically motivated work, and an awful fate for a long cherished example.

Frame Systems in AI

After the systems just described, a new complexity was introduced under the influence of a proposal of Minsky (1975) that the knowledge structures in use in AI – and he was writing about machine vision as well, but here we shall concentrate only on language – should be higher-order structures that he called frames. One can see the sort of thing he was getting at by considering the statement: "John went into a supermarket and put some soap into his basket. On impulse he put a bar of chocolate in his pocket as well, but when he reached the cash desk his face went red and he said 'I didn't mean to take it".

The question that might come up in machine translation is how we know that the "it" refers to the chocolate, and not to the soap. The two words might have different genders in some output language, and so we would have to get the decision right, and in a general and plausible manner. It is easy to see that one might need to have access, even for this apparently simple task, to some complex formalised structure expressing what normally went on in a supermarket, so that one could infer from it that putting buyable items in one's pocket was not normal behaviour. Notice that it would have to be very specific information too, because it would not be enough to know that, in a supermarket, one normally puts buyables into a container, for a pocket is certainly a container. On so general a description of the activity of shopping the "abnormal" act would slip through unnoticed. Only the specification of (cart or basket) will do the trick.

It is just such highly complex and specific knowledge structures that Minsky argued should be called frames, which, in some formalised version, would be essential to any computerised language understanding system.

Let us begin with the standard quotation from Minsky that best captures the general notion of "frame": "A frame is a data-structure for representing a stereotype situation, like a certain kind of living room, or going to a children's birthday party". Attached to each frame are several kinds of information. Some of this information is about how to use the frame. Some is about what one can expect to happen next. Some is about what to do if these expectations are not confirmed.

> "We can think of a frame as a network of nodes and relations. The top levels of a frame are fixed and represent things that are always true about the supposed situation. The lower levels have many terminals ... 'slots' that must be filled by specific instances or data. Each terminal can specify conditions its assignments must meet."

Under the influence of Minsky's proposal, Charniak (1975) produced a frame for shopping in a supermarket (to deal with examples like that about soap and chocolate), while Schank (1975b) produced similar structures but called them scripts. Schank defines a script as "a predetermined causal chain of conceptualisations that describe a normal sequence of things in familiar situation", by which he means some account, capable of simple formalisation, of the normal order of events when visiting a restaurant. He sketches a restaurant script as follows:

Script:
Restaurant roles: Customer; waitress; chef; cashier
Reason: to get food so as to go down in hunger and up in pleasure
scene 1 entering
PTRANS - go into restaurant
MBUILD - find table
PTRANS - go to table
MOVE - sit down
scene 2 ordering
ATRANS - receive menu
ATTEND - look at it
MBUILD - decide on order
MTRANS - tell order to waitress

and so on for scenes 3 eating and 4 exiting. For the reader to get the general idea, we need not go into the precise definitions of the associated primitive actions: entities like PTRANS on the left-hand side (indicating physical movement, in this case) that Schank uses in his underlying semantic conceptualisations of sentences in the computer. Schank's students wrote a program which to take a paragraph-length restaurant story and produce a longer story with the "missing parts" filled in from the script above; and do this in a number of output languages, thus producing a rather new definition of machine translation.

The question is what exactly frames are for in language-understanding systems; what hypothesis their use implicitly appeals to; and whether the benefit they confer could be obtained by other simpler means? There is no doubt they express the dynamic order of events that is part of the meaning of certain concepts, in some intuitive sense.

Moreover, the frame is potentially a powerful device for defining topic context, a problem that has plagued all formal work with language since the earliest machine translation. So, for example, if we see the sentence "John ordered an omelette", we know that it is the "ordering food" sense rather than the "order people about" sense (and these are expressed by different words in French and German, for example, so that for MT the right sense would have to be found). If we are processing a particular text with the aid of the "restaurant script" this problem will already have been settled because the Schankian MTRANS (in the last line of scene 2) will be tied only to the appropriate sense of "order".

This point may be clearer if we think of a language understanding system encountering a word it did not know: suppose it encountered "John ordered scampi", although "scampi" was not in its dictionary. Suppose the system had no restaurant script, but just representations of the senses of "order", including the appropriate one in which ordering was normally done by humans and of physical objects. These normal objects and agents we can call the preferences of the action, because they are not absolute – we can all understand children's stories with sentences like "The dog ordered a bone in the doggy shop" – but they do enable important semantic choices to be made. In "John ordered the numbers", for example, we can reasonably say that we select the mathematical sense of "order" because numbers fit the preferred object for that particular sense, though not the preferred physical object of the sense of "order" appropriate to "ordering things commercially".

Now we can see the payoff from the restaurant script: if we are analysing our sentences with it then we know that even the unknown "scampi" is almost certainly a food, just because that is the preferred object of the sense of the action tied into the script at that point. If we had only the general sense of "order" we could infer only that a physical object was ordered.

Frames or scripts, therefore, will certainly help in determining individual word context, provided that we can reliably decide in advance what is the appropriate frame with which to analyse the given input. This assumes reliable cues (the word "restaurant" for example) which will not always be present ("They stopped off to eat at a little place he knew"), and a way of deciding which of these large-scale information structures to use when several have been cued by a single sentence ("On the way home from the cinema, they stopped off at the supermarket before dropping into Luigi's restaurant"). Problems will also arise as to when to stop following one script and get rid it in favour of another.

The real issue, though, is not technical but concerns what claims are being made by frame users. They are, I think, making what I will call a plot line hypothesis as follows: Humans, or computer understanding systems, can only understand a particular story by seeing how far it follows, or diverges from (as did the chocolate and soap story), the stereotypical story of that type. Or, as Charniak (1975) puts it:

"The primary mechanism in understanding a line of a story is to see it as instantiating one or more frame statements".

The trouble is that the claim is not obviously true, as we can see by making up an imaginary frame about a more remote cultural activity. I have jotted down the following for a male puberty rite in Charniak's (1975) notation one which is more or less self-explanatory:

Frame: male puberty rite
Roles: male child, village elder, helpers, crowd
Reason: placing ritual incisions on back of child
(a) Goal: CHILD is tattooed
(b) HELPERS hold CHILD (by both arms)
(c) ELDER obtains TOOLS
(d) ELDER exhorts CROWD (on proper behaviour)
(e) (general condition) Bad behaviour by CROWD => Activity halts
(f) ELDER checks if CHILD properly purified
(g) (special condition) CHILD not purified => activity halted
(h) ELDER marks CHILD's back
(I) (method suggested) do for all CUT-MARKS

and so on. Again the general idea is clear, and the choice of a remote, and imaginary, culture is not accidental, as I shall now try to show.

Suppose we have three stories contained in three sentences:

{ "Little Kimathis's mother (looked away accidentally)"
"Little Kimathis's mother (dropped her shoga)"
"Little Kimathis's mother (touched his arm) during the puberty rite. The crowd drew back in horror". }

If we wish to understand these stories, do we need the frame above to do it? The frame covers the end of the story with line (e) in some sense, given an adequate list defining bad behaviour accessible from the frame.

And yet it is clear that we understand the sentences perfectly well without the frame. In commonsense terms we could say that we infer from the sentences that the mother touching Kimathi during the ceremony was bad thing. We do not need that information in order to understand.

One might argue that, in order to understand the above, a program should tie two parts of its representation together with some rule equivalent to:

human display alarm => other human has performed bad action.

A Martian lacking any earthly frame could understand the stories so long as he understood this rule and the constituent words. That is, of course, why I chose a puberty rite rather than a restaurant as a frame topic, for most of us are Martians where puberty rites are concerned. If we do understand the stories (and we do) it cannot be from our associated frame, because we do not have one. So we must understand it on the basis of knowledge organised on some simpler principles.

At present there is a tension between those who believe that frames are necessary for language understanding, and those who think whatever is necessary can be provided by a system of cues and inference rules no more complex than the "humans show alarm" rule So, to return to the "ordering scampi" example, provided we had a restaurant cue (which even a frame needs, as we saw) we could have an inference rule tied to that cue that said "ordering is now normally of food". The reply from frame advocates is that these inference rules would be too numerous to be accessed but, as we saw, there are also enormous problems about access to and manipulation of frames, so that this question is not settled, either by argument or by the performance of programs.

Some frame advocates are not urging the "plot line hypothesis" (PLH) in the strong form of "you must have structure X to understand" but are claiming that it is more efficient to understand text from the topmost level down in that way.

However, an efficiency-PLH cannot be assessed in the absence of frame application procedures. Moreover, and this is the important point, an efficiency-PLH almost certainly rests on some statistical assumption about the degree to which texts do in fact follow the frame norms: the PLH would clearly be more plausible if, say, 90 per cent of texts about X were consistent with the knowledge in the frame about X, than if, say, only 5 per cent of texts about X did so.

The Argument that Less-than-Frame AI Systems have a Role in MT

I want to argue that, although Bar-Hillel was wrong, and everyday knowledge can be manipulated in AI systems, nevertheless we may not need to go as far as the frame systems just described in order to alleviate some of the pressing problems of MT. Let me briefly recap the notation of my own semantics-based natural language understanding system (NLUS) (Wilks, 1973a, 1973b).

In other places I have described an NLUS in which rules operate on semantic word-sense descriptions to build up text descriptions. The rules that insert sense descriptions into text descriptions are what I have called "preferential": they seek preferred entities, but will accept the less preferred if necessary. A sense description for the action "drink" might be the formula:

((*ANI SUBJ)(((FLOW STUFF)(OBJE)((*ANI IN)(((THIS(*ANI (THRU PART)))TO)(BE CAUSE)))))

Figure 2.1 is a formal structure of semantic primitives expressing the meaning of the action "drink" (see Wilks 1973a): that drinking is a CAUSing to MOVE, preferably done by an ANImate SUBJect (=agent) and to a liquid (FLOW STUFF), TO a particular ANImate aperture (THRU PART), and INto the SELF (=the animate agent). For short we will write Fig. 2.1 as [drink]. The text structures in this system are semantic templates (together with semantic ties between them): a template is a

((*ANI SUBJ)(((FLOW STUFF)(OBJE)((*ANI IN)(((THIS(*ANI (THRU PART)))TO)(BE CAUSE)))))

Fig. 2.1 A semantic formula for the action of drinking

network of formulas, containing at least an agent, action and object formula. Thus the template for "The adder drinks water" will be written: [the+adder drinks water] for short where the whole of Fig. 2.1 is in fact at the central (action) node of that structure.

The process of setting up the templates allows the formulas to compete to fill nodes in templates. Thus the formula for the (snake-) adder goes to the agent node in the template above in preference to the (machine-) adder because Fig. 2.1 specifies, by (ANI SUBJ), that it prefers to be accompanied in a template by an animate agent formula. However, in the sentence:

My car drinks gasoline

the available formula for the first template node, namely [car], is not for an animate entity, yet it is accepted because there is no competitor for the position.

An important later process is called extraction: additional template-like structures are inferred and added to the text representation even though they match nothing in the surface text. They are "deeper" inferences from the case structures of formulas in some actual template. Thus, to the template for [My car drinks gasoline] we would add an extraction (in double square parentheses in abbreviated form):

[[gasoline in car]]

which is an inference extracted from the containment subformula of Fig. 2.1, (SELF IN). Analogous extractions could be made for each case primitive in each formula in the template for [my car drinks gasoline].

After the programmed version of the system, reported in (Wilks 1978), a structural change (Wilks 1976b) allowed a wider, and more specific, form of expression

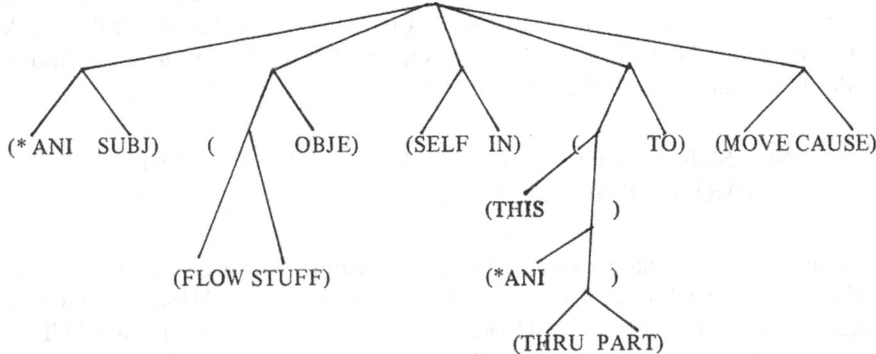

Fig. 2.2 The action formula for drinking installed at the central action node of a semantic template of formulas for "John drinks beer"

in formulas by allowing thesaurus items, as well as primitives, to function in them. No problems are introduced by doing this, provided that the thesaurus items are also themselves words in the dictionary, and so have their formulas defined elsewhere in their turn. One advantage of this extension is to impose a thesaurus structure on the whole vocabulary, and so render its semantic expression more consistent.

Let us now return to two of the examples introduced earlier: first, the complex French noun phrase. Let us imagine that its four key words "analyse", "establish", "simulate" and "understand" (we will ignore the problems of "combustion" and "retraitment", since they are not in the heart of the matter) have as part of their meaning expression inference rules (and those need not be distinct – but merely types of label for nodes on a syntax tree).

1.	[Human analyses X]	→ [Human wants X]	1i
		→ [Human understands X]	1ii
		→ [X has components/parts]	1iii
		→ [Human uses a process/method]	1iv
2.	[Human establishes X]	→ [X does not change]	2i
		→ [Human uses a process/method]	2ii
3.	[Human simulates X]	→ [Human wants X]	3i
	[Human understands X]	→ [X is process/method]	3ii

If we think of these rules, written as template-to-template patterns, chaining across the text under the guidance of a reasonable semantic algorithm, it should be clear that "analyse" chains to "simulation", on plausible grounds, but "etablissement" does not. The appropriate chaining is:

From "analyse" (the rules 1i, 1ii, 1iii are pointed to by that word) we infer by 1ii
[the human (analyser) understands (the method)]
also we infer (backwards up the text) from simulation via 3i and 3ii
[the human (simulator) understands X]

Hence, given this chain, leading to a close match of semantic patterns (after identifying X with method) we infer that it is the analysis that is simulated and hence make the prepositional phrase ("par simulation") depend appropriately and so resolve the syntactic tree ambiguity.

Notice that both 1iv and 2ii (from "analyse" and "etablissement" respectively) are both patterns seeking the one yielded from simulation by 3ii. In other words, both seek a process for achieving their ends (this is equivalent to the simple "process" match which yields no discrimination between the candidates because both matches succeed). It is only the quite separate pattern matching via 1ii and 3ii that succeeds in discriminating, and this one is not reducible to simple marker repetition, hence our method is not reducible to that of Fodor and Katz.

We might even attempt to apply this method of semantic pattern manipulation to Bar-Hillel's favourite example: the box in the pen, given earlier.

First, let us assume two sense formulas for "pen" in the notation given earlier, as trees or primitives.

Let us now consider the treatment of [The box is]/[in the pen] broken in to two templates as shown. The sentence will have been fragmented at the stroke by initial procedures and a template will be attached to each part: the first template having a dummy object place, and the second a dummy agent place, since a formula for "in" becomes the "pseudo-action" of the second template and has no agent.

Thus the parsing phase will have implicitly assigned formula trees to the slots of the two templates as follows:

FIRST TEMPLATE

Agent – formula	Action – formula	Object – formula
[The box]	[is]	Dummy

SECOND TEMPLATE

Agent – formula	Action – formula	Object – formula
Dummy	[in]	{ [playpen] [writingpen] }

There will, of course, be two second templates with the two different trees above at their respective third nodes.

Inference structures called paraplates, specific rules for prepositions, whose nature need not detain us (see Wilks 1978), then seek to link the two templates back together, the paraplate being in effect a case frame that resolves the "in" of this particular sentence as the introducer of the CONTAINMENT case. The application of this paraplate allows the dummy agent of the second template to be "repacked" in this particular containment case frame by the agent of the first template and thus we obtain, by a "repacking inference", a template form in the representation equivalent to [box in pen], which is not, of course, an assertion explicitly present in the text. This "repacked template form" will have a formula for "box" at its agent node and, since we still have two formulas for "pen" in play, not having yet resolved between them, we shall in fact have two repacked templates at this point, both with a formula for "box" at their agent node, and with the two formulas for "pen" at their respective object nodes. Or, expanding the "square bracket", or shorthand form.

[box in pen] and [box in playpen]

[playpen] stands for the formula for "playpen" which will contain the primitive WRAP (for "contain"), and [box] the formula for "box", whose head is the primitive THING.

Lastly we have to remember another very general process within this semantic representation system. When the templates of formulas are first set up for sentence fragments, an attempt is made to see what "semantic preferences", expressed by the formulas are in fact satisfied by the presence of neighbouring formulas in the templates (in which the formulas are now installed).

Thus, in a template for [John drinks gin] the formula [drinks] (Fig. 2.1 above) shows within its tree that drinking is normally done by animate beings (just as the formula tree for "playpen" showed that it normally contains children). So in [John drinks gin] the animate agent "preference" of [drinks] is satisfied by the presence of

[John] (which can be seen to be animate because its head is MAN) at the agent node of the template that has [drinks] at its action node.

The general preference rule of inference in the system is to take, as the provisional semantic representation at every stage, the template with the most satisfied preferences between its constituent formulas.

So now, let us envisage this process re-applied after the application of case paraplates and the consequential repacking. If we do this to the two competing templates we still have for "in the pen", and one turns out to have more preferences satisfied than the other then we shall, by this general rule of inference be able to discard the latter.

The system will consider whether the box is plausibly inside the playpen or writing pen from the inference rule (of the same type as used in the "combustion nucleaire" example above).

$$[X \quad \text{WRAP} \qquad Y] \rightarrow [Y \text{ in} \qquad X]$$

which links, as inverses, the internal structure of the [pen] formulas to the structure of the two templates.

Inside the formula tree for "playpen" we see that playpens prefer to contain children, while writing pens prefer to contain liquids. And, since a box is a physical object (the head of its formula is THING), and so is a child, while a liquid (the head of whose formula is STUFF for substances) is not a physical object. Thus it is clear that the first template with the "playpen" formula, is more satisfied that the other, and so is preferred. To put the matter simply: the application (backwards) of the inference rules prefers a wrapper of objects (the playpen) to a wrapper of liquids (writing pen).

This method can seem ad hoc, designed to deal with a classic cleaver example, and it is. But notice, it cannot be outmanoeuvred by the repeated-writing-marker "inkstand in pen" point of Bar Hillel's mentioned earlier, since the writing pen will also be dispreferred as a wrapper of an object like an inkstand, given that the writing pen prefers to wrap liquids. Furthermore, this solution is somewhat general, for the ambiguity is resolved by the application of the general rules of preference used in setting up the representation, and not in any sense by special rules for the example. Although nothing follows from any particular example in this field, this use of general principles of language that set up the representation itself is, I would argue, a more promising approach to the traditional MT problem than either (a) very large knowledge structures, like frames, that are difficult to motivate and manipulate or the other suggested alternative for this example which is (b) ad hoc size categorizations of physical objects on some 1–10 scale, so that, say, boxes would be 4, writing pens 2 and playpens 5 in which case unaided arithmetic could yield the correct result, since $4 > 2$ and $4 < 5$ (a solution once seriously suggested by Horace Enea).

The conclusion so far is that we should be optimistic, and that AI semantic systems based on general principles like "preference" may relieve at least some pressing MT difficulties, and without claiming to be able to represent all the knowledge in the universe. For about that and its intractability Bar-Hillel was surely right.

Chapter 3
An Artificial Intelligence Approach to Machine Translation

I take Artificial Intelligence to be the enterprise of causing automata to perform peculiarly human tasks, and by appropriate methods, though I do not want to go into great detail about that difficult word "appropriate" here. I will therefore call what follows an Artificial Intelligence (AI) approach to machine translation for three reasons:

First, if fully developed, the system to be described for representing natural language would contain two methods for expressing the content of any given utterance: one logical, the other linguistic, in a broad sense of that term. At the present time (i.e. in 1975) a question outstanding within Artificial Intelligence is which of these general approaches is the most suitable. In that the present system has both representation capabilities, it should be able to compare them with a view to throwing some light on this important dispute.

Secondly, I argued elsewhere (Wilks, 1971) that the space of meaningful expressions of a natural language cannot be determined or decided by any set of rules whatever, – in the way that almost all linguistic theories implicitly assume can be done. That is because. in common sense terms, a speaker always has the option to *make* any string of words meaningful by the use of explanations and definitions. However, any working system of linguistic rules does implicitly specify a class of acceptable expressions, and so, indirectly, a class of unacceptable ones. The only way of combining these two facts of life is to have a modifiable system of linguistic rules, which was implemented in an elementary way in an earlier version of this system (Wilks, 1968).

Another aspect of the AI approach – and my third reason – has been an attraction to methods consistent with what humans think their procedures are, as distinct from more formally motivated methods. Hence the attraction of heuristics in, say, Al approaches to theorem proving. The system to be described is entirely semantics based, in that it avoids the explicit use of a conventional linguistic syntax at both the analysis and the generation stages, and any explicit theorem-proving technique. In the analysis of input, syntax is avoided by a template system: the use of a set of deep semantic forms that seek to pick up the message conveyed by the input string, on the assumption that there is a fairly well-defined set of basic messages that people always want to convey whenever they write and speak: and that in order to analyse and express the content of discourse, it is these simple messages-such as "a certain thing has a certain part" that we need to locate. Again, the overall representation of complex sentences is that of a linear sequence of message forms in a real time order, interrelated by conceptual ties called paraplates, rather than the hierarchical tree structure preferred by linguists. From the very common sense forms of expression I have had to use to express this method of attack, it will be seen that the method itself is one close to ordinary intuitions about how we understand, and somewhat distant from the concerns of formal grammarians.

Next, the French generation is done without the explicit use of a generative grammar, in the conventional sense. The interlingual representation passed from the analysis routines to the generation ones already contains, as part of the coding of the English input words, French stereotypes – strings of French words and functions that evaluate to French words. These functions are evaluated recursively to produce French output, and the stereotypes thus constitute both French output and procedures for assembling that output properly. No other inventory of French words or grammar rules is ever searched. and the stereotypes constitute a principled way of coping with linguistic diversity and irregularity – since individual words have their own stereotypes – without recourse to what Bar-Hillel (1970) calls 'bags of tricks'.

And finally, a point related to the general approaches previously discussed but importantly different is that of the "level of understanding" required for MT. It would certainly be unintelligent to develop any level of understanding more complex than is required for any task, and it is hoped that by the methods described it may be possible to establish a level of understanding for MT somewhat short of that required for question-answering and other more intelligent behaviors.

While agreeing with Michie's (1971) unexceptionable "... we now have as a touchstone the realization that the central operations of the intelligence are ... transactions on a knowledge base", it is hoped that for MT linguistic, or linguistically expressible, knowledge may suffice.

It is the semantic approach that is intended to answer the quite proper question "Why start MT again at all?" The generally negative surveys produced after the demise of most of the MT research of the fifties in no way established that a wholly new approach like the present one was foredoomed to fail – only that the methods tried so far had in fact done so. At this distance in time, it is easy to be unfair to the memory of that early MT work and to over exaggerate its simplistic assumptions about language. But the fact remains that almost all of it was done on the basis of naive syntactic analysis and without any of the developments in semantic structuring and description that have been the most noteworthy features of recent linguistic advance.

One word of warning is appropriate at this point about the semantic method and its relation to the form of this chapter. This is intended to be a practical note, concerned to describe what is being done in a particular system and research project, so it is not concerned to argue abstractly for the value of systems based on conceptual connections: this has been done elsewhere by writers such as (Simmons, 1970) (Quillian, 1969), (Klein, 1968) (Schank, 1971), and myself. I am not concerned to argue for a general method, nor shall I set out much in the way of the now familiar graph structures linking the items of example sentences in order to display their "real structure" for my purposes. I am concerned more to display the information structure I use, and the manipulations the system applies to certain linguistic examples in order to get them into the prescribed form for translation. The display of conceptual or dependency connections between items of real text will only be made in cases where unnecessary obscurity or complexity would be introduced by displaying the same connexions between items of the interlingual representation.

It has become fashionable to claim that "dictionary based" systems cannot find a place within AI. I would like to argue at the outset of this section that this view, pervasive though rarely made explicit, is not helpful, and can only inhibit progress on the understanding of natural language in an AI context.

The rise of this view can, I think, be correlated with the fresh interest being generated among linguists and others by new – i.e. in 1975 – attempts, (such as Montague 1970), to produce a formal logic capable of representing rather more of the forms of language than the classic attempts of Russell, Carnap, Reichenbach, et al. The implicit argument goes as follows: that logical structure provides the real structure of language, and there is no place in a logic for a dictionary, hence. . ..

Insofar as any premise of this argument is made precise, it can then be seen to be highly misleading, if not downright false. The relation of formal logic to language is and always has been a much disputed matter and cannot be discussed here in any detail. But any adequate logic must contain a dictionary or its equivalent if it is to handle anything more than terms with naive denotations such as "chair". Any system of analysis that is to handle sentences containing say, "hand" is going to need to have available in some form such information as that a hand is a part of a body, and that it is something that only human beings have. It does not matter whether this information is explicitly tied to a word name in the form of markers, or is expressed as a series of true assertions, a dictionary is what it is, and if the information is adequately expressed, it must be possible to construct either of those forms from the other, just as an ordinary English dictionary expresses information in a mixture of both forms. On the whole, the "explicit dictionary" is a more economical form of expression.

Those who attack "dictionary based" systems do not seem to see that matters could not be otherwise. Pressed for alternatives that express their point of view, they are now prone to refer to Winograd (1972). But that is absurd: Winograd's work certainly contains a dictionary, although this is not as obvious as it might be because of the highly simplified universe with which he deals and the direct denotational nature of the words it contains. But my point holds even within that simplified world.

To see this one only has to read Winograd's work with the question in mind: how does the system know, say, that a block is "handleable". The answer is put quite clearly in a text figure: by means of a small marker dictionary, of course.

Michie (1971) has written of ". . . the mandatory relationship, ignored by some computational linguists, between what is monadic, what is structural, and what is epistemic", in connexion with his claim that Winograd's work constitutes "the first successful solution of the machine translation problem". I think Michie means by "epistemic" is "concerned with the real world rather than the language", a rather special and non-traditional meaning and one by no means as clear as he thinks. Facts about language are also facts, of course; and many facts about the physical world can equally well be expressed as facts about language. For example, the assertion that "drink" prefers, or requires, an animate agent might seem very close to the assertion that only animals drink, or that most drinkers are animals.

Carnap's proposed translation of statements, from what he called the "material" to the "formal" mode, was a claim about the existence of a general equivalence of this nature. It seems to me that the onus of proof is on the believers – that knowledge about the real world, in some strong sense of those words, is necessary for tasks like MT. It is usual to refer, as Michie does, to examples like Winograd's distinction between the pronoun "they" as in "The City Council refused the women a permit because they feared violence" and "The City Council refused the women a permit because they were communists". But if the epistemic believers mean by "knowledge of the world" the "inductive knowledge of the average man", then they are being over-parochial in accepting such examples at face value; it all depends on whether the City Council is in Washington or Peking, so that an intelligent system might be perfectly right to refuse to assign the anaphora in such trick examples at all.

I am not suggesting, though, that the manipulations to be described here are merely "dictionary based", if that is to be taken to mean having no theoretical presuppositions. There are in fact three important linguistic presuppositions on which the following analysis is based: namely, the use of templates for analysis, and stereotypes for generation, referred to above and described in detail in the body of the paper, and in addition the principle, to be developed below, that by building up the densest, or most connected, representation that it can for a piece of language, the system of analysis will be getting the word senses and much of the grammar right. What I mean by "density of connection" here will be the subject of much that follows. Moreover, I shall argue later that the use of some 'formal' mode for information, even for inductive inferences, avoids certain bottomless pits that may await those who insist on using, possibly false, statements about the physical world in order to do linguistic processing.

Certain kinds of information dictate their form of expression; if it is agreed by all parties that to do MT we need to know that hands have four fingers, then some form of representation at least as strong as set theory or the predicate calculus will be needed to express it. The need for facts of that sort is a disputed one, but it is beyond dispute that we shall need to know that, say; a soldier is a human being. And an important question that arises is, what form of representation is necessary for facts of that sort.

This project is intended to produce a working artefact and not to settle intellectual questions. Nevertheless, because the territory has been gone over so heavily in the past years and because the questions still at issue seem to cause the adoption of very definite points of view by observers and participants alike, it is necessary to make remarks on certain matters before any detailed MT work can get started. In particular, different views are held at the present time as to whether the intermediate representation between two languages for MT should be logical or linguistic in form.

What the key words in that last sentence, "logical" and "linguistic", actually mean is not as clear as might appear; for example, they are almost certainly not exclusive methods of attacking the problem; in that any "logical coding" of text will require a good deal of what is best called linguistic analysis in order to get the text into the required logical form: such as coping with sense ambiguity, case dependency and so on. On the other hand, few linguistically oriented people would deny the need for some analysis of the logical relations present in the discourse to be analysed. However, for the purposes of the present project certain assumptions may be made safely: whatever linguists and philosophers may say to the contrary, it has never been shown that there are linguistic forms whose meaning cannot be represented in any logical system whatever. So, for example, linguists often produce kinds of inferences properly made but not catered for in conventional existing calculi: such as the "and so" inference in "I felt tired and went home", but nothing follows to the effect that such an inference could not be coped with by means of a simple and appropriate adjustment in the rules of inference.

Whatever logicians may believe to the contrary, it has never been shown that human beings perform anything like a logical translation when they translate sentences from one language to another, nor has it ever been shown that it is necessary to do that in order to translate mechanically. To take a trivial example, if one wants to translate the English "is", then for an adequate logical translation one will almost certainly want to know whether the particular use of "is" in question is best rendered into logic by identity, set membership or set inclusion. Yet for the purposes of translating an English sentence containing "is" into a closely related language such as French it is highly unlikely that one would ever want to make any such distinction for the purpose immediately in hand.

The preceding assumptions in no way close off discussion of the questions outstanding: they merely allow constructive work to proceed. In particular, philosophical discussion should be continued on (a) exactly what the linguist is trying to say when he says that there are linguistic forms and common sense inferences beyond the scope of any logic, and (b) exactly what the logician is trying to say when he holds in a strong form the thesis that logical form is the basis of brain coding, or is the appropriate basis for computing over natural language.

There are also interesting comparisons to be made on this point among contemporary academic developments and in particular the drawing together at the present time of the interests and approaches of hitherto separated work: the extended set logic of Montague for example that he claimed coped with linguistic structure better than did MIT linguistics, and, on the other hand, the linguistic work of Lakoff (1970) which claims that the transformationalists in general, and Chomsky in particular, always were seeking for some quite conventional notion of logical form and should have faced up to the fact in their work. But those interesting questions are not issues here, because the aim of the present project is to produce a small artefact that not only translates from one natural language to another but is also, potentially at least, capable of some logic translation and so admitting of question-answering and the additional "understanding" that that implies.

Nowhere here is it being denied that some form of knowledge-based inference will be needed for MT, and I shall describe one below. If one wanted a question-answering facility as well as MT, there can be no real problem about the coexistence of the two forms of coding, logical and linguistic, within a single system, because all but the most dogmatic linguists would admit the need of some logical analysis within any reasonable question-answering system. However, the coexistence might also preclude what one would in fantasy like to have, namely a way of testing against each other the logicist and linguistic hypotheses about MT. Such a test would be precluded because any logical translation (in the sense of translation into logic) within such a system would have much of the work done by the linguistic analysis that the system also contained. So there could be no real comparison of the two paths

ENGLISH → PREDICATE CALCULUS REPRESENTATION → FRENCH ENGLISH → LINGUISTIC CONCEPTUALIZATION → FRENCH

because the first path would also contain quite a bit of the latter in order to get the natural language input into logical form. But it might, as I discuss below, be possible to get translated output by two different paths in a single system and so give some rein to the notion of experimental comparison.

It is important to be clear at this point that the dispute between the logicists and the linguists is often unsymmetrical in form. One holding a strong logicist thesis about MT asserts, it seems to me, that a Predicate Calculus (PC) representation is necessary for the task. The linguist of correspondingly strong commitment denies this, but does not always assert that a linguistic representation is necessary. He may admit that a logical representation is sufficient, denying only that it is necessary. He might argue that a logical representation makes explicit more information in the input text than is necessary. By this he means simply that it is harder to translate into a logical notation than it is into most linguistic ones – a fact well attested to by research projects of the past – in that more access to dictionaries and forms of information outside the text itself is necessary in the logical translation case.

This is what I mean by saying that the logic translation may contain more information than a semantic one, even though the text translated can clearly contain only the information it contains. The additional information comes from the extra-textual dictionaries and axioms. The logicist, on the other hand, will most likely deny that a linguistic representation is even sufficient for MT.

However, one must be a little cautious here about the admission that a logical coding contains more information than a linguistic-semantic one, as those terms are usually understood. Any linguistic representation is going to tie some such marker as MAN or HUMAN to a word like "soldier", so that when "soldier" occurs in a text, that system is going to be just as capable of inferring that a man is being talked about as is a system that contains an explicit predicate calculus axiom

$$(\forall x), \text{SOLDIER}(x) \supset \text{MAN}(x).$$

What is usually meant by an admission that a logical representation may contain more information than a purely linguistic one concerns the notation for variable identification (as in the Winograd "women" example) and the existential quantifier notation. Though, again, there is no reason to think that a linguistic marker notation cannot be adapted to cope with existential information for such purposes as MT.

That there are difficulties about a naive introduction of "inference" into semantics can be seen from a recent paper, where Bierwisch (1970) says that an adequate semantics must explicate how "Many of the students were unable to answer your question" follows from "Only a few students grasped your question". Now, in a quite clear sense it does not follow at all; in that there is no problem about considering students who fail to grasp but nonetheless answer. That should not test anyone's conceptual powers very far, so it cannot be that one follows from the other in the sense that if the premise is true then the conclusion cannot be false. We could call that relationship of propositions "philosophical entailment", and I do not want to defend the status of the notion here, but only to point out that any representation of the sentences in question, logical or linguistic, that allows inferences like that one is going to be potentially useless.

There may indeed be a sense of "answer" in which the axiom

$$\forall x, \forall y, \text{QUESTION}(x), \text{HUMAN}(y), \text{ANSWERS}(y, x) \supset \text{GRASPS}(y. x)$$

would be a good one to apply, in the sense of producing a true result. But there are obviously senses of "answer" in which that is just not so, and to point that out is to demand, from the proponents of only logical representation, some suggestion as to how to cope with the real words people use, and to ask them to consider that perhaps real language is not just an EXTENSION of discussions of coloured blocks. Perhaps the clearest answer to any claim (see Charniak 1973) that a deductive logic must be used to solve problems of anaphora in real texts is to consider a children's story such as the following:

My dog is an animal, naturally. All animals have ears, and my dog has ears. My snake has no ears, therefore it is an animal too. I call it Horace.

Since the story involves a false deduction itself (and why should it not) any deductive analyser must decide that the 'it' refers to the dog, even though any casual reader can see that it is the snake that is called Horace.

The Structure of a Translation System

The diagram below is intended to represent the overall structure of the system under construction. The system represented by the lower half of the diagram is in operation, programmed in LISP at the Stanford AI Laboratory, and is producing good French for small English paragraphs.

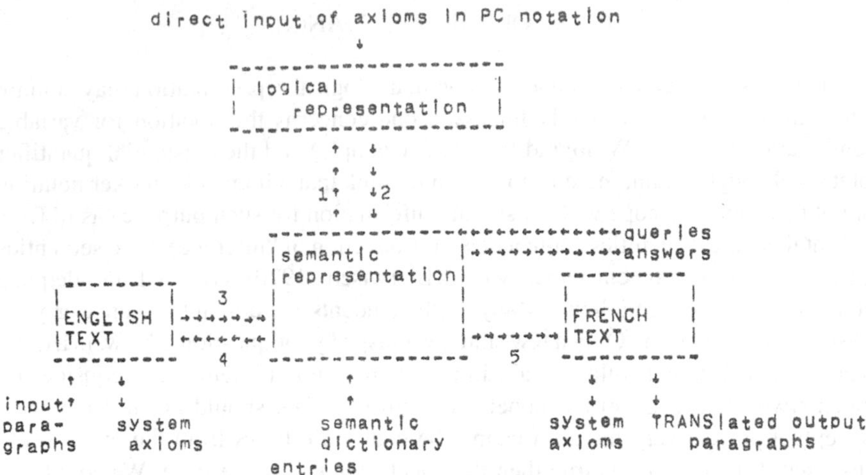

Fig. 3.1 Original graphic for the structure of the Stanford MI system

I assume in what follows that processes 2, 4, and 5 are the relatively easy tasks-in that they involve throwing away information – whereas 1 and 3 are the harder tasks in that they involve making information explicit with the aid of dictionaries and rules.

With all the parts to the diagram and the facilities they imply – including not only translation of small texts via a semantic representation but also the translation of axioms in the PC into both natural languages – it is clear that input to the system must be fairly restricted if anything is to be done in a finite time. There are however, ways of restricting input that would destroy the point of the whole activity: for example, if we restricted ourselves to the translation of isolated sentences rather than going for the translation of paragraph length texts. Whatever Bar-Hillel (1970) says to the contrary about MT being essentially concerned with utterances, I am assuming that the only sort of MT that will impress a disinterested observer will be the translation of text.

In any case, concentration on utterances can easily lead to what is in fact concentration on the trick example sentences of linguistic text books.

So what is to be the general strategy of translation? It is to segment the text in some acceptable way, produce a semantic representation as directly as possible, and generate an output French form from it. This would involve mapping what I call semantic templates directly onto the clauses and phrases of English, and trying to map out directly from the templates into French clauses and phrases, with their relative order being changed where necessary. I assume also, that no strong syntax analysis, in the linguistic sense, is necessary for this purpose and that all that is necessary can be done with a good semantic representation – which leave us with the big question of what is in the semantic box, and how is it different from what is in the logic box?

In the diagram, I am using "semantic representation" narrowly to mean whatever degree of representation is necessary for MT: though not necessarily for question answering (that's what the logic box is for). For this we may well not need the refinements of "is" that I mentioned earlier, nor, say, existential quantification or the analysis of presuppositions given by translation of definite descriptions, though we shall need what I shall call common-sense inference rules. My main assumption here about the difference between the two boxes, logical and linguistic, is that an "adequate" logical translation makes all such matters explicit, and that is why it is so much more difficult to translate into the top box than the bottom one. But the difference between the two remains a pragmatic one; intended to correspond to two "levels of understanding" in the human being.

With the difficult task 1 achieved – translation from semantic representation into a logical one – then it might be possible to have the two paths of translation from English to French: namely 3-5 and 3-1-2-5. The translation through the logic and out again might not be especially illuminating, but it would be a control that should not produce a noticeably worse translation than one achieved by the shorter route.

Inputs to the logic box will be in a Restricted Formal Language (RFL) and it should be possible to input axioms in it direct at a screen or teletype. The RFL will have to be at least as formal as the description in McCarthy and Hayes (1969) if the diagram is to be of any use, for there is no point in having an RFL to ENGLISH translation routine if the RFL is close to English – one might just as well write in English. The Sandewall form (1971), for example, with infixed predicate names is probably already too like English, which no argument against his notation, of course, simply an argument that it might not be worth writing a translator from it to English.

If it should turn out that the level of understanding provided by the semantic coding is inadequate for MT. then the diagram can still apply with the logic box, functioning as the interlingua: the difference being that the semantics will then be effectively a translation stage between natural language input and the logical representation.

If the semantic coding does turn out to be adequate for some form of restricted MT, then the function of the logic box will be to answer questions about the content of what has been translated. In that case, only those statements from the translated text relevant to the question need be translated up into the logic form.

What follows is divided into four parts which correspond to stages on the diagram above: The processing of English input text; The interlingual representation produced; The form of the dictionary used; The generation of French output from the interlingual representation.

The Processing of English Text

The aim of the text processing sections of the overall program is to derive from an English text an interlingual representation that has an adequate, though not excessive, complexity for two tasks: as a representation from which output in another natural language – French in this case – can be computed, and as a representation that can also serve as an analysandum of predicate calculus statements about some particular universe.

A fragmented text is to be represented by an interlingual structure consisting of TEMPLATES bound together by PARAPLATES and CS (or commonsense) INFERENCES. These three items consist of FORMULAS (and predicates and functions ranging over them and sub-formulas), which in turn consist of ELEMENTS. ELEMENTS are sixty primitive semantic units used to express the semantic entities, states, qualities, and actions about which humans speak and write. The elements fall into five classes as follows (elements in upper case):

1. entities: MAN(human being), STUFF(substances), THING(physical object), PART(parts of things), FOLK(human groups), ACT(acts), STATE(states of existence), BEAST(animals), etc.
2. actions FORCE(compels), CAUSE(causes to happen), FLOW(moving as liquids do), PICK(choosing), BE(exists) etc.
3. type indicators: KIND(being a quality). HOW(being a type of action) etc.
4. sorts: CONT(being a container), GOOD(being morally acceptable), THRU(being an aperture) etc.
5. cases: TO(direction). SOUR(source), GOAL(goal or end), LOCA(location), SUBJ(actor or agent), OBJE(patient of action), IN(containment), POSS(possessed by) etc.

FORMULAS are constructed from elements and right and left brackets. They express the senses of English words with one formula to each sense. The formulas are binarily bracketed lists of whatever depth is necessary to express the word sense. They are written and interpreted with – in each pair at whatever level it comes – a dependence of left side on corresponding right. Formulas can be thought of, and written out, as binary trees of semantic primitives. In that form they are not unlike the lexical decomposition trees of Lakoff and McCawley.

Consider the action "drink" and its relation to the formula (also shown as Fig 3.1 above):

((*ANI SUBJ)(((FLOW STUFF)OBJE)((*ANI IN)(((THIS(*ANI (THRU PART)))TO)(BE CAUSE)))))

*ANI here is simply the name of a class of elements, those expressing animate entities namely, MAN, BEAST, and FOLK (human groups). In order to keep a small usable list of semantic elements, and to avoid arbitrary extensions of the list, many notions are coded by conventional sub-formulas: so, for example, (FLOW STUFF) is used to indicate liquids and (THRU PART) is used to indicate apertures.

Let us now decompose the formula for "drink". It is to be read as an action, preferably done by animate things (*ANI SUBJ) to liquids ((FLOW STUFF) OBJE) of causing the liquid to be in the animate thing (*ANI IN) and via (TO indicating the direction case) a particular aperture of the animate thing; the mouth of course. It is hard to indicate a notion as specific as "mouth" with such general concepts. It would be simply irresponsible, I think, to suggest adding MOUTH as a semantic primitive, as do semantic systems that simply add an awkward lexeme as a new "primitive". Lastly, the THIS indicates that the part is a specific part of the subject.

The notion of preference is important here: SUBJ case displays the preferred agents of actions, and OBJE case the preferred objects or patients. We cannot enter such preferences as stipulations, or necessary conditions, as many linguistic systems do, such as Katz's and Fodor's (1963) "selection restrictions", for we can be said to drink gall and wormwood (i.e. which would never be coded as DRINKABLES by selection restrictions), and cars are said to drink gasoline. It is proper to prefer the normal (quite different from probabilistically expecting it, I shall argue), but it would be absurd, in an intelligent understanding system, not to accept the abnormal if it is described – not only everyday metaphors, but the description of the simplest fictions, require it. It is for these reasons that preference should be seen as a quite different form of linguistic coding from selection restrictions, even though the former can indeed select senses.

A formula expresses the meaning of the word senses to which it is attached. This claim assumes a common sense distinction between explaining the meaning of a word and knowing facts about the thing the word indicates. The formulas are intended only to express the former, and to express what we might find – though in a formal manner – in a reasonable dictionary.

So, for example, to know the meaning of "water" we need to know, among other things, that it is a liquid substance. But we do not need to know the law of physics that tells us that it freezes into ice. Many of the world's inhabitants have never seen ice and do not know of its existence even, but they cannot therefore be said to be ignorant of the meaning of whatever the word for water is in their language. This common sense distinction cannot be pushed too far, but it will serve provided we have (as we do have) ways besides formulas of accessing facts about the world.

This flexible method of formula encoding and decomposition, down to any degree of depth necessary to express the meaning of a word, is designed in part to avoid a number of pitfalls, well known in other systems of meaning analysis, such as trying to specify in advance all the ways in which an action or agent can be qualified. In a number of AI approaches there is often no attempt at lexical decomposition or the establishment of semantic primitives. New words "encountered" are simply added as primitives in new "axioms". This leads to an endless proliferation of "primitive" vocabulary, as well as inefficiency of representation. And the inability to generalise and connect clearly connected things (such as two facts differing only by a synonym for example).

Just as elements are to be explained by seeing how they functioned within formulas, so formulas, one level higher, are to be explained by describing how they function within TEMPLATES, the third kind of semantic item in the system. The notion of a template is intended to correspond to an intuitive one of message: one not reducible merely to unstructured associations of word-senses as some have suggested.

A template consists of a network of formulas grounded on a basic actor-action-object triple of formulas. This basic formula triple is found in frames of formulas, one formula for each fragment word in each frame, by means of a device called a bare template. A bare template is simply a triple of elements that are the heads of three formulas in actor-action-object form.

For example: "Small men sometimes father big sons", when represented by a string of formulas, will give the two sequences of heads:

KIND MAN HOW MAN KIND MAN

and

KIND MAN HOW CAUSE KIND MAN

(CAUSE is the head of the verbal sense of 'father"; "to father" is analyzed as "to cause to have life".)

The first sequence has no underlying template; however, in the second we find MAN-CAUSE-MAN which is a legitimate bare template. Thus we have disambiguated "father", at the same time as picking up a sequence of three formulas that is the core of the template for the sentence. It must be emphasized here that the template is the sequence of formulas, and not to be confused with the triple of elements (heads) used to locate it.

It is a hypothesis of this work that we can build up a finite but useful inventory of bare templates adequate for the analysis of ordinary language: a list of the messages that people want to convey at some fairly high level of generality (for template matching is not in any sense phrase-matching at the surface level). The bare templates are an attempt to explicate a notion of a non-atomistic linguistic pattern: to be located whole in texts in the way that human beings appear to when they read or listen.

The present working list of bare templates is stored in the program in Backus Normal Form for convenience of reading. The list (see below) consists of items like |< *ANI ><FEEL >< *MAR >| which says that, for bare templates whose middle action element is FEEL. the first (agent) element must be from the class of elements *ANI. Similarly, the object element must come from the element class *MAR, and therefore be one of the mark elements STATE, SIGN or ACT. All of which is to say that only animate things can feel, and that what they feel (since the notion of tactile feeling is covered by SENSE, not FEEL) are internal states, and acts, or their written equivalents. I would not wish to defend the particular template list in use at any given moment. Such lists are always subject to modification by experience, as are the formulas and even the inventory of basic elements. The only defence is that the system using them actually works, and if anyone replies that its working depends on mere inductive generalization, I can only remind them of Garvin's obvious but invaluable remark that all linguistic generalizations are, and must be, inductive.

Let us now illustrate the central processes of expansion and preference by considering the sentence "The big policeman interrogated the crook", and let us take the following formulas for the four main word senses:

1. "policeman":

   ((FOLK SOUR)((((NOTGOOD MAN)OBJE)PICK)(SUBJ MAN)))

   i.e., a person who selects bad persons out of the body of people (FOLK). The case marker SUBJ is the dependent in the last element pair, indicating that the normal "top first" order for subject-entities in formulas has been violated, and necessarily so if the head is also to be the last element in linear order.
2. "big"

   ((*PHYSOB POSS)(MUCH KIND))

   i.e., a property preferably possessed by physical objects (substances are not big).
3. "interrogates":

   ((MAN SUBJ))((MAN OBJE)(TELL FORCE)))

   i.e., forcing to tell something, done preferably by humans, to humans.
4. a. "crook":

   ((((NOTGOOD ACT)OBJE)DO)(SUBJ MAN))

   i.e., a man who does bad acts. And we have to remember here that we are ignoring other senses of "crook" at the moment, such as the shepherd's.
5. b. "crook":

   ((((((THIS BEAST)OBJE)FORCE)(SUBJ MAN))POSS)(LINE THING)

   i.e., a long straight object possessed by a man who controls a particular kind of animal. The template matching algorithm will see the sentence under examination as a frame of formulas, one for each of its words, and will look only at the heads of the formulas. Given that MAN FORCE MAN is in the inventory of bare templates, then one scan of a frame of formulas (containing formula (4a) for "crook"), will have picked up the sequence of formulas labelled 1, 3, 4a, in that order.

Again, when a frame containing formula (4b), the shepherds' sense of "crook", is scanned, since MAN FORCE THING is also a proper bare template, the sequence of formulas 1. 3. 4b will also be selected as a possible initial structure for the sentence.

We now have two possible template representations for the sentence after the initial match; both a triple of formulas in actor-action-object form. Next, the templates are expanded, if possible. This process consists of extending the simple networks we have so far; both by attaching other formulas into the network, and strengthening the bonds between those already in the template, if possible. Qualifier formulas can be attached where appropriate, and so the formula numbered 2 (for "big") is tied to that for "policeman" in both templates. But now comes a crucial difference between the two representations, one that will resolve the sense of "crook". The expansion algorithm looks into the formulas expressing preferences and sees if any of the preferences are satisfied: as we saw formula 2 for "big" prefers to qualify physical objects. A policeman is such an object and that additional dependency is marked in both templates: similarly for the preference of "interrogate' for human actors, in both representations. The difference comes with preferred objects: only the formula 4a for human crooks can satisfy that preference, the formula 4b, for shepherds' crooks, cannot. Hence the former template network is denser by one dependency, and is preferred over the latter in all subsequent processing: its connectivity is (using numbers for the corresponding formulas, and ignoring the "the"s):

$$2 \rightarrow\rightarrow\rightarrow 1 \rightarrow\leftrightarrow 3 \leftrightarrow\leftarrow 4a$$

and so that becomes the template for this sentence. The other possible template (one arrow for each dependency established; and where "<->" denotes the mutual dependencies between the three chief formulas of the template) was connected as follows

$$2 \rightarrow\rightarrow 1 \rightarrow\leftrightarrow 3 \leftrightarrow 4b$$

and it is now discarded.

Thus the parts of the formulas that express preferences of various sorts not only express the meaning of the corresponding word sense, but can also be interpreted as implicit procedures for the construction of correct templates. This preference for the greatest semantic density works well, and can be seen as an expression of what Joos (1971) calls "semantic axiom number one", that the right meaning is the least meaning, or what Scriven (1972) has called "the trick [in meaning analysis] of creating redundancies in the input". As we shall see, this uniform principle works over both the areas that are conventionally distinguished in linguistics as syntax and semantics. There is no such distinction in this system, since all manipulations are of formulas and templates, and these are all constructed out of elements of a single type.

Matching templates onto sentences in the way I have described is also an initial selection among the possible sense formulas for each word. For example, let us suppose that we have stored two formulas for "winner": one for the sense of a person who wins, and one for the sense of a good thing of its sort, as in "This bicycle is a winner". If we then made a match of that sentence with the template inventory, which we may suppose to contain THING BE THING but not THING BE MAN, then it will be the "good thing" sense of "winner" that will be picked up, clearly, since only its formula has the head THING. So the matching with the template inventory has already, at this early stage of analysis, made the correct selection from among the two senses of "winner".

If the THING-headed (metaphorical) sense of "winner" had not been in the dictionary, however, there would have been no match of the sentence with the template inventory. This is what we would expect to happen when words are used in new or unlikely senses, as in all metaphors. In such cases the system makes up a new template by accepting the combination of senses it is given, but notes that something odd is going on. This is consistent with the general rule of the system, of preferring the usual, but always accepting the unusual if necessary, as an intelligent language analyser should.

The limitation of the illustrative examples, so far, has been that they are the usual short example sentences of linguists whereas what we actually have here is a general system for application to paragraph length texts. I will now sketch in how the system deals with two sorts of non-sentential text fragments with a general template format.

In the actual implementation of the system, an input text is initially fragmented, and templates are matched with each fragment of the text. The input routine partitions paragraphs at the occurrence of any of an extensive list of KEY words. The list contains almost all punctuation marks, subjunctions, conjunctions, and prepositions.

Difficult but important cases of two kinds must then be considered: first, those where a text string is NOT fragmented even though a key word is encountered. Two intuitively obvious non-subordinating uses of "that" are found in "I like that wine", and prepositions functioning as "post verbs" as in "He gave up his post". In these cases there would be no fragmentation before the key words. In other cases text strings are fragmented even though a key word is NOT present. Four cases are worth mentioning:

I. "I want him to go" is fragmented as (I want) (him to go). A boundary is inserted after any forms of the words "say" and "want", and a further boundary is inhibited before the following "to". This seems intuitively acceptable since "want" in fact subjoins the whole of what follows it is that sentence. We shall expect to match onto these fragments bare templates of the form MAN WANT DTHIS and MAN MOVE DTHIS respectively – where the first dummy DTHIS in fact stands for the whole of the next template. The fragmentation functions operate at the lowest possible level of analysis, which is to say they inspect the semantic formulas given for a word in the dictionary, but they cannot assume that the choice among the formulas has been made.

So then, the fragmentation functions can consider only the range of possible senses of a word. However, in this case inspection of any of the formulas for "wants" or "says" enables the system to infer that the act can subjoin a whole template and not merely an object, as in "I want him". A verb like "advise" on the other hand is not of this sort since we can infer "I advise him" in a way we cannot infer "I want him" in the earlier case. So we would expect "I advise him to go" to receive no special treatment and to be fragmented as (I advise him) (to go), on a key word basis.

II. Relative clauses beginning with "that" or "which" are located and isolated and then inserted back into the string of fragments at a new point. For example "The girl that I like left" is fragmented as (The girl left) (that I like); where the final period of the sentence is also moved to close off the sentence at a new point. Thus the partition after " like" is made in the absence of any key word.

III. "The old man in the corner left" is naturally enough fragmented as (The old man) (in the corner) (left). The breach made here between the actor and act of the sentence is replaced later by a tie (see below).

IV. The sentences "John likes eating fish", "John likes eating", "John began eating fish" are all fragmented before "eating", so that these forms are all assimilated to

"John likes to eat fish", (which is synonymous with the first sentence above) rather than to "John is eating fish", which would not be fragmented at all. In template terms "John is eating fish" is to be thought of as MAN DO THING, while "John likes fish" is MAN FEEL DTHIS + DTHIS DO THING, where the first DTHIS refers to the whole of the next template, and the second DTHIS stands in place of MAN (i.e., John).

"Of" is a key word that receives rather special treatment, and is not used to make a partition when it introduces a possessive noun phrase.

After fragmentation, each fragment is passed through an ISOLATE function which looks within each fragment and seeks for the right hand boundaries of "of" phrases and marks them off by inserting a character "FO" into the text. Thus "He has a book of mine" would be returned from the ISOLATE function as "He has a book of mine fo". This is done in all cases except those like "I don't want to speak of him" where "of" effectively functions as a post verb.

It may seem obvious enough why 'of" phrases should remain within the fragment, since "of John" functions as does 'John's", but the demarcation of the phrase with the "FO" character can only be explained by considering the PICKUP and EXTEND routines.

Pickup and Extend

The PICKUP routines have already been described in a general way: they match bare templates onto the string of formulas for a text fragment. As the routines move through the string of formulas, those contained between an OF and a FO are ignored for the purpose of the initial match.

This ensures that "of phrases" are only treated as qualifiers. So, in the sentence "The father of my friend fo is called Jack", the match would never try to make the head of the formula for "friend" into the root of a template matching the sentence, since it is sealed between an "of-fo' pair. To illustrate the results of applying PICKUP I shall set down the bare templates that would be expected to match onto Nida & Taber's (1969) suggested seven basic forms of the English indicative sentence. (In this note I describe only the indicative mood as it is implemented in the trial version of this system. Queries and imperatives, like passives, are dealt with by the appropriate manipulation of the template order.)

In each case I give the basic sentence, the bare template, and a diagramatic representation of the corresponding dependencies implied between the text items, where " ↔ " again links those words on which the bare template is rooted or based, and " → " links a dependent word to its governor.

The establishment of this dependency by EXTEND is discussed next.

A natural question at this point is what exactly is this inventory of bare templates to be used in the analysis of input language? No detailed defense is offered of the inventory used nor, I believe, can one be given. The fact is that one uses the inventory that seems empirically right, revises it when necessary, in operation or under criticism, and concludes that that, alas, is how things must be in the real world of practical language analysis.

i. John ran quickly.

MAN MOVE DTHIS

John ↔ ran ↔ [DTHIS]

↑

quickly

ii. John hit Bill.

MAN DO MAN

John ↔ hit ↔ Bill

iii. John gave Bill a ball.

MAN GIVE THING

John ↔ gave ↔ ball

↑ ↑

(to) Bill a

Fig. 3.2 Correspondence of template head triples to sentence words

The inventory used can be reconstructed from the table of rules set out below in Backus Normal Form. It is set out in terms of the action designating semantic elements, such as FORCE, and the classes of substantive designating elements (such as *SOFT meaning STUFF. WHOLE, PART, GRAIN, AND SPREAD) that can

iv. John is in the house.

MAN BE DTHIS DTHIS PBE THING

John ↔ is ↔ [DTHIS] [DTHIS] ↔ in ↔ house

↑

the

v. John is sick

MAN BE KIND

John ↔ is ↔ boy

↑

a

iv. John is a boy

MAN BE MAN

John ↔ is ↔ father

↑

my

Fig. 3.3 Correspondence of template head triples to sentence words

precede such an action as a subject, and follow it as an object to create a three element bare template.

<bare template>: :=

<*PO> <DO> <*EN> |<*PO><CAUSE> <*EN> |<*PO> <CHANGE> <*EN> | <*AN> <FEEL> <*MA> |<*EN><HAVE><*EN>| <*AL><PLEASE><*AN>| <*AL><PAIR><*EN>| <*PO><SENSE><*EN>|<*PO><WANT><*EN>|<*PO><~SE><*EN>| <*PO><TELL><*MA>| <*PO><DROP><*EN>| <*PO><FORCE><*EN>| <*EN><MOVE><DTHIS>| <*PO><GIVE><*EN>| <*AL><WRAP><*EN>| <*AN><THINK><*MA>| <*SO><FLOW><DTHIS>| <*PO><PICK><*EN>|<*PO><MAKE><*EN>|<*AL><BE><same member of *AL as last occurrence>

The following are examples of the names of classes of elements:

<*AL>::=<DTHIS|THIS|MAN|FOLK|GRAIN|PART|WORLD|STUFF|THING |BEAST|PLANT|SPREAD|LINE|ACT|STATE> (*AL means all substantive elements)

<*EN>::=<DTHIS|THIS|MAN|FOLK|GRAIN|PART|STUFF|THING |BEAST|PLANT|SPREAD|LINE> (*EN means elements that are entities)

<*AN>::=<MAN|FOLK|BEAST|GRAIN> (*AN means animate entities, GRAIN is used as the main element for social organizations, like The Red Cross)

<*PO>::=<DTHIS|THIS|MAN|FOLK|GRAIN|PART|STUFF|THING|ACT| BEAST |PLANT|STATE> (*PO means potent elements, those that can designate actors. The class cannot be restricted to *AN since rain wets the ground, and the wind opens doors)

<*SO>::=<STUFF|PART|GRAIN|SPREAD>

<*MA>::=<ACT|SIGN STATE> (*MA designates mark elements, those that can designate items that themselves designate like thoughts and writings)

It will be noticed that I have distorted BNF very slightly so as to write the bare templates containing BE in a convenient and perspicuous form. The forms containing MOVE and FLOW also contain a DTHIS (i.e. they are “dummy templates”) indicating that there cannot be objects in those bare templates. Thus MOVE is used only in the coding of intransitive actions and not to deal with sentences like “I moved all the furniture round the room”.

There are dummy templates not included in this list for several occur in the preceding description of the Nida and Taber sentences. The remaining rules specifying them are intuitively obvious, but may be found in detail in (Wilks, 1972), where I also give important ancillary rules which specify when dummies are to be generated in matching sentences. Naturally a dummy MAN BE DTHIS is generated for the first fragment of (John is) (in the house) simply because a proper three element bare template cannot be fitted on to the information available. But in other cases, where a three element template can be fitted, dummies are generated as well, since subsequent routines to be described may want to prefer the dummy to the bare template. For example, in the analysis of the first fragment of (The old transport system) (which I loved) (in my youth) (has been found uneconomic), a reasonably full dictionary will contain formulas for the substantive sense of "old" and the action sense of "transport". Thus, the actor-action-object template FOLK CAUSE GRAIN can be fitted on here but will be incorrect. The dummy GRAIN DBE DTHIS will also be fitted on and will be preferred by the EXTEND procedures I describe below. Such slight complexity of the basic template notion are necessary if so simple a concept is to deal with the realities of language. This matter is described in greater detail in (Wilks, 1972).

The matching by PICKUP will still, in general, leave a number of bare templates attached to a text fragment. It is the EXTEND routines, working out from the three points at which the bare template attaches to the fragment, that try to create the densest dependency network possible for the fragment, in the way I described earlier, and so to reduce the number of templates matching a fragment, down to one if possible.

I explained the role of EXTEND in general terms earlier: it inspects the strings of formulas that replace a fragment and seeks to set up dependencies of formulas upon each other. It keeps a score as it does so, and in the end it selects the structuring of formulas with the most dependencies, on the assumption that it is the right one (or ones, if two or more structurings of formulas have the same dependency score).

The dependencies that can be set up are of two sorts: (A) those between formulas whose heads are part of the bare template, and (B) those of formulas whose heads are not in the bare template upon those formulas whose heads are in the bare template.

Consider the sentence "John talked quickly" for which the bare template would be MAN TELL DTHIS, thus establishing the dependency [John] ~ [talked] ~ [DTHIS] at the word level. Now suppose we expand out from each of the elements constituting the bare template in turn. We shall find that in the formula for "talked" that there is the preference for an actor formula whose head is MAN, since talking is generally done by people. This preference is satisfied here, where we can think of it as establishing a word dependency of "John" on "talked", which is a type A dependency. Expanding again from the element TELL, we have a formula for "quickly" whose head is HOW, and HOW-headed formulas are proper qualifiers for actions. Hence we have been able to set up the following diagramatic dependency at the word level:

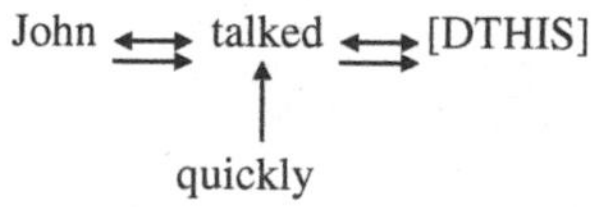

John ⇄ talked ⇄ [DTHIS]
↑
quickly

Fig. 3.4 Dependencies between sentence words, where the upper line are words corresponding to template formula heads, including a dummy (DTHIS) (where "⇆" indicates a bare template connectivity strengthened by a direct semantic dependency, springing from the preference of "talked" for a human actor in this case) and we would score two for such a representation. Furthermore, the formulas having type B dependence would be tied in a list to the main formula on which they depend. The subtypes of dependence are as follows:

A. among the formulas whose heads constitute the bare template

i. preferred subjects on actions
"John talked".
ii. preferred objects of actions on actions
"interrogated a prisoner.

B. of formulas not constituting bare templates on those that do,

i. qualifiers of substantives on substantive
"red door"
ii. qualifiers of actions on actions
"opened quickly"
iii. articles on substantives
"a book"
iv. of – fo phrases on substantives
"the house of my father fo"
v. qualifiers of actions on qualifiers of substantives
"very much"
vi. post verbs on actions
"give up"
vii. indirect objects on actions
"gave John a . . . ".
viii. auxiliaries on actions
"was going"
ix. "to" on infinitive form of action.
"to relax".

The searches for type B dependencies are all directed in the formula string in an intuitively obvious manner:

1. goes leftwards only:
2. goes right and left:
3. leftwards only:
4. leftwards only:
5. leftwards only:
6. rightwards only:
7. rightwards only:
8. leftwards only.

The purpose of the score of dependencies established can be illustrated here with regard to an example normally considered part of "syntax" rather than "semantics":

the indirect object construction. Let us take the sentence "John gave Mary the book", onto which the matching routine PICKUP will have matched two bare templates as follows, since it has no reason to prefer one to the other:

John	gave	Mary	the	book
MAN	GIVE	MAN		
MAN	GIVE			THING

EXTEND now seeks for dependencies, and since the formula for "gave" has no preferred actors or objects, the top bare template cannot be extended at all and so scores zero. In the case of the lower bare template. Then a GIVE action can be expanded by any substantive formula to its immediate right which is not already part of the bare template. Again "book" is qualified by an article, which is not noticed by the top bare template. So then, by EXTENDing we have established in the second case the following dependencies at the word level and scored two (of the "∼" dependencies). Two scores higher than zero and the second representation is preferred. This is another application of the general rule referred to earlier as "pick up the most connected representation from the fragment", applied to a superficially "syntactic" matter, though in this system with its uniform principle of choice and a single set of elements, there is no real distinction between syntactic and semantic questions.

The auxiliary of an action also has its formula made dependent on that of the appropriate action and the fact scored, but auxiliary formulas are not listed as dependent formulas either. They are picked up by EXTEND and examined to determine the tense of the action. They are then forgotten and an element indicating the tense is attached directly to the action formula. In its initial state the system recognises only four tenses of complex actions.

PRES:does hide/is hiding/did hide/are hiding/am hiding IMPE:was hiding/were hiding/PAST:did hide/had hidden FUTU:will hide/will be hiding/shall hide/shall be hiding

In the negative tense of any of these, the word "not" is deleted, and an atom NPRES, NIMPE, NPAST, or NFUTU is attached to the appropriate action formula instead. At present, the system does not deal with passives, although I indicate later how they are dealt with within the template format.

The third and last pass of the text applies the TIE routines, which establish dependencies between the representations of different fragments. Each text fragment has been tied by the routines described so far to one or more full templates, each consisting of three main formulas to each of which a list of dependent formulas may be tied. The interlingual representation consists, for each text fragment, of ONE full template together with up to four additional items of information called Key, Mark, Case, and Phase respectively. The interlingual representation also contains the English name of the fragment itself. The Key is simply the first word of the fragment: if it occurs on the list of key words; or, in the cases of "that" and "which", a key USE of the word.

The Mark for a given key is the text word to which the key word ties the whole fragment of which it is the key. So, in (He came home) (from the war), the mark of the second fragment is "came", and the second fragment is tied in a relation of dependence to that mark by the key 'from". Every key has a corresponding mark, found by TIE, unless (a) the key is "and" or "but", or (b) the fragment introduced by the key is itself a complete sentence, not dependent on anything outside itself. The notion will become clearer from examining the example paragraph set out below.

From the point of view of the present system of analysis, the case of a fragment, if any, generally expresses the role of that fragment in relation to its key and mark: it specifies the SORT of dependence the fragment has upon its mark. There is one important case, OBJECT, whose assignment to a case does not depend on the presence of a key. So, in the sentence (I want) (her to leave), the latter fragment would be assigned the case OBJECT and would be tied to the action "want" as the mark of that fragment, even though there is no key present. (The case markers used are the same as those that occur as elements within formulas.)

Phase notation is merely a code to indicate in a very general way to the subsequent generation routines where in the "progress of the whole sentence" one is at a given fragment. A phase number is attached to each fragment on the following basis by TIE, where the stage referred to applies at the beginning of the fragment to which the number :attaches.

0 –> main subject not vet reached
1 –> subject reached but not main verb
2 –> main verb reached but not complement or object
3 –> complement or object reached or not expected

The TIE routines then apply PARAPLATES to the template codings. Using the same density techniques one level further up, as it were. Paraplates have the general form: (list of predicates. . .list of generation items and functions. . .list of template predicates). The paraplates are attached, as ordered lists, to key words in English.

Let me give an example of semantic resolution, and simplify matters at this stage by writing not the French generation items in the paraplates, but a resolved version of the English. Consider the following three schematic paraplates for "in":

((20BCAS INST GOAL)(PRMARK *DO)IN(into)(FN1 CONT THING)(PRCASE DIRE)) ((20BHEAD NIL)

(PRMARK *DO) IN(make part) (PRCASE LOCA))

(PRMARK *DO) IN(into) (FN1 CONT THING) (PRCASE DIRE))

*DIRE is a direction case marker (covering TO, mentioned above, and FROM), 20BCAS and 20BHEAD are simply predicates that look at both the object formulas of the template in hand, and at the subject formula of the preceding template, i.e. at two objects. 20BHEAD is true if the two have the same head, and 20BCAS is true if they contain the same GOAL or INSTRUMENT subformula. The lower case words simply explain which sense of "in" is the one appropriate to the paraplate in which it occurs. For translation, of course, these will in general be different French prepositions.

Now consider the sentence "The key is / in the lock, 'fragmented at the stroke as shown. Let us consider that two templates have been set up for the second fragment: one for "lock" as a fastener, and one for the raising lock on a canal. Both formulas may be expected to be CONTainers. If we apply the first paraplate first, we find that it fits only for the template with the correct sense of "lock" since only there will 20BCAS be satisfied as the formulas for "lock" and "key" both have a subformula under GOAL, or INST, indicating that their purpose is to close something. The third paraplate will fit with the template for the canal sense of "lock" but the first is a more extensive fit (indicated by the order of the paraplates) and is preferred. This preference has simultaneously selected both the right template for the second fragment and the right paraplate for further generation.

If we take "He put the number / in the table ' we shall find it fails the first paraplate but fits the second, thus giving us the "make part of" sense of "in", and the right (list) sense of 'table", since formulas for "number" and (list) ' table" have the same head SIGN, though the formula for (flat. wooden) "table" does not. Similarly, only the third paraplate will fit "He put the list / in the table", and we get the 'into" sense of "in" (case DIRECTION) and the physical object sense of "table". Here we see the fitting of paraplates, and choosing the densest preferential fit, which is always the highest paraplate on the list, determining both word sense ambiguity and the case ambiguity of prepositions at once.

The application of paraplates is an extension of the preference for greater semantic density described in detail within fragments: the higher up the list of paraplates the greater the density achieved by applying it successfully. Extensions of this formalism cover anaphora (the correct referent leads to greater semantic density for the whole), and the common-sense inference rules mentioned earlier.

The common-sense inference rules are needed to cover difficult cases of representation where some form of more explicit world knowledge is required. There is no disputing the need of such knowledge for translation, and its absence was one of the major causes of failure of the early MT efforts, as well as of the irrelevance of much modern linguistics. A simple example will establish the need: consider the sentence already mentioned: "The soldiers fired at the women, and I saw several of them fall". Anyone who writes that sentence will be taken to mean that the women fell, so that when, in analysing the sentence, the question arises of whether "them" refers to "soldiers" or "women" (a choice that will result in a differently gendered pronoun in French) we will have to be able to infer that things fired at often fall, or at least are much more likely to fall than things doing the firing. Hence there must be access to inferential information here, above and beyond the meanings of the constituent words, from which we could infer that hurt things tend to fall down.

Such rules are intended to cover not only "world knowledge" examples like the "women fall" just mentioned, but also such cases as "In order to construct an object, it usually takes a series of drawings to describe "it", where to fix the second "it" as "object" and not "series" (though both give equivalent semantic densities in

EXPAND), we need an inference rule that can be loosely expressed as "an instrument of an action is not also an object of it". The point of such rules is that they do not apply at a lexical level like simple facts (and so become an unmanageable totality), but to higher level items like semantic formulas and cases. Moreover, their "fitting" in any particular case is always a "fitting better than" other applicable rules, and so is a further extension of the uniform principle of inference, based on density, discussed above.

In more straightforward cases of anaphora such as "I bought the wine, /sat on a rock / and drank it", it is easy to see that the last word should be tied by TIE to "wine" and not "rock". This matter is settled by density after considering alternative ties for "it", and seeing which yields the denser representation overall. Here it will be "wine" since "drink" prefers a liquid object.

The Interlingual Representation

What follows is a shorthand version of the interlingual representation for a paragraph, designed to illustrate the four forms of information for a paragraph: key, mark, case and phase – described above. The schema below gives only the bare template form of the semantic information attached to each fragment – the semantic formulas and their pendant lists of formulas that make up the full template structure are all omitted, as is mention of the paraplates applied to achieve this form. The French given is only illustrative, and no indication is given at this point as to how it is produced. The point of the example is to illustrate the (Speer, 1970) application of the general method to complex material, above and beyond simple example sentences. CM denotes a comma and PD a period.

(later CM)
  (PLUS TARD VG)
[nil:nil:nil:0:No Template]
(DURING THE WAR CM)
(PENDANT LA GUERRE VG)
(DURING GAVEUP:location:0:DTHIS PBE ACT]

(HITLER GAVE UP THE EVENING SHOWINGS CM)
(HITLER RENONCA AUX REPRESENTATIONS DU SOIR VG)
[nil:nil:nil:0:MAN DROP ACT]

(SAYING)
(DISANT)
[nil:HITLER:nil:3:DTHIS DO DTHIS]

(THAT HE WANTED)
(QU'IL VOULAIT)
[THAT:SAYING:object: 3:MAN WANT DTHIS]

(TO RENOUNCE HIS FAVORITE ENTERTAINMENT)
(RENONCER A SA DISTRACTION FAVORITE)
[TO:WANT:object:3:DTHIS DROP ACT]

(OUTOF SYMPATHY)
(PAR SYMPATHIE)
[OUTOF:RENOUNCE:source 3:DTHIS PDO SIGN]

(FOR THE PRIVATIONS OF THE SOLDIERS PD)
(POUR LES PRIVATIONS DES SOLDATS PT)
[FOR:SYMPATHY:recipient:3:DTHIS PBE ACT]

(INSTEAD RECORDS WERE PLAYED PD) (A LA PLACE ON PASSA DES DISQUES PT)
[INSTEAD:nil:nil:0:MAN USE THING](comment:template is made active)

(BUT)
(MAIS)
[BUT:nil:nil:0:No Template]

(ALTHOUGH THE RECORD COLLECTION WAS EXCELLENT CM)
(BIEN QUE LA COLLECTION DE DISQUES FUT EXCELLENTE VG)
[ALTHOUGH:PREFERRED:nil:0:GRAIN BE KIND]

(HITLER ALWAYS PREFERRED THE SAME MUSIC PD)
(HITLER PREFERAIT TOUJOURS LA MEME MUSIQUE PT)
[nil:nil:nil:0:MAN WANT GRAIN]

(NEITHER BAROQUE)
(NI LA MUSIQUE BAROQUE)
[NEITHER:MUSIC:qualifier:0:DTHIS DBE KIND]

(NOR CLASSICAL MUSIC CM)
(NI CLASSIQUE VG)
[NOR:INTERESTED:nil:0:GRAIN DBE DTHIS]

(NEITHER CHAMBER MUSIC
(NI LA MUSIQUE DE CHAMBRE)
[NEITHER:INTERESTED:nil:0:GRAIN DBE DTHIS]

(NOR SYMPHONIES CM)
(NI LES SYMPHONIES VG)
[NOR:INTERESTED:nil:0:GRAIN DBE DTHIS]

(INTERESTED HIM PD!
(NE L'INTERESSAIENT PT)
[nil:nil:nil:l:DTHIS CHANGE MAN]

(BEFORELONG THE ORDER OF THE RECORDS BECAME VIRTUALLY FIXED PD)

(BIENTOT L'ORDRE DES DISQUES DEVINT VIRTUELLEMENT FIXE PT)
[BEFORELONG:ni':nil:0:GRAIN BE KIND]

(FIRST HE WANTED A FEW BRAVURA SELECTIONS)
(D'ABORD IL VOULAIT QUELQ ES SELECTIONS DE BRAVOURE)
[nil:nil:nil:0:MAN '.VANT PART]

(FROM WAGNERIAN OPERAS CM)
(D'OPERAS WAGNERTENS VG)
[FROM:SELECTIONS:souroe:3:DTHIS PDO GRAIN]

(TO BE FOLLOWED PROMPTLY) (QUI DEVAIENT ETRE SUIVIES RAPIDEMENT)
[TO:OPERAS:nil:3:MAN DO DTHIS](comment:shift to active template again may give a different but not incorrect translation)

(WITH OPERETTAS PDI)
(PAR DES OPERETTAS PT)
[WITH:FOLLOWED:ni':3:DTHIS PBE GRAIN]

(THAT REMAINED THE PATTERN PD)
(CELA DEVINT LA REGLE PT)
[nil:nil:nil:0:THAT BE GRAIN](comment:no mark because 'that ties to a whole sentence)

(HITLER MADE A POINT OF TRYING)
(HITLER SE FAISAIT UNE REGLE D'ESSAYER)
[nil:nil:nil:0:MAN DO DTHIS]

(TO GUESS THE NAMES OF THE SOPRANOS)
(DE DEVINER LES NOMS DES SOPRANOS)
[TO: TRYING: object: 2: DTHIS DO SIGN]

(AND WAS PLEASED)
(ET ETAIT CONTENT)
[AND:HITLER:nil:3:DTHIS BE KIND]

(WHEN HE GUESSED RIGHT CM)
(QUAND IL DEVINAIT JUSTE VG)
[WHEN:PLEASED:location:3:MAN DO DTHIS]

(AS HE FREQUENTLY DID PD)
(COMME IL LE FAISAIT FREQUEMMENT PT)
[AS: GUESSED: manner: 3: MAN DO DTHIS]

It is assumed that those fragments that have no template attached to them – such as (LATER) – can be translated adequately by purely word-for-word means. Were it not for the difficulty involved in reading it, we could lay out the above text so as to display the dependencies implied by the assignment of cases and marks at the word level. These would all be of dependencies of whole fragments on particular words.

The interlingual representation described, as the result of the analysis of English text, and illustrated above in bare template form, is the intermediate form handed, as it were, from the English analysis programs to the French generation ones.

However, this intermediate stage is, as it must be, an arbitrary one in the English-French processing, yet it is helpful here to do a cursory examination for expository purposes and not only in the coded form. There is often a misunderstanding of the nature of an interlingua, in that it is supposed that an intermediate stage like the present interlingual representation (IR for short) must contain "all possible semantic information" in some explicit form if the IR is to be adequate for any purpose.

But the quoted words are not, and cannot be, well defined with respect to any coding scheme whatsoever. The IR must contain sufficient information so as to admit of formal manipulations upon itself adequate for producing translations in other natural or formal languages. But that is quite another matter of course. The fallacy is analogous to that committed by the computationally illiterate who say that "you can't get more out of a computer than you put in, can you?", which is false if it is taken to exclude computation upon what you put in. A more traditional parallel is the Socratic argument about whether or not the premises of an argument "really" contain all possible conclusions from themselves already, in that to know the premises is already to know the conclusions.

Analogously, the IR for translation need not contain any particular explicit information about the text. The real restriction is that. In creating the IR, no information should have been thrown away that will later turn out to be important. So, if one makes the superficial but correct generalization that one of the difficulties of English-French MT is the need to extend and make explicit in the French things that are not so in the English, then it is no answer to say there is no problem since, whatever those things are, the IR, if adequate, must contain them anyway. It is then argued that if there is a problem it is a general one about deriving the IR from English and has nothing at all to do with French.

But this, as I have pointed out, need not be true of any particular IR, since any IR must be an arbitrary cut-off stage in going from one language to another; a slice taken at a particular point for examination, as it were.

Consider the sentence "The house I live in is collapsing" which contains no subjunction "that", though in French it MUST be expressed explicitly, as by "dans laquelle". There need not be any representation of "that" anywhere in the IR. All that is necessary is that the subordination of the second fragment to the mark "house" is coded, and generation procedures that know that in such cases of subordination an appropriate subjunction must occur in the French output. It is the need for such procedures that constitutes the sometimes awkward expansion of English into French, but the need for them in no way dictates the explicit content of the IR.

The Dictionary Format

The dictionary is essentially a list of sense-pairs: the left-hand member of each sense pair is a formula, expressing the sense of some English word, and the corresponding right-hand member is a list of STEREOTYPES, from which French output is to be generated. Thus each formula that is pulled into the IR by the analysis procedures described, has pulled with it the stereotypes for the corresponding French. As will be seen, the stereotypes are in fact implicit procedures for assembling the French, so the role of the generation routines is simply to recursively unwrap, as it were, the package of the interlingual representation. So for example, the French words "rouge" and "socialiste" might be said to distinguish two senses of the English word "red", and we might code these two senses of "red" in the dictionary by means of the sense pairs:

(((WHERESPREAD)KIND)(RED(ROUGE)))((((WORLDCHANGE)WANT) MAN)(RED(SOCIALISTE))).

The French words 'rouge" and 'socialiste" are enclosed in list parentheses because they need not have been, as in this case, single French words. They could be French words strings of any length: for example, the qualifier sense of "hunting" as it occurs in a "a hunting gun" is rendered in French as "de chasse", hence we would expect as the right hand member of one sense pair for "hunting" (HUNTING(DE CHASSE)). Moreover, as we shall see below, a formula may require more than one stereotype in the list attached to it.

This simplified notion of stereotype is adequate for the representation of most qualifiers and substantives.

The general form of the full stereotype is a list of predicates, followed by a string of French words and functions that evaluate to French words, or to NIL (in which case the stereotype fails). The functions may also evaluate to blank symbols for reasons to be described.

The predicates – which occur only in preposition stereotypes – normally refer to the case of the fragment containing the word, and to its mark respectively. If both these predicates are satisfied, the program continues on through the stereotype to the French output.

Let us consider the verb 'advise", rendered in its most straightforward sense by the French word "conseiller". It is likely to be followed by two different constructions as in the English: I advise John to have patience, and, I advise patience. Verb stereotypes contain no predicates, so we might expect the most usual sense pair for 'advise" to contain a formula followed by

(ADVISE(CONSEILLER A (FNl FOLK MAN)) (CONSEILLER (FN2 ACT STATE STUFF)))

The role of the stereotypes should by now be clearer; in generating from an action, the system looks down a list of stereotypes tied to the sense of the action in the full template. If any of the functions it now encounters evaluate to NIL, then the whole stereotype containing the function fails and the next is tried. If the functions evaluate to French words then they are generated along with the French words that appear as their own names, like "conseiller".

The details of the French generation procedures are discussed in the following section, but we can see here in a general way how the stereotypes for "advise" produce correct translations of sentences i and ii. In sentence i, in the form of two fragments (I advise John)(to have patience), the program begins to generate from the stereotype for the formula in the action position in the first fragment's template. It moves rightwards as described and begins to generate "conseiller a". Then (FN1 FOLK MAN) is evaluated, which is a function that looks at the formula for the third, object, position of the current template and returns its French stereotype only if its head is MAN or FOLK – that is to say if it is a human being that is being advised. The formula for "John" satisfies this and "Jean" is generated after "conseiller a". Proper names are translated here for illustrative purposes only, so we obtain the correct construction "Je conseille a Jean".

Had we been examining the sentence "I advise patience", this first stereotype for "advise" would have failed since (FN1 FOLK MAN) would not have produced a French word on being applied to the formula for "patience", whose head is ACT. Hence the next stereotype would have been tried and found to apply.

The stereotypes do more than simply avoid the explicit use of a conventional generative grammar (not that there is much precedent for using one of those) in a system that has already eschewed the use of an analysis grammar. They also direct the production of the French translation by providing complex context-sensitive rules at the point required, and without any search of a large rule inventory. This method is, in principle, extensible to the production of reasonably complex implicit rephrasings and expansions, as in the derivation of "si intelligent soit-il" from the second fragment of (No man)(however intelligent)(can survive death), given the appropriate stereotype for "however".

Prepositions are taken as having only a single sense each, even though that sense may give rise to a great number of stereotypes. Let us consider, by way of example, "outof" (considered as a single word) in the three sentences:

1. (It was made)(outof wood)
2. (He killed him)(outof hatred)
3. (I live)(outof town)

It seems to me unhelpful to say that here are three senses of "outof" even though its occurrence in these examples requires translation into French by "de". "par" and "en dehors de" respectively, and other contexts would require "parmi" or "dans."

Given the convention for stereotypes described earlier for actions, let us set down stereotypes that would enable us to deal with these examples:

Si. ((PRCASE SOUR)(PRMARK *DO) DE (FN1 STUFF THING))
Sii. ((PRCASE SOUR)(PRMARK *DO) PAR (FN2 FEEL))
Siii. ((PRCASE LOCA) EN DEHORS DE (FN1 POINT SPREAD))

Where *DO indicates a wide class of action formulas: any, in fact, whose heads are not PDO, DBE or BE.

One thing that should be made clear at this point, to avoid confusing anyone who has noticed the similarity of paraplates and these full stereotypes for prepositions, is that they are in fact the same thing. In the analysis section, for ease of presentation, I described the application of a list of paraplates, tied to a key word like a preposition, and the selection of the correct one from context in order to determine the case of the tie between templates. This process is also the selection of the correct stereotype for generation from the same structure. There is no pause, as it were, in the operation of the whole system: when the interlingual representation is finished, the procedure passes directly into generation. So, what was described earlier as the successful evaluation of a function in a paraplate, thus showing that the paraplate 'fitted', is in fact the evaluation of that function to a French word string that itself becomes the output from the whole process.

Thus the same theoretical objects can be seen in analysis as paraplates, being items that tie a meaning representation together, and, in generation as stereotypes being implicit procedures producing output strings as values.

In sentence fragments (It was made) (outof wood), when the program enters the second fragment it knows from the whole interlingual representation described earlier that the case of that fragment is SOURCE and its mark is "made". The mark word has DO as its head, and so the case and mark predicates PRCASE and PRMARK in the first stereotype are both satisfied. Thus 'de" is tentatively generated from the first stereotype and FNl is applied, because of its definition, to the object formula in this template, that is to say, the one for "wood". The arguments of FN1 are STUFF and THING and the function finds STUFF as the head of the formula for "wood" in the full template, and is satisfied and thus generates "bois" from the stereotype for "wood".

In the second fragment of (He killed him) (outof hatred), the two predicates of the first stereotype for 'outof" would again be satisfied, but (FNl THING STUFF) would fail with the formula for "hatred" whose head is STATE. The next stereotype Sii would be tried; the same two predicates would be satisfied, and now (FN2 FEEL) would be applied to (NOTPLEASE(FEEL STATE)) the formula for "hatred". But FN2 by its definition examines not formula heads, but rather seeks for the containment of one of its arguments within the formula. Here it finds FEEL within the formula and so generates the French word stereotype for "hatred".

Similar considerations apply to the third example sentence involving the LOCATION case; though in that case there would be no need to work through the two SOURCE stereotypes already discussed since, when a case is assigned to a fragment during paraplate analysis, only those stereotypes are left in the interlingual representation that correspond to the assigned case.

The Generation of French

Much of the heart of the French generation has been described in outline in the last section, since it is impossible to describe the dictionary and its stereotypes usefully without describing the generative role that the stereotypes play.

To complete this brief sketch all that it is appropriate to add is some description of the way in which generations from the stereotype of a key and of the mark for the same fragment interlock – the mark being in a different fragment – as control flows backwards and forwards between the stereotypes of different words in search of a satisfactory French output. There is not space available here for description of the bottom level of the generation program – the concord and number routines – in which even the simplest need access to mark information, as in locating the gender of " heureux" in (John seems) (to be happy) translated as "Jean semble etre heureux". Again, much of the detailed content of the generation is to be found in the functions evaluating to French words that I have arbitrarily named FN1 and so on. Some of these seek detail down to gender markers. For example, one would expect to get the correct translations "Je voyageais en France" but ". . . au Canada" with the aid of functions, say, FNF and FNM that seek not only specific formula heads but genders as well. So, among the stereotypes for the English "in" we would expect to find (given that formulas for land areas have SPREAD as their heads): . . . A (FNM SPREAD)) and . . . EN (FNF SPREAD)).

It is not expected that there will be more than twenty or so of these inner stereotype functions in all. Though it should be noticed at this point that there is no level of generation that does not require quite complicated semantic information processing. I have in mind here what one might call the bottom level of generation, the addition and compression of articles. An MT program has to get " Je bois du vin" for " I drink wine" but to "J'aime LE vin" for "I like wine". Now there is no analog for this distinction in English and nothing about the meanings of "like" and "drink" that accounts for the difference in the French in a way intuitively acceptable to the English speaker. At present we are expecting to generate the difference by means of stereotypes that seek the notion USE in the semantic codings – which will be located in "drink" but not in "like", and to use this to generate the "de" where appropriate. The overall control function of the generation expects five different types of template names to occur:

1. *THIS *DO *ANY where *THIS is any substantive head (not DTHIS)
   *DO is any real action head (not BE, PDO, DBE)
   *ANY is any of *DO or KIND or DTHIS. With this type of template the number. person, and gender of the verb are deduced from the French stereotype for the subject part.
   1a. type *THIS BE KIND is treated with type 1.
2. DTHIS *DO *ANY These templates arise when a subject has been split from its action by fragmentation. The mark of the fragment is then the subject. Or, the template may represent an object action phrase, such as a simple infinitive with an implicit subject to be determined from the mark.
3. *THIS DBE DTHIS Templates of this type represent the subject, split off from its action represented by type 2 template above The translation is simply generated from the stereotype of the subject formula, since the rest are dummies, though there may arise cases of the form DTHIS DBE KIND where generation is only possible from a qualifier as in the second fragment of (I like tall CM) (blond CM) (and blue-eyed Germans).

4. DTHIS PDO *REAL Templates of this type represent prepositional phrases and the translation is generated as described from the key stereotype, after which the translation for the template object is added (*REAL denotes any head in *THIS or is KIND).

The general strategy for the final stages of the MT program is to generate French word strings directly from the template structure assigned to a fragment of English text. The first move is to find out which of the five major types of template distinguished above is the one attached to the fragment under examination.

So then, for a fragment as simple as "John already owns a big red car", the program would notice that the fragment has no mark or key. Hence, by default, the generation is to proceed from a stereotype that is a function of the general type of the template attaching to the fragment. The bare name-of the template for this one fragment sentence is MAN HAVE THING and inspection of the types above will show this to be a member of type I. whose general form is *THIS *DO *ANY. The stereotype is a function for any particular template type (let us call it FTEMP) and, to conform with the general format for stereotypes described earlier, this can be thought of as being one of the stereotypes for the "null word", since we have no mark or key word to start from here.

In this case the generation of French is simplicity itself: the function FTEMP evaluates to a French word string whose order is that of the stereotypes of the English words of the fragment. This order is directed by the presence of the first type of template comprising an elementary sequence subject-action-object. This is done recursively so that, along with the French words generated for those English words whose formulas constitute the bare template (i.e. "John", "own", and "car") are generated those whose formulas are merely dependent on the main formulas of the template – in this case the formulas for "already", "big", and "red".

If complex stereotypes are located while generating for any of the words of the fragment – "complex", meaning full stereotypes which have constituents that are functions as well as French words – then generation from these newly found stereotypes immediately takes precedence over further generation from the last stereotype at the level above.

Here, then, "own" creates no problems since it is a completely regular French verb, and its stereotypes contain nothing but French words. In general, it is only irregular French verbs that contain complexity in their stereotypes so as to dictate the form of what follows them in a sentence. (It should be understood that I am using "irregular" here to mean irregular with respect to this system of classification – my usage is not intended to correspond to the standard opposition of "regular" to irregular" in French grammars).

Now suppose we consider the two fragment sentence ' r order John to leave". The fragments will be presented to the generation program in the form described earlier: with Key, Mark, Case, and Phase information attached to each fragment:

(I order John) nil:nil:nil:O
(to leave) to:order:OBJE:2

Also attached to the fragments will be full templates whose bare template names in this case will be MAN TELL MAN and DTHIS MOVE DTHIS respectively.

The generation program enters the first fragment which has no mark or key; so it starts to generate, as before, from the stereotype for the null word which again is one for the first template type. This gets them subject right: "je" from the stereotype for "1", later to be modified to "j" by the concord routine. It then enters the stereotypes for the action: the first being

(ORDONNER A (FN I MAN FOLK)).

The head of the formula for "John" is MAN, and FN I here is an arbitrary name for a function that looks into the formula for the object place of a template and, if the head of that formula is any of the function's arguments, it returns the stereotype value of that formula. In this case the function FNl is satisfied by "John", so by definition that stereotype for "order" is satisfied, and the program generates from it the sequence "ordonner a Jean", giving the correct sequence "Je$ ordonner$ a Jean" – where $ indicates the need for further minor processing by the concord routine. The stereotype has now been exhausted – nothing in it remains unevaluated or ungenerated. Similarly the fragment is exhausted since no words remain whose stereotypes have not been generated, either directly or via the stereotype from some other word, and so the program passes on to the second fragment.

The program enters the second fragment and finds that it has a mark, namely "order". It then consults the stereotypes in hand for 'order" in fragment (i) to see if it was exhausted or not. It was, and so the program turns to the stereotypes for "to", the key of (ii). Among those whose first predicate has the argument OBJE will be the stereotype

((PRCASE OBJE)(PRMARK FORCE TELL) DE (FNINF *DO)).

If we remember that the head of the current formula for "order", the mark of fragment ii, is FORCE, and that PRMARK seeks and compares its arguments with the head of the mark formula, then the predicates are seen to be satisfied and the program generates "de" after seeing that FNINF is satisfied, since an action formula for "leave" follows, whose head MOVE is in the class *DO.

FNINF on evaluation finds, where necessary, the implicit subject of the infinitive. That is unnecessary here, but would be essential in examples only slightly more complex, such as "Marie regrette de s'etre rejouie trop tot". Finally FNINF itself evaluates to the French stereotype selected for "leave". This might itself give rise to more searching if the use of "leave" dictated its own sequents as in "I order John to leave by the first train". Here however the evaluation terminates immediately to "partir" since the sentence stops. The program makes no attempt now to generate for "lcavc" again, since it realises it has already entered its stereotype list via the "to" stereotype. Thus the correct French string "Je$ ordonne$ a Jean de partir" has been generated.

The last example was little more than a more detailed re-description of the processes described in the dictionary section in connexion with the example "I advise John to have patience". However, now that we have dealt fully with a fairly standard case and shown the recursive use of stereotypes in the generation of French on a fragment-by-fragment basis, we can discuss a final pair of examples in which a more powerful stereotype, as it were, can dictate and take over the generation of other fragments.

If we were to consider in detail the generation of French for the two fragment sentence (I throw the ball) (outof the window), we should find the process almost identical to that used in the last example. Here, too, the main stereotype used to generate the French for the first fragment is that of the action – "throw" in this example. The stereotype for "throw" is exhausted by the first fragment, so that nothing in that stereotype causes the program to inspect the second fragment.

Now consider, in the same format, (I drink wine) (outof a glass). Following the same procedures as before, we shall find ourselves processing the stereotype for "drink" which reads

(BOIRE (FN1 (FLOW STUFF)) (FNX1 SOUR PDO THING) | DANS (FNX2 THING))

where "|" indicates a halt-point. The program begins to generate tentatively, evaluating the functions left to right and being prepared to cancel the whole stereotype if any one of them fails. FN1 is applied to the formula for "wine" and specifies the inclusion in its formula, not of one of two elements, but of the whole conventional subformula for liquids (FLOW STUFF). This it finds, is satisfied, and so evaluates to "vin", to be modified by concord to "du vin".

The program now encounters FNX1, a function which by definition applies to the full template for some following fragment. At this point the program evaluates FNX1 which returns a blank symbol if and only if it finds a following (though not necessarily immediately following) fragment with a SOURce case and a template, the last two elements of whose bare name are PDO THING. It is, therefore, a preposition type fragment with a physical object as the object of the preposition. This situation would not obtain if the sentence were "I drink the wine out of politeness". If FNX1 is satisfied, as it is here, it causes the generation from this stereotype to halt after generating a blank symbol. Halting in an evaluation is to be taken as quite different from both exhausting (all functions evaluated to French word strings or a blank) and failing (at least one function evaluates to NIL).

The main control program now passes to the next fragment, in this case "outof a glass". It asks first if it has a mark, which it has, namely "drink", and looks at the stereotype in hand for the mark to see if it is exhausted, which it is not, merely halted. The program therefore continues to generate from the same stereotype, for "drink", producing "du vin", then "dans", followed by the evaluate of FNX2, namely "verre", thus giving the correct translation "Je bois$ du vin dans un verre".

The important point here is that the stereotypes for the key to the second fragment, "outof", are never consulted at all. The translations for all the words of the second fragment will have been entered via a stereotype for the previous fragment, the one for "drink". The advantage of this method will be clear: because it would be very difficult, conceptually and within the framework I have described, to obtain the translation of "outof" as "dans" in this context from the stereotype for "outof", because that translation is specific to the occurrence of certain French words, such as "boire", rather than to the application of certain concepts. In this way the stereotypes can cope with linguistic idiosyncrasy as well as with conceptual regularity. It should be noted, too, that since "dans" is not generated until after the halted stereotype restarts, there is no requirement that the two example fragments be contiguous. The method I have described could cope just as well with (I drink the wine) (I like most) (outof a silver goblet).

The point here (about what words are generated through the stereotypes for what OTHER words) can perhaps be made a little clearer with a diagram in which lines connect the English word through whose stereotype a generation is done to the word for which output is generated. All generations conventionally start from 0, the null word mentioned above. It is, by convention, the word for which the five basic stereotypes are the stereotype.

The general rule with action stereotypes is that the more irregular the action, the more information goes into its stereotype and the less is needed in the stereotypes for its sequents. So, for example, there is no need for a stereotype for "outof" to contain DANS at all. Again, just as the regular "I order John to leave" produced the translation "J'ordonne a Jean de partir" by using the stereotype for the key "to", the less regular "I urge John to leave" which requires the quite different construction "J'exhorte Jean a partir", would be dealt with by a halting stereotype for "urge" whose form would be

(EXHORTER (FNl MAN FOLK) (FNX1 OBJE *DO) | A (FNXINF *DO))

with the stereotype for "to" never being consulted at all.

Finally, it should be admitted that in the actual analysis and generation system, two items described, "case" and "mark", shrink in importance, though by no means disappear. Their role has been overstressed in this chapter, in order to make a clear distinction between the analysis and generation routines and so present a clear interlingual representation whose format is independent of the algorithmic techniques employed. What I sought to avoid was any reference to a "seamless computational whole" all of whose levels seem to presuppose all of the other levels, and which even if it works, cannot be inspected or discussed in any way.

The assignment of the case and mark information demands access to the French stereotypes. It would clearly be absurd to consult the stereotypes to assign this information and then, later, consult them again in order to make use of it in the generation of French. In fact, the analysis and generation routines fuse at this point, and the case and mark are located during the generation of the French output. The change in the format that this requires is that the mark predicate PRMARK is not now simply a predicate that checks whether the already assigned mark for the fragment in hand meets the specification: it is a predicate that at the same time actively seeks for a mark meeting that specification. And, as with the stereotype functions already described, the failure to find such a mark fails the whole stereotype containing it. There will now be a number of mark predicates fulfilling different roles. The case predicate, conversely, is not diversified but vestigial, because there is now no previously assigned case to a fragment for the predicate to check, and the case is now just a label in the dictionary of stereotypes to aid the reader.

A last, quick look at a previous example should make all this clear. Consider again (He hit the boy)(with the wooden leg) as contrasted with the alternative second fragments (with a stick) and (with long hair). Let us consider the analysis routines terminating with the provision of full templates for fragments (and phase information), and let us consider everything that follows that a French generation.

Let us now consider the generation program entering the second fragment, armed with the following list of stereotypes for "with:"

((PRMKOB	*ENT)	(POSS)	A	(FN *ENT))
((PRMARK	*DO)	(INST)	AVEC	(FN THING))
(PRMARK	*ENT)	(POSS)	A	(FN *REAL))

PRMKOB is a directed predicate that seeks for a mark in a preceding fragment (within a range of two fragments). It looks only at candidates whose heads are in the class *ENT, that is, THING, MAN, FOLK, BEAST, or WORLD; entities that can in some sense have parts In the same sense the heads ACT, STATE, POINT, etc., are not attached to word senses that we can speak of as having parts. PRMKOB compares the formulas for potential marks in the third, object, template position of preceding fragments with the formula for the object in the template for the fragment in hand. And it is true if and only if the latter formula indicates that it ties to a word sense that can be a part of the entity tied to the "candidate mark" formula.

So, in the case of (He hit the boy)(with the wooden leg) PRMKOB finds itself comparing the formulas for "boy" (head MAN) and "leg" (which contains the sub-formula (MAN PART). In this case PRMKOB is satisfied and the generation continues through the first stereotype, correctly generating "à" for "with" and then the output for "wooden leg". The *REAL in the function in the first stereotype merely indicates that any object in that fragment should then have its stereotype generated (any substantive head is in the class *REAL), because its appropriateness has already been established by the satisfaction of PRMKOB.

Following exactly the procedures described in other examples, it will be seen that (with a stick) fails the first but is translated by the second stereotype, while (with long hair) fails the first two but is correctly generated by the third.

Afterword in 2008: this paper was published in 1973, and much of the above detail may seen odd after thirty years and far too closely tied to the formal syntax of LISP. The logic versus linguistics debate, much in evidence at the beginning of this paper, has never been settled but has grown tired and lifeless. Now that part-of-speech tagging is a reality, it may seem bizarre that a system like this would go to such lengths to keep processes within the semantic sphere that might have been much simpler if carried out upon part-of-speech tags with some minimal syntactic machinery. However, I believe it can still be argued that, given a language with so little morphological in formation as English, it is remarkable how much can be done with only semantic codings and that the system above contains principles which have been constantly rediscovered (e.g. Jacobs et al., 1991) within NLP in the intervening years. The general principles of this generation model have, I believe, appeared in a range of other approaches, such as Whitelock's ‘Shake and Bake” model (Whitelock, 1992).

The paper was one the earliest to present a functioning interlingual system, and for many years part of its LISP code was displayed in the Computer Museum in Boston. Moreover, and as we shall see in a later chapter, Japanese commercial systems were later built, such as Fujitsu's, that made interlingual systems a reality, and indeed contained internal codings in a form of English primitives very like those of this chapter. So, though this chapter describes only a historical and small scale system, it and others of the same type, such as Schank's (1975b), were not without influence.

The paper should be seen as part of a movement in the 1970s (other participants were Schank, Simmons, Klein and Quillian among others) to argue that if computational linguistics, and MT in particular, were to revive – MT after the ALPAC report of 1966 – some central role must be assigned to semantics, in a way that Chomskyan linguistics assigned it no such role. The paper is also quite different from the graphical/visual methods used by some of those mentioned above for displaying linguistic content; its assumption was that semantics methods should be plainly procedural methods (like “preference”) over lexical information structures, and in that last respect the paper was prescient for the future of NLP/CL work like that of Pustejovsky (1993) and his generation.

Chapter 4
It Works but How Far Can It Go: Evaluating the SYSTRAN MT System

Introduction

To this day the SYSTRAN system (Toma, 1976) remains the existence proof of machine translation (MT). When people argue (as they sometimes still do) that usable MT (of a quality that benefits a large class of consumers) does not exist, one can simply point to the existence of SYSTRAN and, in particular, to its forty year history at the Federal Translation Division in Dayton, Ohio, where it still translates large numbers of Russian scientific and engineering theses every month.

There has been a resurgence of MT research since 1990 based only, or largely, on text data and statistics at IBM, New York, a revived technique (Brown et al. 1990, see Chapter 7 below) that has attracted both interest and funding, as well as a spread of the techniques used beyond MT to all areas of language processing. The 1990 claim from that IBM, let by Fred Jelinek, that MT can and should be done on the basis of correlations of English and foreign words, established between very large bilingual corpora, assumed that "symbolic", non-quantitative, MT cannot do the job. The quick answer to them is again SYSTRAN, which IBM's "proportion of sentences correct" percentage (40% versus SYSTRAN's 60–70% success rate) lags far behind, with no evidence that that gap could ever be closed. One should be cautious about the future, as always, but Jelinek later moved his group, before its dissolution, towards the investigation of how to model more conventional linguistic resources such as lexicons and grammars with data, so one should take the figures above as referring to SYSTRAN versus the original IBM system, based on text statistics directly via a simple "equation of MT" (see again Chapter 7 below).

A more detached observer might say of this clash of opinion that, while SYSTRAN has forty years of work to its name, the IBM results would *still* be important even if all they could do was reach the same levels of accuracy as SYSTRAN, simply because the original IBM procedures would be wholly automatic, requiring no linguistics, translations, text marking, rules, dictionaries, or even foreign language speakers.

However, the weakness of that response is that it ignores SYSTRAN's long history of tackling the most obvious language pairs (English-French, English-Japanese, etc.). The purported economic gain for statistical methods would have to be found in less common language pairs (in terms of translation volume): but these are, almost by definition, the very pairs for which the very large bilingual corpora the IBM method requires will not be available. So the assumption, even if true, will not yield much, at least until large bilingual corpora involving more remote languages have been developed.

The IBM researchers originally claimed that their method would eventually out-perform SYSTRAN, but it now seems clear that this will not be the case, and there is little or no support now for the statistics-only methodology of the first CANDIDE system. It may well be that the IBM statistical techniques – unaided by the modelling of additional linguistic structures – have already done all they can, and that their original success rate (46%) of correctly translated sentences is simply inadequate to be a useful product, remarkable through it may be given their non-standard assumptions. The influence of the IBM methodology, of seeking to model from data the intermediate linguistic structures needed for MT, has been so great that most effective new systems since 2000 have been of this type: Yarowsky's and Knight's being among the best known in the US. In the evaluations conducted by NIST since 2002, these post-Jelinek data-driven systems have indeed overtaken SYSTRAN in controlled experiments, but have not yet been deployed in forms that threaten SYSTRAN's established market. It seems to be the case that newer language pairs being added to established webpage translation systems are being developed by these methods, even when older, more common, language pairs available from the same web source remain SYSTRAN-like.

I do not wish to suggest that the only challenge to SYSTRAN in MT comes from the use of statistical techniques. On the contrary, a number of researchers in linguistics and artificial intelligence (AI) (e.g. Sergei Nirenburg) continue to claim that advances in linguistics, semantics and knowledge representation during the past decades now permit the construction of a wholly new MT system that will be able to break through the quality ceiling of about 65–70% correctly-translated sentences established by SYSTRAN.

The last effort to surpass SYSTRAN on a substantial scale was EUROTRA (Johnson et al. 1985). While one must admit that its results were undistinguished, this can be largely attributed to failures in the management of an overly large-scale international cooperative venture, and to the inappropriateness of using classical linguistic methods, as opposed to AI or knowledge-based methods. But as with everything else, time will tell whether those efforts will bear fruit or not.

The purpose of this pocket history of MT is to emphasize SYSTRAN'S continuing role, as *the* point of reference in MT, a role that has been strengthened by the World Wide Web and its use as the basis of the widely used Babelfish system for web-page translation. Forty years after its inception, SYSTRAN is still the European Community's rough translator of memoranda: it is used in Luxembourg on a daily basis, while EUROTRA is not. In spite of all its advantages, however, SYSTRAN's methods and nature are both in dispute, as is the quality of its repeated performance evaluations. This shadow of doubt has many sources, including the suspicious nature of many early MT demonstrations; some doubt clings to any system, like SYSTRAN, whose origins go back to those days.

Yet since that time, there have been many evaluations of SYSTRAN, in the course of which it has performed well, and it is one of these (which I carried out for the US Airforce in 1979–1980) that I wish to describe in this chapter, since I believe it to have been of considerable importance (I have received repeated requests for it over the years). This was not only because of continuing interest in SYSTRAN, but because it was an evaluation that assumed on the basis of long experience that SYSTRAN already performed MT at a level suitable for some class of customers – the most numerous being US readers of science theses and books in Russian – and sought further to investigate the issue of how far revisions to the system – done for a new type of text (in this case, political texts as opposed to the scientific Russian texts upon which the SYSTRAN Russian-English system had been built) – transferred to more (unseen) texts of that second type.

This test answered what is to me the key question about MT systems: how improvable are they, and what are their optimization ceilings; when do new errors introduced by revisions to the lexicon or grammar equal or outweigh their benefits (i.e. sentences worsened versus those improved)? In other words, it demonstrated that, while all MT systems are certain to fail in many cases, what counts is their flexibility and improvability. In this and other ways, I believe, SYSTRAN has discovered answers while evolving methods more familiar to AI than to linguistics proper. This may sound to some an absurd remark since, by conventional standards, SYSTRAN has neither conventional linguistic-syntactic rules, nor any explicit representation of world knowledge of the kind found in many AI systems. This is because, as I argued elsewhere (Wilks, 1990), SYSTRAN confirms two "principles" of MT:

Any theory (however absurd) can be the basis of an MT system, and MT systems, if they have substantial coverage, normally do not operate by means of their stated principles.

While SYSTRAN translates to a reasonably high degree of proficiency, it has no underlying theory that a theoretical linguist would acknowledge as such: hence we have (a) above. SYSTRAN has been the subject of few published descriptions most of which have described it in terms of multiple passes through texts and the extraction of phrases and clauses by a "partial parser". But, in fact, there is good reason to believe that SYSTRAN'S original Russian-English performance is as good as it is because of the very large number of long word-collocations in Russian (about 300K, together with a 300K word stem vocabulary): hence we have principle (b) above.

One can view this as an early application of what in AI is now called "case-based techniques": the storage of very large numbers of individual cases of usage. Again, partial parsing is a technique that is constantly being rediscovered in AI e.g. (Jacobs et al., 1991), as are techniques for controlling and keeping in use large bodies of usable but antique software whose internal structure is no longer modifiable. Donald Michie once argued in a lecture that a major future role of AI and – not one it had ever foreseen – would be to proved intelligent "wrappers" so as to keep old, unmodifiable, but critical software functioning.

In the case of SYSTRAN, of course, it is its core routines that are no longer modifiable, but which are simply imported *en bloc* when a new language pair is started. It is for this reason (the reusability of blocks of analysis and generation software, even if they have little function in reality) that SYSTRAN has been described by its current owners as a *transfer* rather than a direct system, even though in fact it has no true separable transfer lexicon for a language pair.

In conclusion, the power of SYSTRAN lies in its well-established and relentless, system of lexicon modification and augmentation in the face of bad translation results. It is these cycles that yield its subsequently high performance levels; the role of the following experiments was to see how far the process could go when SYSTRAN's capabilities were applied to a totally new subject area.

Background: Assessment of the FTD/MT Systems

What follows is different from previous assessments of the SYSTRAN system in two ways:

1. The subject matter tested (political articles and books) differs greatly from the scientific areas for which the SYSTRAN FTD/MT system was originally designed.
2. The methodology of the present study differs from all existing studies with the exception of the Battelle Memorial Institute report (1977), henceforth referred to as (BR).

The present project's goals in evaluating the US Foreign Technology Division's (FTD) version of SYSTRAN committed it to the (BR) methodology, at the core of which is an important and valuable point (we shall touch on some of BR's shortcomings later). Given a realistic and developing system like SYSTRAN, a sensible questionnaire would not demand that evaluator assign an arbitrary value to a translated sentence (such as 6 or 7 on a scale of 10), but rather would reduce evaluator judgments to the form:

Sentence *X* is better than sentence *Y* in terms of quality *Z* where *Z* might be translation accuracy or some other wholly internal quality to the target language material, such as intelligibility or naturalness of the language.

Such a method is appropriate to system like FTD's SYSTRAN which is constantly being updated and improved in the face of new requirements (i.e. new Russian language usages). According to (BR), it is reasonable to ask an evaluator: "Is version *X* better than version *Y* in terms of quality *Z*?" where *X* and *Y* are two different target language translations of the same source language string (English, we shall assume here, translated from Russian) and Y was produced in after the correction of errors found in a body of sentences that may or may not have included *X*. If the corpus whose errors were corrected did include X, then the improvement of *Y* over *X* is to be expected. If *X* was *not* in the corpus update but *Y* improved anyway, then that would be very interesting to us, indeed, and this is the heart of the BR method.

Our testing method had two such corpora: texts that were updated with corrections after a "first run", and whose corrections were fed into the system's dictionaries and rules, and those whose improvement was *not* examined after the first run, but after second run only. This latter was the *control text*, the most significant for our study: if great translation improvements were subsequently achieved in this non-updated corpus that would indicate that a continually expanding and updating MT system may be economically viable.

Restricting oneself to this form of qualitative assessment, as the BR method does, rules out the use of some of the more original methods of MT assessment, such as Carroll's (1966), in which an evaluator judged whether a translation from FTD was informative by comparing it to a normative (correct) translation. The assumption there was that if the translation was informative (compared to the original) it must be, to that degree, wrong. Monolinguals could perform that function, and bilinguals could compare the machine translation to the original source text as well. Carroll's method was only appropriate for relatively small text samples for which high quality normative translations could be given, however. More importantly, his methodology also assumed that the question "How well does the FTD/MT system translate?" had been answered elsewhere. The present study assumes the same, and that, having satisfactorily answered that question, we are free to discover how far updating improves the translation of unseen sentences.

A key element in the BR methodology was the prominence given to monolinguals. The origin of such an emphasis can be found in the following passages from the ALPAC Report (1966).

"The results from the ratings by bilinguals contribute nothing more to the differentiation of the translations than is obtainable with the monolinguals' ratings ... one is inclined to give more credence to the results from the monolinguals because monolinguals are more representative of potential users of translations and are not influenced by knowledge of the source language" (ibid., p. 72).

This passage will undoubtedly elicit conflicting reactions in modern readers: on the one hand, given that a high correlation between fidelity and intelligibility is well established with regard to translations, that seems reasonable enough. And as we shall see, some of the bilinguals' odd behavior in the present study can only be explained if we, too, assume that they are adversely influenced by their knowledge of the source text when making certain judgments. On the other hand, it is quite risky to base one's judgment of MT largely on the performance of monolinguals, if only because sentences may be intelligible and coherent without being faithful translations, something a monolingual would have no way of spotting. But the above correlation, and anecdotal experience, suggest that a fully intelligible but quite wrong translation is a very rare thing indeed.

In this study, we used three monolinguals and six bilinguals and, despite the discrepancies amongst the former group's judgments, all agreed upon the improvements of the control text sentences. It turned out that our results relied more heavily than we expected upon the evidence provided by the bilingual evaluators. It also should be noted that nothing in our study challenged the hypothesized correlation between fidelity and intelligibility: The statistics for the present study were not analyzed in such a way as to allow that to be tested for individual sentences.

The Battelle Report: Its Methodology and Shortcomings

The (BR) had two objectives: it surveyed existing methods of machine translation evaluation, and then applied a version of the updating methodology sketched above to a sample of scientific texts. In this section we will examine their discussion of monolingual evaluation and its relation to categories such as intelligibility.

The arguments for monolingual evaluation in the (BR) survey of evaluation methods were twofold: first, that estimates of the fidelity (correctness) of a translation strongly correlate to estimates of its quality in monolingual judgments of the output. And, secondly, that a monolingual expert can be expected to judge the overall coherence of an output text since, as a text lengthens, the chances of its being both coherent and incorrect approach zero.

BR counted as distinct the following three concepts that they completely failed to distinguish, namely: intelligibility, comprehensibility and readability (pp. 10–11). At first glance, it might seem that the difference between these categories is one of scale (with only *comprehensibility* applying to entire texts), but the intelligibility test is also applied by them to long sequences of output. Likewise, readability which "measures the appropriate overall contextual cohesiveness" of a text (p. 14) has little obvious contrast to the previous two categories. Indeed, the three separate tests given (one rating output on a "clarity scale", the second asking questions about the content of the output, and the third "Cloze technique" requiring a subject to fill in word gaps left at regular intervals in the output) could be applied equally to any of the three concepts with no change in the results. What is actually being discussed here are three different methods of measuring *coherence*, nothing more.

Battelle also seem to miss the significance of their essentially monolingual tests when they assert:

> "Although results obtained from these methods may correlate well with quality of translation [*monolingual quality assessment: YW*], many of them do not really test the correctness of translation, the basic purpose of both an MT system and an evaluation method". (p. 23) completely contradicting their earlier remark that, in a significant class of cases, monolingually-judged quality and correctness of translation correlate strongly.

Despite these ambiguities, Battelle's survey of monolingual tests gives us a useful notion of test coherence that can be assessed by experts ignorant of the source language. Moreover, we can be confident that the results of such tests may well continue to correlate strongly with bilingually-assessed translation correctness, which brings us to our adaptation of their experimental design.

Methodology of the Present Test

The test had the following stages:

1. Text materials containing one-and-a-half million Russian words were sent from FTD to LATSEC, the SYSTRAN company in California.

2. Of these, 150,000 were chosen by a random procedure and divided into two roughly equal groups of documents: the object or update text (0) and the control text (C).
3. Both texts were keypunched and the object text translated by an existing copy of the FTD/MT Russian-English MT system.
4. The control text was left unexamined and untouched, while errors in the translation of the object text were analyzed at LATSEC, and dictionary and program corrections implemented for them. This process took four and a half months, during which 2,750 stem dictionary entries and 2,800 expression dictionary entries were updated.
5. With the update system inserted, a second version of the MT program was created which was then run on both object and control texts.
6. The first copy of the MT system (without the updating) was then run on the control text, thus creating four sets of output: first runs of object and control texts and second runs of both.
7. A comparator program took the first and second runs of each text and listed only those sentences that were changed between runs.
8. The two outputs of the comparator program (one object, one control) were each divided into three parts.
9. Evaluators were chosen at three sites as follows:

   A. At Essex University, two bilinguals familiar with Russian-English translation but not with MT, plus one monolingual with qualifications in political science were named A1, A2, A3, respectively.
   B. At FTD, three bilinguals familiar with MT were named B1, B2, B3, respectively.
   C. At LATSEC, the inverse of (A) was done: one non-MT bilingual plus two monolinguals familiar with the subject matter were chosen, called C3, C1, C2, respectively.

10. Each evaluator with a given digit in their name code received that same one-third of the changed object and control text.
11. Each evaluator received the same instructions and questionnaire (see below). The sentences came to them in the form of a Russian sentence, a first-run English sentence, or a second-run English sentence. These last two sentences were randomly ordered, so as to avoid any assumption the second was "better". For each of three questions the evaluator was asked to choose one of four answers A, B, C or D. Their choice was indicated by circling one of the letters on a computer form containing the number of the sentence and the letters A through D. Answer sheets were mailed directly back to LATSEC.
12. A totalizator program compiled the results from each evaluator for each set of texts, plus monolingual and bilingual totals and these in turn were subjected to statistical analysis.
13. The evaluators were asked to give their reactions to the test and questionnaire, and some were asked to review sample sentences, answering with different

choice orders, and to count the Russian words that survived translation (for the significance of this, see questionnaire below)

Precautions Taken Against Bias and to Ensure Security of the Data

For any observer, especially one sceptical about MT or the FTD/MT system in particular, it is critical to be sure that none of the updatings were performed on the control text, for the "unplanned" improvement of the control-text (or carry-over effect) is at the very heart of the study. And while no methodology is foolproof, we believe that ours took all reasonable precautions against obvious sources of bias in its results, and against any criticisms that must inevitably arise about the security of the control text.

Test Selection

A keypuncher at LATSEC prepared a card for each document in the one-and-a-half million word Russian corpus. On each card was punched the number of one of the documents and a random number (these being taken from the standard library copy of a random number table, starting on the first page with the first number, and continuing in order from that page). The pack of cards prepared for all the documents in the corpus went to Teledyne Ryan who ran it through a standard program that sorts random numbers in ascending order. LATSEC then keypunched the Russian documents by taking their numbers from the ordered list provided by Teledyne Ryan (taking the document numbers in turn which corresponded one-to-one in that they are on the same card) to the random numbers, now in numerical sequence.

For security, the original card pack was then sent to FTD so that the whole procedure could be verified later with any standard sorting program. We believe this procedure gave a random selection of 150K Russian words by LATSEC, keypunching down the list until that total was reached (the first 75K becoming the object text so that translation and updating could start immediately, and the second 75K becoming the control text). While this method was perhaps overly detailed, it yielded a significant sample of the corpus by any normal statistical criteria, one which compared very well in terms of sample size with experiments referred to in other surveys.

Anonymity and Spread of Evaluators

The nine evaluators were marked on the totalized output by their code names only (Al, ... C3). They communicated directly with LATSEC, and their identities were not divulged to the project director. As previously noted, the evaluators were not only of three types, but were from three sites; six out of nine had no previous connection with LATSEC.

Order of A, B, C, D Choices and 1, 2, 3 Questions

To prevent the order of questions, and answer types within questions, influencing the evaluators (such as the suggestion that both translations might be too poor to assess their relationship), the evaluators at FTD answered the questions in the orders (2 1 3) (3 2 1) (3 2 1), while all other evaluators used orders (1 2 3); Essex evaluators further re-did a sample of their answers to the questions with the choices re-ordered as BCDA.

Order of Presentation of the English Translations

An obvious source of bias would have been the ordering of first-and second-run English translations in regular patterns, creating an order bias in quality assessment. To avoid such a bias, the two translations were presented in random order on the data sheets, and the input answers corrected for this by the totalizator program question by question.

Security of the Control Text

The first-run MT program was copied and sent to FTD so that it could be tested later to ensure that it was in fact the program that ran on the control text. More substantially, each sheet used by LATSEC in updating the object text (like all the originals, these were sent to FTD at the end of the project) was labelled by the text and sentence number that gave rise to update for later reference.

Finally, FTD was sent a copy of all the updates made during the project for incorporation into their system, so that they could run the following small scale check: taking a number of updates from the whole set, they traced back (via the hand-marked sheets and the texts) to ensure that they did indeed arise from a text in the object sample rather than the control text.

Results of the Study and Their Significance

Let us begin by asking the main question: has this procedure improved translation quality as judged by bilinguals?

Question 1: Fidelity of Translation as Judged by FTD and Non-FTD Bilinguals

Of 3,655 sentences analyzed by both FTD and non-FTD bilinguals, the standard application of confidence intervals around any of the percentages for responses A through D, shows them to be statistically significant, due to the large sample size of the texts (see the Appendix for the A, B, C, D codes). Using the orthodox formula for confidence intervals yielded a maximum error (at the 95% confidence level) of less than 2% either way for any of these categories. It was thus established that the technique did improve the translation, with an improvement rate of $47 \pm 2\%$.

The pattern and significance levels were the same for both FTD and non-FTD evaluators, with a large variance within both sets of results. The percentage of C codes given varied inside both teams by around 14%. The FTD team had a high of 53% improvement by one evaluator, while the non-FTD team went from 51% to 38% accuracy, a difference that cannot be accounted for by the varying difficulty of the text batches (the batch which for B2 improved by 38% caused A2 to find 47% improvement).

These differences of proportion (Z test = 5.89) are statistically significant at any known level. As the frequency of B code judgments also varied (though not as much), the most obvious measure of success (percentage improved minus percentage made worse) fluctuated considerably. The table below shows this:

Evaluator	C code%	B code%	Balance of improvement (= C–B%)
A1	53	11	42%
A2	47	10	37%
C3	41	6	35%
B1	45	7	38%
B2	38	15	23%
B3	51	13	38%

The average, it should be noted, was for a net improvement rate of 36%. We now turn to the Control Text results for the carry-over effect on question 1.

Once more, the basic table shows us the consistency between the aggregate results of the two teams, how the results demonstrated a statistically significant improvement, and that the A/D distinction was an unreliable one, although the combined A+D response categories were nearly constant between the two teams (a matter we shall return to below).

Non-FTD Team

Answer codes	A	B	C	D
%	44	10	29	17

Total sentences analyzed: 3,127

FTD Team

Answer codes	A	B	C	D
%	42	13	31	14

Total sentences analyzed: 3,127

(The margin of error for any of these percentages was again less than ± 2%.)

The fluctuation range was much the same over evaluators as before, though its net impact is less important. The table below gives the balance, and of course displays the range of fluctuation:

Evaluator	B code%	C code%	Balance of improvement (= C–B%)
A1	21	42	21%
A2	9	30	21%
C3	41	6	35%
B1	14	35	21%
B2	12	25	13%
B3	13	38	25%

Question 2: Intelligibility

The results may be summarized as follows:

	Object Text Codes				Control Text Codes			
Team	A	B	C	D	A	B	C	D
Non-FTD	32	8	46	14	37	9	31	23
FTD	27	11	51	11	21	18	44	17
Mono	10	13	48	29	12	11	28	50

These results generally confirm that for both O and C texts, there was a significant improvement in the second translation. For the O text, this should be assessed as 44%–53% improvement. (All C code percentages have a margin of error of no more than 2%.) Little attention should be paid to the monolingual value (especially where it differs in the C text), for the three monolinguals disagreed with each other sharply.

The overall result for the bilinguals can be seen by pooling the FTD and non-FTD teams as follows:

O Text = 6,304 judgments

A	B	C	D
29	10	50	11

C Text = 5,003 judgments

A	B	C	D
25	16	40	19

(All percentages accurate to ± 1%.)

This shows us an average improvement (C–B%) of 40% for the object text, and 24% for the control text, subject to the limits shown.

Question 3: Naturalness of the English

In some ways, these were the most interesting results, in that they clearly showed the difference between monolinguals and bilinguals. The table below gives the percentages for the two bilingual teams and the monolinguals separately:

	O Text				C Text			
	A	B	C	D	A	B	C	D
NoN FTD	61	4	22	13	65	5	18	12
FTD	71	5	20	4	88	3	7	2
C1	4	15	57	23	3	23	49	24
C2 mono's	3	16	59	23	9	18	46	27
A3	23	9	32	37	18	9	23	15

(All percentages in this table have a statistical margin of error of less than 5%.) Here we see that bilinguals were unprepared to treat the sentences as good enough to make judgments about them on this dimension, although they did judge there to be a significant improvement (20%). The monolinguals, on the other hand, found the judgment relatively easy to make, and found nearly 50% improvement for the O text, reduced to just under 40% for the C text (we shall return to this contrast later.)

To summarize the results in one great table: (see Appendix for the questions asked):

PROPORTION OF IMPROVEMENTS (i.e., column C responses, not improvement balance C–B)

	UPDATE (OBJECT) TEXT			CONTROL TEXT		
Group	Qu1	Qu2	Qu3	Qu1	Qu2	Qu3
Non-FTD	48%*	46%	22%*	29%*	31%	18%
	(3,655)	(3,655)	(3,655)	(3,127)	(3,127)	(3,127)
FTD	45%	51%	20%*	29%*	31%	18%
	(3,654)	(3,654)	(3,654)	(3,127)	(3,127)	(3,127)
Mono	–	48%	52%	–	28%	37%
	–	(2,645)	(2,645)	–	(1,876)	(1,876)
All	–	45%	30%	–	34%	21%
					(9,381)	(9,381)

(All these figures were subject to very small error margins (1.5–2.5%), and are statistically significant. The slots followed by an asterisk are those in which the FTD/non-FTD differences are insignificant.)

The Effect of Question and Choice Order

The complete results show us that inter-evaluator disagreement was high and that question order might have been one cause of this, since the FTD bilinguals answered not in order (1 2 3) but (2 1 3) (3 2 1) and (3 2 1), respectively. While question order as one possible cause of the variance cannot be ruled out, I do not believe it explains much of it. The table below demonstrates that there is no significant difference between improvement percentages among any of the orderings in question 1.

Group and ordering	Percent in each category			
	A	B	C	D
A1, A2 and C3 (1 2 3)	31	9	47	13
B1 (2 1 3)	41	7	45	7
B2 and 3 (3 2 1)	34	14	45	8

One might argue that the difference in question 3's results was dependent on ordering: those who answered it last (non-FTD and B1 at FTD) were less likely to find improvement (in only 18% of the cases), while B2 and 3 (at FTD), who answered it first, found a 28% improvement. But if we look further, we find that there was actually more disagreement within this order group (B2 = 19%, B3 = 33%) than between the two groups! And furthermore, A3 (non-FTD) found as high an improvement score (32%) as did B3 (FTD), while C3 (non-FTD) found an even higher one (38%).

To investigate the effect of choice order, the Essex (A) group re-did a large sample of their data sheets in the choice order B C D A. The average difference they found was around 4%: most likely an insignificant figure.

Evaluator Variance

As already noted, a striking feature of the results is the high level of evaluator variance. The standard deviation of the 24 individual judgments made by 9 evaluators on 3 questions (monolinguals did not answer the first question) is very high: 17.2% (19.4% for the control text) for the proportion deemed judgeable (the sum of B+C%). While this is unfortunate, it is compensated for by the much lower standard deviation for those judgments that were made, around 4.8–4.9%. In other words, we should attach little importance to the figures when a sentence translation pair (i.e. first run, second run) could not be judged as different, but considerable reliability to the 70–80% figure for improvement when a decision could be made. Thus while the average unjudgeable (A+D) proportion was 50% for O text and 60% for C text, the range within which the true figure lies is much greater, for the margin of error was +7%. But for the actual judgments, we can confidently state that the error range was less than 2%. This is reassuring because had the reverse result occurred (i.e. had the evaluations of improvement varied greatly in a subjective way), we would have cause to doubt our entire methodology of evaluation.

Further confirmation of our method came from examining correlations between evaluations of O and C texts. Reassuringly, the correlation coefficient over the 25 judgments made on each text is not significantly different from zero. On the other hand, the tendency to deem sentences unjudgeable was shown to arise from evaluators' individual differences in outlook; the correlation between each evaluator's unjudgeability evaluations for each question between O and C text was amazingly high (.913). As this clearly did not represent any actual link between such evaluation items (the texts having been drawn at random), the average level and the variance of these decisions should not concern us.

Shortcomings of the Present Study

After the completion of their task, the evaluators were invited to comment on the questionnaire and the entire study in which they had taken part. Their comments are distilled in the following discussion of a number of interconnected problems:

The A/D Choice

Even for the bilinguals, the distinction between codes A and D seemed unreliable (monolinguals had no way of expressing their preference for a D-choice sentence, as the bilinguals could by choosing A, for instance). The FTD team found 7% more sentences to be unjudgeable because of translation errors (choice A), and 7% fewer sentences undifferentiable (choice D). This pattern was further highlighted by the individual evaluator's distinctions: there was a high negative correlation (–O.715) between categories A and D. The ambiguity follows from the fact that the choices Code A (either i: both English sentences are so bad as translations that no choice can be made between them; or ii: both English sentences contain Russian words) or Code D (iii: no preference) are subjective. (ii) is an objective assessment, while (i) and (iii) are not mutually exclusive. Our assumption was that choice D applied to two equally acceptable translations, and choice A to two equally unacceptable translations, but, unfortunately, the evaluators appear not to have acted according to our assumption.

The basic error here was not a lack of strict definition for the categories (as some monolinguals felt), but asymmetry between mono and bilinguals. This may have contributed to the wide variance (and hence downgrading) of the monolinguals' evidence. To compensate for this effect, we simply combined choices A+D into an "unjudgeable" category, leaving us with three possibilities: worsened, improved and unjudgeable translations.

The "Question 3 Effect"

Certainly, the strong negative correlation between choices A and D cannot be explained away by a mistaken blurring of the two categories (as can be seen by the strikingly different A/D behavior of the monolinguals and bilinguals between questions 2 and 3). As we remarked earlier, in responding to question 3 the bilinguals simply declined to judge the naturalness of the English, and often took refuge in choice A, even though they were quite prepared to accept these same translations in question 2 on the basis of intelligibility (A choices for question 2 for the two bilingual groups were 37% and 21% versus 65% and 88% for question 3), while the monolinguals had no problem making the choice, a fact that confirms the value of monolingual judgements.

C. The Original Sampling of O and C Texts

Our process standardized the total number of words in the documents, but not the number of documents in each sample. Thus, if document length varied greatly, word samples drawn from a smaller number of long texts would be chosen alongside word samples drawn from a large number of short texts, which creates a problem if there is in fact a relationship between the length of a text and the nature of its language. By making the documents sampled units, a random selection could have represented them proportionately to the frequency with which different text lengths co-occurred in the corpus. But happily, no such problem arose.

The "Russian Word Problem"

Part of the A choices refer to the presence of (untranslated) Russian words in the output but, as we saw with B1, an evaluator may be tempted to interpret this loosely (considering the word's meaning obvious, or unimportant), or deeming it a Cyrillic misspelling not a Russian word. On the other hand, some monolinguals can guess the meaning of a Russian word, especially if it is close to the Latin spelling, as in N'YUSDEY ("Newsday" in 78054/177). Furthermore, the questionnaire forces the monolingual to choose the sentence without Russian words as more natural English. Finally, there were many sentences where the program translated a proper name into English, also creating confusion in the mind of the monolinguals, who might well believe that (wholly) English sentence contain Russian words.

In summary, what it meant for a sentence to contain a Russian word was not made totally clear, presenting a genuine difficulty for clarity. Since less than 10% of the sentences contained Russian words, this had a negligible effect on our results. In future tests, the problem could be avoided by removing untranslated items in the sentences from the date seen by the evaluators.

Monolingual Expertise

It is generally accepted that the value of monolingual evaluation in scientific subjects depends on monolingual subject expertise. While our monolingual evaluators all had some expertise in the field of political science, this simply did not transfer from

Russian to English in the way that a universally understood area like physics would. To some degree, this explains the high variance among the monolinguals, and their consequently diminished role compared to the (BR) study of scientific texts.

Conclusion: Summary of Findings

1. While the Battelle Report was poorly argued and statistically flawed, it provided us with the methodological basis for a new study.
2. The most significant finding was the 20% carry-over effect from updated to control text (balance of improvement: 30% of sentences improved minus 10% worsened) in a very different subject area from the one for which the system was originally developed.
3. There was a very high variance among evaluators, especially monolinguals. This was reduced to a significant result by distinguishing between sentences deemed judgeable and, of those judgeable, taking those deemed improved. While variance as to what was judgeable remained high, in the vital category of which judgeables were improved, variance was minimal: a strong, indirect confirmation of our methodology.
4. Since the question of naturalness of English output produced an odd response in the bilinguals, it is better ignored, especially since this notion is of little importance to the ultimate monolingual user, in any case.

Appendix: Notes For Evaluators

IT IS MOST IMPORTANT THAT YOU STUDY THESE NOTES AND THE QUESTIONNAIRE BEFORE READING THE DATA.

In the body of the data you will find sets of three items: a Russian sentence followed by two English sentences. IF YOU DO NOT KNOW ANY RUSSIAN, you should simply ignore the former, and concentrate on the latter. The English sentences which contain items that are not really in English (those that contain numbers, for instance) are easily spotted, and will be referred to in the questions as Russian words, even though they are written mostly in the English alphabet.

When looking at the English sentences you should ignore all questions of stylistic nicety, such as differences between British and American English, and think only in terms of what is natural English for you.

When looking at both the Russian and the English, you should be careful not to assume that the sets of sentences form coherent, continuous texts; rather, you should treat each triplet individually. Also, do not assume that the second English sentence is better than the first: the order of the sentence pairs is entirely random.

The difference between "understandable" and "natural" can be illustrated as follows: the sentences *To John gave I the apple* and *I want you go now* are both understandable, but not natural English.

QUESTIONNAIRE

Each line on the form corresponds to one sentence triplet (one Russian and two English) by number. Each numbered section below corresponds to a column on the answer form. You should circle one and only one letter (A, B, C, or D) for each question and then do that for each sentence triplet in the data.

1. (enter in column 1 for each triplet)
   Look at the set of three sentences and consider (if you can) whether the English sentences are accurate translations of the Russian one.
   Circle
   . A
   if you do not speak Russian, OR if you speak Russian and consider both English sentences to be such bad translations that no choice can be made between them, OR if you speak Russian and can see that BOTH English sentences contain Russian words.
   . B
   if you prefer the first sentence as an accurate translation
   . C
   if you prefer the second sentence
   . D
   if you have no preference

2. (enter in column 2 for each triplet)
   Now look at only the English sentences in the triplet, and ask yourself if you can comprehend them as such, accounting for your knowledge of the subject matter.
   Circle
   . A
   if you speak Russian, but consider both texts to be such bad translations that you decline to form a judgement, OR if both English sentences contain Russian words. (This option is available to non-Russian speakers, as well.)
   . B
   if you prefer the first sentence for its understandability
   . C
   if you prefer the second sentence
   . D
   if you have no preference

3. (enter in column 3 for each triplet)
   Consider the English sentences alone once more, and judge their naturalness of language (word order, word choice, and so forth).
   Circle
   . A
   if you speak Russian and consider both sentences such bad translations of the Russian that you decline to make this judgment, OR if both English sentences

contain Russian words (once again, you can select this if you do not speak Russian, but should NOT do so if only one of the English sentences contains Russian words)

. B

if you prefer the first sentence for naturalness of its English

. C

if you prefer the second sentence

. D

if you have no preference

Afterword on MT Evaluation

I have found myself arguing for years, only semi-facetiously, that the evaluation of MT is more developed than MT itself. The point of this remark is to bring home that there were, and are, many radically different theories of MT but, given an MT system, and a substantial quantity of output from it, by whatever method it was produced, there is a range of pretty well established techniques with which to evaluate it. Since radical disagreement on method is often a measure of the scientific immaturity of a field, the original comment about MT and its evaluation follows. MT is the oldest part of natural language processing (NLP), and one which still has strong commercial implications; it reaches back to the common history of AI and NLP, when Prolog was developed (by Colmerauer) in France to do MT, a fact very few AI researchers are aware of. Constant evaluation, often in hostile situations, sometimes following upon excessively optimistic proposals and funding, has been integral to its progress and credibility. But the recent dominance of NLP by issues related to evaluation has a different and more recent source. It dates from the major DARPA programs of the 1980s: speech recognition (including ATIS), information retrieval (TREC), message understanding (alias Information Extraction or IE: and the evaluations known as (MUCK, MUC and TIPSTER), and in the 1990s, MT itself again. There have been related, unofficial, competitive evaluations for part of speech tagging, PARSEVAL (for syntactic parsing) and most recently, since 1998, SENSEVAL for word-sense tagging of text words. These programs have made substantial use of machine learning techniques, based on a markup-train-model- test paradigm, and, although the DARPA competitions have been essentially open to all comers, DARPA recipients have understood that entry in the relevant competition was expected.

Some of the evaluations involved domain-based tasks, plausibly close to those in the real world (e.g. the DARPA ATIS task for speech recognition within a full airline reservation domain, with associated dialogue and knowledge bases). Others, like syntactic parsing, were evaluations of isolated NLP modules, about whose ultimate usefulness there was no general agreement: many of the MUC Information Extraction systems did not have a linguistic parsing module at all but worked with a general form of pattern recognition over surface language forms. Within some evaluation regimes, the DARPA slogan of "Don't worry about your initial figures, just benchmark and improve from there" produced some absurd situations, where evaluation deadlines were set at or near the start of a contract, which encouraged researchers to cobble together any random system at all at the start so as to meet such deadlines. It was not always possible to get off the evaluation treadmill later and design or restructure the original ad hoc assembly; it was just optimized upwards and some were amazed how far it sometimes went. But there was a general feeling around that this was not the way to get a well-designed well-motivated state of the art system.

Proponents of that way of doing research, wholly driven by evaluations (and they were often the US funders themselves), assumed that this method had worked well for speech and must therefore work for NLP; only this methodology, many assumed, would drag NLP away from the toy systems with tiny vocabularies that were believed to be the bad part of its inheritance from AI. This development regime also produced very fragile systems, due in part to classic inbreeding of systems, and encouraged by the very good DARPA requirement that all tools and resources developed should be shared among competing groups. This made it hard, and for a different reason, to redesign or rethink a system for any task; another evaluation was always coming and the differences between methods, tools, and resources available to the competing groups were very small.

It was this overall situation that was almost certainly to the explanation of the successes of non – American groups entering the competitions for the first time: the ENTROPIC speech system from Cambridge, England, and the fact that two of the five tasks in MUC7 were won by British groups. They were, in effect, exogamic entrants to an inbred tribe: a situation that often gives short-term advantage. All this must been seen against a background of extraordinary improvement in performance at a range of NLP tasks over the last decade: some of them real, objective, tasks like MT and IE, and some only defined linguistically, like parsing and part-of-speech and sense tagging. It was this scenario that caused the non-DARPA part of the NLP universe, especially the European Commission, to become hostile to all organised NLP evaluation; they saw only the duplication of effort and funding, and failed to see the gains and the weeding out of poor research. There is something in such implied criticism, well known within the DARPA community as well, but it fails too to discern the cooperation in the US system, behind the overt competition, especially over resources and tools, and between not only academic researchers but companies as well.

In the European Commission's Fifth and Sixth Framework research programs, there was a slightly stronger and more prominent role to NLP evaluations, and just at the moment when DARPA's love of it was weakening a little. Much of difference between the attitudes of the two continental systems towards evaluation can be explained in terms of the EC's commitment to industry-directed research, versus the US model of the Department of Defense as the main consumer of paid NLP contract work, even though, of course, the US also has far more industry-based NLP as well. Inevitably, an industry-directed program cannot make evaluation central, since it is, in principle the market that decides all evaluation issues, so how could industrial users agree on a common domain, tools, resources etc. with which the general evaluation would run? Only a single consumer like the US Department of Defense, one for whom immediate application is not crucial, could do that. Given the absolute centrality of the evaluation paradigm in the NLP of the last decade, it is surprising how little of the general literature has been devoted to it.

Little has been written, within a general analytical scheme, about MT evaluation since the classic text by Lehrberger & Bourbeau (1988). Since then, Sparck Jones and Galliers' (1996, and SJG from now on) is almost certainly the first and only book to try to bring together NLP evaluation schemes, methods and issues as a whole, as opposed to evaluations within one NLP area, or system type, such as MT.

SJG put strong emphasis on what they call the "setup" (an unfortunately ambiguous choice for a key term, perhaps) that combines an NLP system and its setting or user-determined environment and application. I doubt they are wholehearted about the centrality of setups, because they also give a great deal of space and discussion to the ideas of those on the theory-expert side, e.g. those in the EAGLES evaluation group in Europe who are argue strongly for "glass box" evaluations (where you can see how your own theoretical structures are doing in a system evaluation) as opposed to those who prefer black boxes (where only the final output, such as a translation, counts, no matter how it was obtained, which is very close to what I take a setup to be). I will return to this in a moment; it is an issue which I consider to be close to an "anti-evaluation" theme found in some researchers, and I will discuss how SJG deal with it.

Vexed issues like test-suites in MT evaluation are not really discussed in SJG, only described: this is the notion, much favored by the EAGLES group in the EU, that evaluation should not be done using real corpora but rather sets of sentences (the test suites) written and chosen to display particular syntactic structures. This is a position very close to that favoring glass-box evaluations: it is again theory-driven and derives, I believe, from the EUROTRA disaster, the largest MT experiment ever, which cost $75 million in the 1980s, and with no discernible results. Among its bad has been an anti-evaluation culture that that has prized theoretical advance in MT itself and seeks evaluation methods that detect conformity to theory (through glass, as it were) rather than seeking real experimental results. Test suites continue this tradition directly, and it is rarely if ever asked whether test suite sentence types occur with serious frequency is actual texts.

Another example of issues not being central for SJG would be when they discuss an experiment by the present author to evaluate the US MT system SYSTRAN (see the earlier part of this chapter above): they have a generous discussion (pp. 79–80) in which they mention the methodological assumption, made there and elsewhere, that since fidelity of translation (i.e. accuracy) correlates highly with intelligibility (i.e. the output prose quality), then one can use the latter to measure the former and MT could be assessed by monolinguals, people knowing only the output language and not the language the translation came from. But this, if true, is a bizarre fact and leads to an interesting methodology of MT evaluation, quite different from anything else. But it is only mentioned in passing and no analysis or discussion is given. In their discussion of later ARPA MT evaluations (p.81) there is again only mention and no analysis of the vexed and contentious issue of whether you can assess MT systems and machine-aided human translation systems in the same competition as ARPA did.

SJG makes use of an analytic device in evaluation that is original but I think misleading for MT. Karen Sparck Jones has had a separate and distinguished career in Information Retrieval (IR), an area whose relevance to NLP is disputed but which has undoubtedly had firm evaluation methodologies for many years. SJG, and this must surely be Sparck Jones herself, present an early subchapter "The Information Retrieval Experience" (2.2 pp.20ff.) which contains useful material but has the effect of slanting the book towards a comparison with, and influence from, IR in NLP evaluation. There is something to be said for this, since IR evaluation is well established and its key measures, particularly precision and recall, also have application in areas of NLP, like IE, that attempt by linguistic methods to extract the relevant from the irrelevant, while delivering as a little of the latter as possible.

But there are two drawbacks to this device: first, although much of the recent impetus in NLP towards evaluation has come from speech research in the US, there is an older tradition of evaluation, namely that of MT, as I noted at the beginning of this chapter. That methodology is as established and well founded as that of IR but, as I again noted at various points, suffers a lack of focus and discussion booking SJG which may be due to the prominence given to the relationship of NLP to IR. The modern link of NLP to IR is, in my view, not through evaluation at all, but through seeing IR and IE as a pair of close and intertwined information access techniques. Anyone reading current NLP papers with their obligatory self-evaluation will often see uses of precision and recall measures in inappropriate places. One use is as a measure of the performance of machine learning algorithms, used in an NLP application, such as automatic word-sense tagging. The problem with this usage is that, from those two parameters, one cannot calculate the only one that really matters, namely the proportion of text words, or content words, or multi-sensed words, correctly sense tagged.

This measure is derived from the MT tradition of the proportion of text sentences correctly translated. Wider use of the classic IR measures in NLP areas other than IE has led to a situation where it is increasingly hard to understand the meaning of results. To take a case at random, some researchers in, say, word-sense tagging will quote results as: precision = correctly sense tagged words/words attempted to be tagged and recall = correctly tagged words/all ambiguous words present in the text often normalized to a percentage in each case. One could argue that this is a pernicious influence of IR on NLP methodology, since precision and recall have no application within a task like this that has no analogue to the prior division of an IR space into the relevant and irrelevant. IE has this required property, but virtually no other NLP task does: in the case of word-sense tagging there is no space of irrelevant but ambiguous words retrieved in error. For most purposes, recall, as defined above, measures correctness, and those that are not recalled are not the relevant-but-missed (as in IR) but simply those that are retrievable but not solved.

Anyone puzzled should try to draw the standard Euler diagrams used to illustrate the basic IR use of the terms and see that they cannot easily be reinterpreted for the NLP case (outside the special case of IE). The real motive behind this odd use is,

I think, to justify selecting small samples from texts, such as a handful of word types to be sense resolved and, for those who think one should perform a task on all the words of a text or none, this is a bad argument supported by misleading measures. No one, for example, uses precision and recall in part-of-speech tagging where there is no question of just sampling the words. This discussion of evaluation in MT has not been intended as a full coverage of the contemporary situation in MT, but as comments on developments of what one might call classic MT evaluation methods, since those I tried on SYSTRAN in a neo-classic experiment discussed in the body of this chapter., The only real innovation in MT evaluation in recent years, and since SJG wrote the standard book I discussed above, has been the "bleu" algorithm. This I shall discuss at the end of the book as a part of the contemporary MT scene.

Part II
MT Present

Chapter 5
Where Am I Coming From: The Reversibility of Analysis and Generation in Natural Language Processing

Introduction

The two general issues discussed in this chapter are:

1. the symmetry (or otherwise) of analysis and generation in natural language processing, and
2. from what structure should generation come?

These related questions are contained within the well-known fable Wittgenstein tells in his *Remarks on the Foundations of Mathematics* (1956), where he imagines entering a room in which a very old man is counting "...5, 4, 3, 2, 1, 0...whew!" Asked why he is so exhausted, the old man responds that he has just finished counting down the natural numbers from infinity. The question implied is why this story seems more absurd to us than a symmetrical story of someone starting off from zero upwards, since the two tasks are essentially the same?

Although both tasks are impossible, we can in this case spot the difference fairly quickly whereas, in the case of analysis and generation, the situation is hardly the same. Both these tasks are possible (we are all existence proofs of that) and we think we have a much clearer idea of what the starting representation is than in the number case. Moreover, few researchers think those two tasks are as asymmetrically reversible as in the fable.

There has been a revival of interest in the reversibility issue in recent years (see, for example, Landsbergen, 1987; Jacobs, 1988; Appelt, 1989; Russell et al. 1990; Dymetman and Isabelle, 1990; Neumann and van Noord, 1993; and well as Strzalkowski's edited book, see Neumann and van Noord above) but the roots are much further back. The original sources of symmetry and asymmetry in computational linguistics (CL) seem to be: (a) fallacious Chomskyan arguments and (b) the long-standing tendency in CL to trivialize generation in a way that was impossible for analysis. Winograd's SHRDLU (1972) is a paradigm of the latter, as of so many other trends, with his heavy-weight, knowledge-based analysis, followed by a fairly trivial word-in-slot-pattern-based generation. It is hard to imagine how this trivialization could have been done the other way around. I believe this very simple fact has been a powerful (if implicit) argument for the asymmetry of the tasks, as well as for the systematic down-grading of generation as a CL enterprise.

On the other hand, Chomsky's original transformational-generative (TG) grammar project (1957) served as an explicit argument for symmetry, though in a way that gave no comfort to any position in CL. The reason for this was that Chomsky always insisted that no procedural interpretation could be imposed on the operation of a TG: that it bound sentence strings to underlying representations statically, in much the same way that a function binds arguments to values without any assumptions about their direction. Functionality was Chomsky's own metaphor and it turned out to be, of course, incorrect.

Sentence strings and "underlying representations" may have a relationship that can be technically expressed as a relation, but it cannot be a function for the same reason that SQUARE-ROOT cannot, namely, that an argument like 4 is bound by the relation to the two values [plus and minus 2] and a function (as every child knows) can yield only a single value. The relationship between underlying representation and surface string is one-to-many in both directions (to speak in the way Chomsky wished to eradicate) and so cannot be functional unless one credits success to the efforts that Ross and others made twenty years ago to constrain or reinterpret transformations so that that relationship was more or less one to one. Another such attempt was that of Lakoff (1970), who tried to reinterpret the relation of "generation" (in the procedural, non-Chomskyan, sense of "down-the-page-towards-the-sentence-string") as one of deduction. That effort guaranteed asymmetry in an even stronger way than Lakoff could have needed in order to make a firm break with Chomsky's, views, since implication/deduction, whatever they are, are certainly not symmetrical. Had Lakoff been correct, no analysis could ever have been performed on Generative Semantics principles (which is to say, in the reverse direction from string to representation). Even the current vogue for abductive notions could not alter that fact.

Much of this debate is long dead, however, because it became clear that Chomsky's position (i.e. that generation was non-directional and did not necessitate sentence synthesis) was motivated by antipathy toward computation and processes, which most linguists of today do not share. Also, the revival of phrase structure grammar methods during the last decade has made the questions of how TG's were best described, and whether or not they could be reversed to do analysis, a matter of less pressing interest.

Nevertheless, I believe that, historically speaking, Chomsky's insistence on the importance of abstract symmetry, taken together with the fact that real TG's at the time were in fact, and plainly, asymmetrical and directional, were powerful motivations for the resurgence of interest in phrase-structure grammars (PSG's). With the return of PSG's came abstract non-directional syntactic specification and well-known algorithms for running them either way (e.g. Kay, 1984).

Then followed the arbitrarily arranged, yet fecund, marriage between revived PSG's and what one might call the "prolog movement". This dynamic duo held out the promise of abstract, declarative, symmetry between analysis and generation from the same grammar, as well as the possibility of real reversible processes, what one might call "running the prolog code backwards", i.e. either:

Provide The String To The Top-Level Predicate And Get The Structure
or
Provide The Structure And The Predicate Provides Its Own Argument, The Initial String.

This could not be a functional relationship for the same reasons as before, but it promised real magic and true symmetry between analysis and generation. Before very briefly posing the question, "was the magic real or mere sleight of hand?" let us pause in order to demonstrate why arriving at this point was significant by itself.

First of all, any demonstration of this symmetry helped the case of those who were actually interested in natural language generation. In other words, if the processes of analysis and generation were symmetrical or even identical, then generation would be as "interesting" as analysis (whatever that means), no matter how much greater the weight of research traditionally devoted to language analysis.

None of those considerations were relevant to those committed to natural language generation, but, from the point of view of the CL field as a whole, the recent growth of interest in generation needs some explanation. Let me put it this way: it needs explanation unless you believe that CL and AI are mainly driven by considerations of fashion. At least, it needs more of an explanation than one given by a distinguished colleague who wrote last year that since "the problems of analysis are settled, the outstanding issues are now in generation". Since the assumption is false, this cannot serve as an explanation, however true its conclusion.

Let us now return to the prolog-PSG marriage, and ask whether it has yielded any real symmetry of processes (alias "reversible prolog code"). This question is not as straightforward as it appears to some. For instance, at NMSU-CRL, we built a multilingual machine translation program called TRA (Farwell and Wilks, 1990) and, for the five languages it deals with (Chinese, Japanese, German, Spanish and English), we say we have "reversible code", meaning that by judicious predicate arrangement and avoidance of cuts, etc., the system is able to run a single chunk of prolog code for the analysis and generation of each language.

Moreover, our claim is not trivial, in that there is in fact a single set of syntactic rules for each language which can be used for both analysis and generation. In other words, the top level predicate does not simply hide a disjunction of two programs.

Nevertheless, the claim is still "cheap reversibility" insofar as it is only behavioral, specifying the minimum behavior required by the top-level predicate. There is certainly no claim that exactly the same set of predicates is evaluated in reverse order during analysis and generation of the same sentence, which would probably be impossible to achieve (even though the highest level sub-predicates in ULTRA do obey that reverse order condition). I mention this only to pose the more serious question: supposing one can have a certain amount of reversibility like that (and hence symmetry in the sense we started with), why should one want it, what benefit does it bring and what independent arguments are there in support of it?

To say it has been a long-held human dream, like going to the Moon or climbing Mt. Everest, is an insufficient explanation and says no more than that we do it to prove that we can.

Arguments for and against Symmetry

I think the abstract arguments for symmetry are:

1. the (half-forgotten) "abstract symmetry" argument inherited from Chomsky which I already mentioned;
2. a simple-minded use of Occam's razor, which forbids multiplying entities beyond necessity (although he said nothing about processes or modules or grammars).

Against the case for symmetry of generation and analysis are the following considerations:

3. that independent modules should be separated wherever possible. I know of no serious evidence for this, as an abstract matter, as opposed to programming practice, or some vague reference to Simon's (1969), "decomposability" notions for robustness or Jacobs' (1988) wish that modules should "use as much shared knowledge as possible". This was also the sort of argument some transformationalists used in support of keeping syntax and semantics as separate modules, although the very same argument told against their own desire to hold analysis and generation together under a single description;
4. the psycholinguistic evidence suggests that analysis and generation are separate cognitive processes. One cannot get a single view on this from the literature, but we all know common-sense versions of it, such as the skills of a dialect speaker who can analyze standard English, but hardly generate any. "Passive vs. active competence" is a well-attested notion in the field of language education and implies strictly separate cognitive skills.

Again, it seems obvious to many researchers that the choices required in analysis, which are largely of structural and lexical ambiguity, cannot be the same as the choices presented during generation because the latter are not mandatory. A good (if tired) example is a sentence containing the word "bank", where the hearer has to decide, consciously or unconsciously, which meaning is intended. It is usually assumed that it is not necessary to do that in order to use (generate) the word "bank" appropriately in a sentence. I shall return to this later, but for now the traditional symmetry argument seems less persuasive after examination and the fact that some non-trivial reversibility of code, such as that one described above, is possible, tells against it.

Considerations of style, at the lowest level of choice, namely word paradigms, are similarly relevant. Consider the following:

- *Roast fish (vs. meat)
- *Rancid meat (vs. fats and oils)

These are pretty clear phenomena for native speakers of English (what I would call "word preferences") but ones whose violation does not impede their comprehensibility in the least.

In the "roast fish" case, one could re-express the asymmetry argument as follows: we understand it without difficulty but most would not choose to generate it, preferring to say "baked or broiled fish" instead.

Do the analysis and generaction activities for this phrase result from the same static information (what I am calling the word-preference of "roast")? It seems so. Are they done by the same processes in reverse? On the face of it, it seems they are not, because only analysis goes through the process of noting that "roasting" requires "meat" to follow it and that "fish" does not satisfy that requirement, though it has access to enough relevant properties of fish to allow the creation of a combination meaning.

But if speaking a language is to utter new and creative metaphors all the time as many researchers assert, then we can also presume that a language generator must have access to the inverse of that very same process, since many metaphors have exactly the form of "roast fish", e.g. "rubber duck". If so, another apparent argument for asymmetry weakens in front of our very eyes. Nothing I am saying here calls into question the large-scale textual demonstrations by Church et al. (1989), and others which show how such references are frequently violated in real text. These conventions are not overthrown by distribution any more than the standard generation of metaphors in the sentences of actual speakers overthrows the type-preferences they "violate".

Nothing said here *proves* that the same procedures are accessed in both direct directions. But the same issues arise in connection with plans as well as word-preferences. Jacobs (1990) has used considerations similar to these to argue that plans are not used in language generation, as many have believed when they assumed that a speaker first decides what to say and then plans how to do it. He uses examples like "He answered he door", which is understood in preference violation terms as we described earlier (though Jacobs would probably not use quite that language), but which, he argues, is hard to explain in generation-as-planning terms, since it is hard to see why any planner would choose to generate that form at the word level. Jacobs position is (like the final position of the present paper) basically a symmetricist one, which sees no strong need for plans in either process.

Finally, we might look for further evidence for asymmetry by asking the question: is a "connectionist-based generation system" a contradiction in terms? Perhaps it should be, if it means training a system by feeding it hand-crafted sentence-pairs and representational structures. A connectionist system would lend credence to the symmetry case only if a single network could function for both purposes, but can that actually be done? One can imagine a network that yields strings for structures as well as structures for strings, but there remains a problem of how one would describe such training. Simmons and Yu (1990) reported a connectionist yet symmetrical system, though it is not yet clear (to this author) whether or not it is of this form.

Is Semantic Parsing (SP) an Argument for Asymmetry?

Semantic parsing, you may recall, is a method claiming that text can be parsed to an appropriate representation without the use of an explicit and separate syntactic component. It was normally assumed (by Schank 1975 and others) that generation from a representation, however obtained, required the use of syntactical rules to generate the correct forms, even though a principal feature of SP was its claim to be the most appropriate method for analyzing (ubiquitous) ill-formed input without such rules. SP became reformed sinner when it came to generation. But is that assumption correct? Can we be sure that the so-called "arbitrary" choices made in generation are more or less arbitrary than those made in analysis?

Consider the following argument which demonstrates that the processes must be more or less symmetrical even for SP:

John loves Mary

In this (all-time favorite) example it can be argued that determining the identity of the agent and the patient is the same process for both analysis and generation. This argument is quite separate from an earlier one I made about lexical and structural ambiguity. Indeed, the present argument turns out to be none other than the traditional anti-SP argument that says that, if any system is able to distinguish the left-right order of symbols in a string, then the system has a syntax component. This argument is right about syntax only in Tarski's sense of abstract symbols, but not in the sense of a set of linguistics-style rules. SP proponents considered left-right order to be their own linguistic province as much as anyone else's.

The counter-examples to the "John loves Mary" argument for symmetry were other favorites like:

Economics, I like
Over the wall came a sturdy youth

In these examples, word order is less important to the interpretation than the fitting of entities to the preferences for the verbs. The first example would have the same meaning even if English did not the mark the nominative case of the personal pronoun. By the same token, the reason you cannot make

John loves Mary
Or
Man eats chicken

mean their order inverses is not their syntax so much as the particular argument symmetry of these verbs, (so that the inverses "make perfect sense") which cannot be said of "like" and "come".

Now, SP might yield the symmetry of generation and analysis if a generation system based on coherence and best-fit slot filling were possible. In fact, on one occasion I designed a generation system for French (the Stanford MT project, see Chapter 3 above), that did have just that form. An SP (a preference semantics analysis of English) produced a "maximally coherent" structure of semantic objects from which a complex of corresponding French objects was produced. This was then "unwrapped" in such a way as to discard much of its content while separating out the most coherent subset that could be in a one-to-one relationship with a well-formed string of French words. On reconsidering that work, I realized that SP does not necessarily lead to a position in favor of asymmetry, as I had previously assumed. At that time, I argued that the structure at the intermediate representation level (in which French information replaced English) could itself be interpreted as a structure of gists, or messages, that the original conveyed. But nothing in the process, including whether the French output was an adequate equivalent of the English input, depended on that interpretation. Indeed, one could argue that a symmetrical SP (an SP followed by an inverted-SP generation) is compatible with a case in which there is no interpretable content at all.

This is the crucial point that brings us back to the second aspect of Wittgenstein's story mentioned earlier. As we can see, what matters there is not the directionality of the counting, but our inability to imagine where the counting began. Classic natural language generation, on the other hand, starts from a structure which is simultaneously arbitrary and interpretable.

A traditional linguistics approach that utilizes a logical predicate structure as an underlying representation is closest to that ideal, while a connectionist system, where the lack of any internal representation is a virtue, is at the other extreme. The symmetrical SP I have described falls somewhere in the middle and could, in fact, go either way.

There has been much continued scepticism about such an interpretable intermediate representation both in AI and in philosophical thought related to it. Dennett, for example (1978), has remained sceptical about it. His original metaphor for language generation was that of a President's public relations officer who hands his leader a statement which is simply read aloud. Such a President may have no message he wants to convey; rather, he will simply say what "comes" to him.

A more succinct version is E.M. Forster's famous quip: "How do I know what I mean till I see what I say?" This takes the argument a step further and effectively concedes primacy to generation in the process of understanding. The philosopher and novelist both want to deny that there is any other code to be understood apart from (generated) natural language.

One can then raise the objection, what difference can all this scepticism about cognitive representations and our access to them possibly make? After all, AI is an abductive science and has never been deterred by any such lack of access to "human cognitive representations": normally it just invents such structures.

Nevertheless, one can retain a degree of healthy scepticism about them not only on the basis of lack of access, but rather on the logical nature of the structures classically proferred. Suppose that one felt sceptical about any internal representation (i.e. a message that represented what we "want to say" and from which we are able to generate) that was not in a real, natural, language. Dennett's public relations example is consistent with this point of view, although it is not normally used in support of it.

This supposition is also a form of Fodor's Language of Thought (LOT) hypothesis (1976), if the latter could be considered a natural language (NL) at all. Fodor has always been coy about revealing what exactly properties LOT may share with NL, though much of his writing implicitly claims that LOT is, in fact, a natural language (one which falls within a class defined by the parameters of Chomsky's Universal Grammar) that we simply do not have access to right now. It is obvious that, if the LOT hypothesis is true, then generation is, quite literally, a form of translation, albeit from a language we are unfamiliar with. An LOT could in principle be Italian or Aymara.

This is an important subject in itself but, in conclusion, I would argue that all this suggests that generation is not an independent computational subject like machine translation. In the latter case, one has true access to what one wants to say (the source language) and a firm sense of direction: one is familiar with both the source and target languages and the direction in which one is headed. Generation may then turn out to be a set of techniques that cannot be separated from a greater whole. But the same would hold true of analysis (as a separate subject) if we accept the earlier conclusion that the processes are fundamentally symmetrical. Yet everyone retains some nostalgia for asymmetry, certain that heading to some unknown destination is less disconcerting than coming from it.

The attempts I have made here to demonstrate that the two processes, of analysis and generation, are asymmetrical (as I would have wanted on my initial, unexamined, SP assumptions) have failed, and therefore to the credit of generation as an intellectual task, even if not an independent one.

Chapter 6
What are Interlinguas for MT: Natural Languages, Logics or Arbitrary Notations?

What are interlinguas, and does the answer have any practical effect on the usefulness, success, or otherwise of interlingual MT, a paradigm that still has life left in it, and some practical and commercial successes, certainly in Japan, with, for example the commercial Fujitsu system.. In this brief chapter, I will focus what I have to stay on the interlingual representation language, as you might expect to find it in an MT system – normally some pidginised version of English with a counterintuitive syntax – but what I have to say applies more generally to symbolic knowledge representations, including those applied to MT (e.g. KBMT: Knowledge Based MT) and those in the mainstream AI tradition.

If we take the view that these can be arbitrary notations then many more systems come within the class of interlingual machine translation systems than would normally be thought the case: certainly SYSTRAN in its earlier periods (before the point at which it was declared a transfer system) had the results of a source language analysis stored in a complex system of register codes and, most importantly, this was done for more than one source language; thus the storage codings, which were largely arbitrary in conventional linguistic terms and certainly without comprehensible/readable predicates, had a degree of linguistic "neutrality" that is thought to be part of what is meant by an interlingua. This is an important point, given that SYSTRAN, before its recoding as a transfer system, was always thought of as a "direct" system; but an interlingual MT system is also in that sense direct, the only difference being whether or not the intermediate coding is shared by language pairs.

Taken more strictly, SYSTRAN was not an interlingual system because its power came largely from its bilingual dictionaries, and, as a matter of definition, a bilingual dictionary is language-pair dependent, and therefore a transfer, device. At that level of strictness, there have been very few truly interlingual MT systems, (i.e. without a bilingual dictionary). Probably the only historical candidate is Schank's MARGIE system of 1972, which did some English-German MT via a conceptual dependency (CD) representation. Schank's CD representation is also much closer to the normal view of an interlingual representation, having a range of English-like predicates (TRANS being the best remembered) within a specified syntax and, in his case, a diagrammatic notation.

My own small English-French MT system (see chapter 3 above), contemporary with Schank's and produced in the same AI laboratory at Stanford, was therefore not interlingual, even though our representations had much in common. I always believed a bilingual dictionary essential, and that the interlingual representation and its associated algorithms selected the correct equivalent from among a set of candidates the lexicon provided. Schank denied that any such crypto-transfer mapping as a bilingual dictionary was needed, but only the source-to-interlingua and interlingua-to-target translators. It was Charniak who later supplied arguments that no level of coding at such a grain, and without a prior bilingual dictionary to constrain choices, could be expected to distinguish among English output forms such as sweat, sneeze, dribble, spit, perspire, as well as a range of less attractive possibilities associated with the Schankian primitive EXPEL, taken along with a coding for LIQUID. All those English verbs could plausibly be generated by an interlingual coding expressing "expelling a liquid through a body aperture", so only a prior bilingual dictionary offering related choices, could constrain that.

The issue of grain here was obviously a function of the richness of the interlingual vocabulary (Schank then had about 14 primitive actions and I about 100 primitives of different syntactic types). If the interlingua had had the full resources of some natural language, then those distinctions could have been made, which of course focuses exactly the question of what it would mean for an interlingua to have the resources of a natural language, as opposed to being a formal language with primitives that may appear to be language-like, as Schank's certainly did, but which their authors (including Schank) deny are language items at all, let alone English words.

That position of denial is to be found not only in the 1970s: Schank's position is essentially that of Mahesh and Nirenburg (1995), when supporting Mikrokosmos as a "language-neutral body of knowledge about the world", in contrast to the "recurring trend in the writings of scholars in the AI tradition toward erasing the boundaries between ontologies and taxonomies of natural language concepts".

This dispute can take unhelpful forms such as "Your codings look like natural language to me" followed by "No they don't". Moreover, it is not clear that any settlement of this issue, for either side, would have effect whatever on the performance or plausibility of interlingual MT systems. One can also filter out more full blooded versions of the NL-IL (natural language vs. intermediate language) identity, such as the Dutch MT system based on Esperanto (an NL for the purposes of this argument) and the reported systems based on the South American language Aymara, said to be without lexical ambiguity (see below) and therefore ideal for this role. These cases, whether or not they work in practice, fall under the criticism of Bar-Hillel in the earliest discussions of interlingual MT: that having an NL in the interlingual role would simply double the work to no benefit by substituting two MT task – source-to-interlingua, followed by interlingua-to-source – for the original one.

The interesting issue, given that we can all concede that ILs do not normally look quite like NLs, and do certainly have some superficial features of formal languages (brackets, capitalization, some non-linguistic connectives etc.) is whether they have any significant features of NLs, above and beyond the simple appearance of a number of NL words in their formulas, normally drawn from English. English words already appear in profusion in many computer programs, particularly those that encourage arbitrary predicate naming, such as LISP and Prolog, from which fact one could not of course conclude that programs in those languages were IN ENGLISH. Appearance of words is not enough, or French could be declared English, or vice versa, or Bulgarian Turkish.

The feature I would seize on in discussion is whether the primitives of interlingual formalisms suffer ambiguity and progressive extension of sense as all known NLs do (except perhaps Aymara, but that may reflect only a lack of study of the language). Some formal languages can tolerate substantial ambiguity of symbols – early LISP, which functioned perfectly well, is now conventionally said to have had a key symbol (NIL) three-ways ambiguous. LISP programs presumably implicitly resolved this ambiguity in context, or did they?

It is widely believed that NLs have their ambiguities resolved in use, up to some acceptable level, and that extensions of sense take place all the time, whether rule governed (e.g. as in Pustejovsky's generative lexicon (1995)), or, as in the old AI/NLP tradition, by means of manipulations on lexicons and knowledge structures that were general procedures but not necessarily equivalent to lexical rules. What would it be like, and I have no clear answer, to determine that the primitives of an IL representation were in this position, too? Schank did, after all split the early TRANS into MTRANS, ATRANS and then others, so the suggestion has precedent.

An answer might require a trip through the more empirical aspects of recent NLP/CL and ask what evidence we have that any given symbol in its occurrences in corpora has more than one sense? Has this any empirical, non-circular answer, that does not require appeal to existing polysemous dictionaries or contrastive translations? I believe the answer is yes, and that an IL does have this key feature of an NL and that no disastrous consequence follows from thus viewing ILs as reduced NLs, rather than full ones. This has for me more intuitive plausibility than continuing to maintain that what seem to be NL features of ILs are not in fact but are language independent. That claim always seems to me one that it is impossible to defend in detail but is a clear residue of the hypnotic power of intuition in an age of empiricism and calculation. One place to look for empirical answers to this question is Guo's (1992) work analysing the defining primitives of LDOCE (Procter et al., 1978): LDOCE is a dictionary for English learners where each word is defined in terms of 2000 English words, which function as primitives. Guo explored the degree to which defining words in LDOCE have more than one sense such that the ambiguity can be (temporarily at least) eliminated by replacing such a word (e.g. "state" used in LDOCE to cover nation states and states of matter) by combinations of other, non-ambiguous LDOCE primitives.

Note: This article originated at 1996 AMTA SIG-IL Preworkshop on Interlinguas, held in Montreal, a series which continues.

Chapter 7
Stone Soup and the French Room: The Statistical Approach to MT at IBM

A Preface in 2008

This chapter was written about 1992 soon after the team at IBM under Jelinek and Mercer had shocked the NLP world with their statistical machine translation system; although their system was never able to translate more than half of its sentence sample accurately, it caused a revolution in the field, and the methods they deployed have since been used to advance computation at every linguistic level of analysis. Some of the predictions in this chapter turned out true and some not; I will return to them again at the end of this chapter and in the final chapter of the book.

Some History

Like connectionism, statistically-based MT is a theory one was brought up to believe had been firmly locked away in the attic, but here it is back in the living room. Unlike connectionism, it carries no psychological baggage, in that it seeks to explain nothing and cannot be attacked on grounds of its small scale as connectionist work has been. On the contrary, that is how it attacks conventional symbolic approaches. Fifty years ago Gilbert King wrote:

> "It is well known that Western Languages are 50% redundant. Experiment shows that if an average person guesses the successive words in a completely unknown sentence he has to be told only half of them. Experiment shows that this also applies to guessing the successive word-ideas in a foreign language. How can this fact be used in machine translation". (King 1956).

Alas, that early article told us little by way of an answer and contained virtually no experiments or empirical work. Like IBM's approach it was essentially a continuation of the idea underlying Weaver's original memorandum on MT: that foreign languages were a *code* to be cracked. I display the quotation as a curiosity, to show that the idea itself is not new and was well known to those who laid the foundations of modern representational linguistics and AI.

I personally never believed Chomsky's arguments in 1957 against other theories than his own any more than I did those supporting his own proposals: his attacks on statistical and behaviorist methods (as on every thing else, like phrase structure grammars) were always in terms of their failure to give explanations, and I will make no use of such arguments here, noting as I say that how much I resent IBMs use of "linguist" to describe everyone and anyone they are against. There is a great difference between linguistic theory in Chomsky's sense, as motivated entirely by the need to explain, and theories, whether linguistic/AI or whatever, as the basis of procedural, application-engineering-orientated accounts of language. The latter stress testability, procedures, coverage, recovery from error, non-standard language, metaphor, textual context, and the interface to general knowledge structures.

Like many in NLP and AI, I was brought up to oppose linguistic methods on exactly the grounds IBM do: their practitioners were uninterested in performance and success at MT in particular. Indeed, the IBM work to be described here has something in common with Chomsky's views, which formed the post-1957 definition of "linguist". It is clear from Chomsky's description of statistical and Skinnerian methods that he was not at all opposed to relevance/pragmatics/semantics-free methods (he advocated them in fact) it was only that, for Chomsky, the statistical methods advocated at the time were too simple a method to do what he wanted to do with transformational grammars. More recent developments in finite state (as in Phrase Structure) grammars have shown that Chomsky was simply wrong about the empirical coverage of simple mechanisms (see Langendoen and Postal, 1984).

In the same vein he dismissed statistical theories of language on the ground that sentence pairs like:

$$\text{I saw a} \left\{ \begin{matrix} \text{the} \\ \text{triangular whale} \end{matrix} \right\}$$

are equally unlikely but significantly different in that only the first is ungrammatical.

Is the Debate about Empiricism?

Anyone working in MT, by whatever method, must care about success, in so far as that is what defines the task. Given that, the published basis of the debate between so-called rationalism and empiricism in MT is silly: we are all empiricists and, to a similar degree, we are all rationalists, in that we prefer certain methodologies to others and will lapse back to others only when our empiricism forces us to. That applies to both sides in this debate, a point I shall return to.

An important note before continuing: when I refer to IBM machine translation I mean only the systems such as Brown et al. (1989, 1990). The IBM Laboratories, as a whole, support many approaches to MT, including McCord's (1989) prolog-based symbolic approach, as well as symbolic systems in Germany and Japan.X

Is the Debate about How We Evaluate MT?

In the same vein, I shall not, as some colleagues on my side of the argument would like to do, simply jump ship on standard evaluation techniques for MT and claim that only very special and sensitive techniques (usually machine-aided techniques to assist the translator) should in future be used to assess our approach.

MT evaluation is, for all its faults, probably in better shape than MT itself, and we should not change the referee when we happen not to like how the game is going. Machine-aided translation (MAT) may be fine stuff but IBM's approach should be competed with head on by those who disagree with it. In any case, IBM's method could in principle provide, just as any other system could, a first draft translation for a translator to improve on line. The only argument against that is that IBM's would be a less useful first draft *if a user wanted to see why certain translation decisions had been taken*. It is a moot point how important that feature is. However, and this is a point Slocum among others has made many times, the evaluation of MT must in the end be economic not scientific. It is a technology and must give added value to a human task. The ALPAC report in 1966, it is often forgotten, was about the economics of contemporary MT, not about its scientific status: that report simply said that MT at that time was not competitive, quality for quality, with human translation.

SYSTRAN won that argument later by showing there was a market for the quality it produced at a given cost. We shall return to this point later, but I make it now because it is one that does tell, in the long run, on the side of those who want to emphasize MAT. But for now, and for any coming showdown between statistically and non-statistically based MT – where the latter will probably have to accept SYSTRAN as their champion for the moment, like it or not – we might as well accept existing "quasi-scientific" evaluation criteria, Cloze tests, test sets of sentences, improvement and acceptability judged by monolingual and bilingual judges etc. None of us in this debate and this research community are competent to settle the economic battle of the future, decisive though it may be.

Arguments Not to Use Against IBM

There are other well known arguments that should not be used against IBM, such as that much natural language is mostly metaphorical and that applies to MT as much as any other NLP task and statistical methods cannot handle it. This is a weak but interesting argument: the awful fact is that IBM cannot even consider a category such as metaphorical use. Everything comes out in the wash, as it were, and it either translates or it does and you cannot ask why. Much of their success rate of sentences translated acceptably is probably of metaphorical uses. There may be some residual use for this argument concerned with very low frequency types of deviance, as there is for very low frequency words themselves, but no one has yet stated this clearly or shown how their symbolic theory in fact gets such uses right (though many of us have theories of that). IBM resolutely deny the need of any such special theory, for *scale* is all that counts for them.

What is the State-of-play Right Now?

Aside from rumor and speculation; what is the true *state of play* at the moment, namely 1992? In recent reported but unpublished DARPA-supervised tests the IBM system CANDIDE did well, but significantly worse than SYSTRAN's French-English system over texts on which neither IBM nor SYSTRAN had trained. Moreover, CANDIDE had far higher standard deviations than SYSTRAN, which is to say that SYSTRAN was far more consistent in its quality (just as the control human translators had the lowest standard deviations across differing texts). French-English is not one of SYSTRANs best systems but this is still a significant result. It may be unpleasant for those in the symbolic camp, who are sure their own system could, or should, do better than SYSTRAN, to have to cling to it in this competition as the flagship of symbolic MT, but there it is.

IBM have taken about 4 years to get to this point. French-English SYSTRAN was getting to about IBM's current levels after 3–4 years of work. IBM would reply that that they are an MT system factory, and could do the next language much faster. We shall return to this point.

What is the Distinctive Claim by IBM about How to do MT?

We need to establish a ground zero on what the IBM system is: their rhetorical claim is (or perhaps was) that they are a pure statistical system, different from their competitors, glorying in the fact that they did not even need French speakers. By analogy with Searle's Chinese Room (Searle, 1980), one could call this theirs a French Room position: MT without a glimmering of understanding or even knowing that French was the language they were working on! There is no space here for a detailed description of IBM's claims (see Brown et al. 1990, 1991). In essence, the method is an adaptation of one that worked well for speech decoding (Jelinek and Mercer 1980).

The method establishes two components: (a) a trigram model of the sequences in the target language; (b) a model of quantitative correspondence of the parts of aligned sentences between French and English. The first is established from very large monolingual corpora in the language, of the order of 100 million words, the second from a corpus of *aligned* sentences in a parallel French-English corpus that are translations of each other. All were provided by a large machine-readable subset of the French-English parallel corpus of Canadian parliamentary proceedings (Hansard). (1) is valuable independent of the language pain and could be used in other pairings which is why they now call the in model a *transfer* one. In very rough simplification: an English sentence yields likeliest equivalences for word strings (sub strings of the English input sentence) i.e. French word strings. The trigram model for French re-arranges these into the most likely order, which is the output French sentence. One of their most striking demonstrations is that their trigram model for French (or English) reliably produces (as the likeliest order for the components) the correct ordering of items for a sentence of 10 words or less.

What should be emphasized is the enormous amount of pre-computation that this method requires and, even then, a ten word sentence as input requires an additional hour of computation to produce a translation. This figure will undoubtedly reduce with time and hardware expansion but it gives some idea of the computational intensity of IBM's method.

The facts are now quite different. They have taken in whatever linguistic has helped: morphology tables, sense tagging (which is directional and dependent of the properties of French in particular), a transfer architecture with an intermediate representation, plural listings, and an actual or proposed use of bilingual dictionaries. In one sense, the symbolic case has won: they topped out by pure statistics at around 40% of sentences acceptably translated and then added whatever was necessary from a symbolic approach to upgrade the figures. No one can blame them: it is simply that they have no firm position beyond taking what ever will succeed, and who can object to that?

There is then no theoretical debate at all, and their rhetorical points against symbolic MT are in bad faith. It is Stone Soup: the statistics are in the bottom of the pot but all flavor and progress now come from the odd trimmings of our systems they pop into the pot.

They are, as it were, wholly pragmatic statisticians: less pure than, say, the Gale group (e.g. Gale & Church, 1990) at AT&T: this is easily seen by the IBM introduction of notions like the one they call "informants" where a noun phrase of some sort is sought before a particular text item of interest. This is an interpolation of a highly theoretically-loaded notion into a routine that, until then, had treated all text items as mere uninterpreted symbols.

One could make an analogy here with localist versus distributivist sub-symbolic connectionists: the former, but not the latter, will take on all kind of categories and representations developed by others for their purposes, without feeling any strong need to discuss their status as artefacts, i.e. how they could have been constructed other than by handcrafting.

This also makes it hard to argue with them. So, also, does their unacademic habit of telling you what they've done but not publishing it, allegedly because they are (a) advancing so fast, and (b) have suffered ripoffs. One can sympathize with all this but it makes serious debate very hard.

The Only Issue

There is only one real issue: is there any natural ceiling of success to pure statistical methods? The shift in their position suggests there is. One might expect some success with those methods on several grounds (and therefore not be as surprised as many are at their success):

1. there have been substantial technical advances in statistical methods since King's day and, of course, in fast hardware to execute such functions, and in disk size to store the corpora.
2. The redundancy levels of natural languages like English are around 50% over both words and letters. One might expect well-optimised statistical functions to exploit that to about that limit, with translation as much as anything other NLP task. One could turn this round in a question to the IBM group: how do they explain why they get, say, 40–50% or so of sentences right, rather than 100%? If their answer refers to the well-known redundancy figure above, then the ceiling comes into view immediately.
   If, on the other hand, their answer is that they cannot explain anything, or there is no explaining to do or discussions to have, then their task and methodology is a very odd one indeed. Debate and explanation are made impossible and, where that is so, one is normally outside any rational or scientific realm. It is the world of the witch-doctor: look I do what I do and notice that (sometimes) it works.
3. according to a conjecture I propounded some years ago, with much anecdotal support, *any theory whatever no matter how bizarre will do some MT*. Hence my surprise level is always low.

Other Reasons for Expecting a Ceiling to Success with Statistics

Other considerations that suggest there is a ceiling to pure statistical methods are as follows:

1. A parallel with statistical information retrieval may be suggestive here: it generally works below the 80% threshold, and the precision/recall tradeoff seems a barrier to greater success by those methods. Yet it is, by general agreement, an easier task than MT and has been systematically worked on for over 35 years, unlike statistical MT whose career has been intermittent. The relationship of MT to IR is rather like that of sentence parsers to sentence recognisers. A key point to note is how rapid the early successes of IR were, and how slow the optimization of those techniques has been since then!
2. a technical issue here is the degree of their reliance on alignment algorithms as a pre-process: in (Brown et al., 1991) they claimed only 80% correct alignments, in which case how could they exceed the ceiling that that suggests? On the other hand, the IBM group did not put a great deal of research effort into alignment techniques, and other groups have produced much better results since then.
3. Their model of a single language is a trigram model because moving up to even one item longer (i.e. a quadgram model) would be computational prohibitive. This alone must impose a strong constraint on how well they can do in the end, since any language has phenomena that connect outside the three item window. This is agreed by all parties. The only issue is how far one can get with the simple trigram-model (and, as we have seen, it gives a basic 40%),

and how far can distance phenomena in syntax be finessed by forms of information caching. One can see the effort to extend the window as enormously ingenious, or patching up what is a basically inadequate model when taken alone.

The Future: Hybrid Approaches

Given the early success of IBM's methods, the most serious and positive question should be what kinds of *hybrid* approach will do best in the future: coming from the symbolic end, plus statistics, or from a statistical base but inducing, or just taking over, whatever symbolic structures help? For this we can only watch and wait, and possibly help a little here and there. However, there are still some subsidiary considerations.

IBM, SYSTRAN and the Economics of Corpora

In one sense, what IBM have done is partially automate the SYSTRAN construction process: replacing laborious error feedback with statistical surveys and lexicon construction. And all of us, including SYSTRAN itself, could do the same. However, we must always remember how totally tied IBM are to their Hansard text, the Rosetta Stone, one might say, of modern MT. We should remember, too, that their notion of word sense is only and exactly that of correspondences between different languages, a wholly unintuitive one for many people.

The problem IBM have is that few such vast bilingual corpora are available in languages for which MT is needed. If, however, they had to be constructed by hand, then the economics of what IBM has done would change radically. By bad luck, the languages for which such corpora are available are also languages in which SYSTRAN already has done pretty well, so IBM will have to overtake, then widen the gap with, SYSTRAN's performance a bit before they can be taken seriously from an economic point of view. They may be clever enough to make do with less than the current 100 million word corpora per language, but one would naturally expect quality to decline as they did so.

This resource argument could be very important: Leech has always made the point, with his own statistical tagger, that any move to make higher-level structures available to the tagger always ended up requiring much more text than he had expected.

This observation does not accord with IBM's claims, which are rather the reverse, so an important point to watch in future will be whether IBM will be able to obtain adequate bilingual-corpora for the domain-specialized MT that is most in demand (such as airline reservations or bank billings). Hansard has the advantage of being large but is very very general indeed.

However, even if IBM did ever equal SYSTRAN's level of performance, it is not clear what inferences we should draw. If it turned out that that result had been achieved with less manpower and time than SYSTRAN took on the same pair, then we could call the result SYSTRAN Without Tears, the automation of the vast amount of human labor that went into that SYSTRAN language pair. But, even so, and great achievement as that would have been by the IBM team, we must always remember (and this is my second point) that they need millions of words of parallel text even to start. But that the French-English Hansard corpus (that they use as the basis for their French-English system) may be unique, in that it will be very hard to find a parallel corpus of that length for any other pair of languages (apart, of course, from the Bible, see Philips (2001). But, if such another pair were found, one would be surprised if it were not for a language pair that SYSTRAN had already tackled. In which case, even if they succeed, it may be that there are no other language pairs for IBM to move to that SYSTRAN has not already dealt with, at about the same level of accuracy (ex-hypothesi). To move to new pairs in that case it will be necessary to construct the parallel corpora from scratch, in which case the whole basis for costing IBM lower than SYSTRAN in the first place will almost certainly be destroyed.

Many have been reduced to intellectual paralysis at seeing IBM do so much better than anyone could have expected, and done it with some charm and a great deal of frankness about the problems they encountered. But, let us remember, this is not a wholly new approach to language processing: Markov chain models (Mandelbrot, 1962) were seriously discussed in the sixties and, in one sense, and ignoring the flashing hardware, nothing has changed. The problems noted then were of longer distance dependencies: prepositional phrases, anaphora, word-sense choice based on phenomena distant in a sentence, and so on. It may well be that French and English, as in the Canadian Hansard, were a lucky choice for their method, since they have roughly the same span of distant dependencies, as English and German (with its verb-final-in-main clause feature) do not. It is not obvious that the method will work as well between those two languages, though there are differing views on this but, happily, it is again an empirical question.

Somers (1993) has argued, with regard to current Russian MT, that if IBM[1]s method has any virtue, then the Russians could leap forward fifteen or so years without the errors and drudgery of the West. I sympathise with his point but fear it cannot happen, any more than countries are able, whatever their dreams and rhetoric, to leap over the unpleasant phases of industrial development in other countries and head straight for the clean, electronic, uplands. Yet, if IBM's statistical method were to prove an MT panacea, they could do just that, since the Russians are as able as anyone in that formal area, and could reproduce such results very rapidly. Which is again, for me, a reason for thinking that outcome very unlikely indeed. Perhaps the drudgery of SYSTRAN cannot be by-passed which, if so, is a depressing thought, akin also to Dreyfus' point about intelligence and environments: intelligent organisms must, he argued, pass though phases where they learn and have experiences and cannot just be loaded up with knowledge as some AI theorists seemed to claim.

Why the AI Argument About MT Still has Force

The basic AI argument for knowledge-based processing does not admit defeat and retreat, it just regroups. It has to accept Bar Hillel's old anti-MT argument (Bar-Hillel 1960) on its own side – i.e. that as he said, good MT must in the end need knowledge representations. One version of this argument is the primitive psychological one: humans do not do translation by exposure to such vast texts, because they simply have not had such exposure, and in the end how people do things will prove important. Note that this argument makes an empirical claim about human exposure to text that might be hard to substantiate.

This argument will cut little ice with our opponents, but there may still be a good argument that we do need representations for tasks in NLP related to MT: e.g. we cannot really imagine doing summarization or question answering by purely statistical methods, can we? There is related practical evidence from message extraction: in the MUC competitions (Lehnert & Sundheim 1991), the systems that have done best have been hybrids of preference and statistics, such as of Grishman (Grishman and Sterling, 1989) and Lehnert, and not pure systems of either type.

There is the related argument that we need access to representations *at some point* to repair errors: this is hard to make precise but fixing errors makes no sense in the pure IBM paradigm; you just provide more data. One does not have to be a hard line syntactician to have a sense that rules do exist in some linguistic areas and can need fixing.

Hard Problems Do Not Go Away

There remain, too, crucial classes of cases that seem to need symbolic inference: an old, self-serving, one will do, yet again, such as "The soldiers fired at the women and I saw several fall". (Wilks 1997)

I simply cannot imagine how any serious statistical method (e.g. not like "pronouns are usually male so make 'several' in a gendered translation agree with soldiers"!) can get the translation of "several" into a gendered language right (where we assume it must be the women who fall from general causality). But again, one must beware here, since presumably any phenomenon whatever will have statistically significant appearances and can be covered by some such function if the scale of the corpus is sufficiently large. This is a truism and goes as much for logical relations between sentences as for morphology. It does not follow that that truism leads to tractable statistics or data gathering. If there could be 75,000 word long Markov chains, and not merely trigrams (which seem the realistic computational limit) the generation of whole novels would be trivial. It is just not practical to have greater-than three chains but we need to fight the point in principle as well!

Or, consider the following example (due to Sergei Nirenburg):

Priest is Charged with Pope Attack

A Spanish priest was charged here today with attempting to murder the Pope. *Juan Fernandez Krohn*, aged 32, was arrested after *a man armed with a bayonet* approached the Pope while he was saying prayers at Fatima on Wednesday night.

> "According to the police, *Fernandez* told the investigators today he trained for the past six months for the assault. He was alleged to have claimed the Pope 'looked furious' on hearing *the priest's* criticism of his handling of the church's affairs. If found guilty, *the Spaniard* faces a prison sentence of 15–20 years".
>
> (The Times, 15 May 1982)

The five underlined phases all refer to the same man, a vital fact for a translator to know since some of those phrases could not be used in any literal manner in another language (e.g. "the Spaniard" could not be translated word-for-word into Spanish or Russian). It is hard to imagine multiple identity of reference like that having *any* determinable statistical basis.

Is the Pure Statistics Argument What is Being Debated?

Everything so far refers to the *pure statistics argument*, from which IBM have now effectively backed off. If the argument is than to be about the deployment of hybrid systems and exactly what data to get from the further induction of rules and categories with statistical functions (e.g. what sort of dictionary to use) then there is really no serious argument at all, just a number of ongoing efforts with slightly differing recipes. Less fun, but maybe more progress, and IBM are to be thanked for helping that shift.

IBM as Pioneers of Data Acquisition

I can add a personal note there: when I worked on what I then called Preference Semantics (Wilks, 1973c) at McCarthy's Stanford AI Lab he always dealt briefly with any attempt to introduce numerical methods into AI – statistical pattern-matching in machine vision was a constant irritation to him – by saying "Where do all those numbers come from?"

I felt a little guilty as Preference Semantics also required at least link counting. One could now say that IBM's revival of statistical methods has told us exactly where some of these numbers come from! But that certainly does not imply that the rules that express the numbers are therefore useless or superseded.

This touches on a deep metaphysical point: I mentioned above that we may feel word-sense is a non-bilingual matter, and that we feel that there *are* rules that need fixing sometimes and so on. Clearly, not everyone feels this. But it is our culture of language study that tells us that rules, senses, metaphors, representations etc. are important and that we cannot imagine all that is a just cultural artefact. An analogy here would be Dennett's (1991) restated theory of human consciousness that suggests that all our explanations of our actions, reason, motives, desires etc. as we articulate them may be no more than fluff on the underlying mechanisms that drive us.

IBM's work induces the same terror in language theorists, AI researchers and linguists alike: all their dearly-held structures may be just fluff, a thing of schoolmen having no contact with the reality of language. Some of us in AI, long ago, had no such trouble imaging most linguistics was fluff, but do not want the same argument turned round on us, that *all* symbolic structures may have the same status.

Another way of looking at this is how much good IBM are doing us all: by showing us, among other things, that we have not spent enough time thinking about how to acquire, in as automatic a manner as possible, the lexicons and rule bases we use. This has been changing lately, even without IBM's influence, as can be seen from the large-scale lexical extraction movement of recent years. But IBM's current attempts to recapitulate, as it were, in the ontogeny of their system, much of the phylogeny of the AI species is a real criticism of how some of us have spent the last twenty years.

We have not given enough attention to knowledge acquisition, and now they are doing it for us. I used to argue that AIers and computational linguists should not been seen as the white-coated laboratory assistants of linguistic theorists (as some linguists used to dream of using us). Similarly, we cannot wait for IBMers to do this dirty work for us while we go on theorizing. Their efforts should change how the rest of us proceed from now on.

Let Us Declare Victory and Carry On Working

Relax, go on taking the medicine. Brown et al.'s retreat to incorporating symbolic structures shows the pure statistics hypothesis has failed. All we should all be haggling about now is how best to derive the symbolic structures we use, and will go on using, for machine translation.

We have good historical reasons for believing that a purely statistical method cannot do high-quality MT, unless all the arguments about the knowledge-basedness of MT, and language understanding in general, are wrong. That, of course, would mean Bar-Hillel (1960) being wrong as much as the proponents of an MT based on some degree of semantics or world knowledge.

- The IBM effort is in the past, and the team that did the work has dispersed; we can now ask what its effect has been on MT and computational linguistics in general. The obvious alternatives are the following:
- Going on with theoretical linguistic development, which one could deem "linguistics as chemistry", in search of the correct and devastating formula that will "solve" MT.

- pursuing Machine-aided translation, which supplements computational lacunae by having a human in the translation loop, and has been much used in commercial systems;
- Keep on hacking in the hope that, like SYSTRAN, a system can grow to an acceptable level of performance, perhaps by blending the best of statistical and symbolic components.

There are systems, still under development, in both commercial environments and research laboratories that have adopted all these latter day strategies, sometimes more than one at once. All those strategies agree on most of the following morals that can and have been drawn from MT experience for future MT systems:

- unaided statistical methods will probably not be sufficient for any viable system, commercial or otherwise, since they do not lead to a ‚system that beats SYSTRAN, which is already available for a large range of languages.
- One should be more sceptical than ever about a system that produces a small amount of demonstration output, because all MT systems work to some degree, whatever their assumptions: word-for-word MT as much as pure statistical MT. Broad coverage is as much a criterion as quality of translation. This is no more than a repetition of Suppes 1970s remark that, to be taken seriously, an MT system must do an unseen book!
- There are proven bags of tricks for doing MT, as Bar-Hillel always argued (1960) and no amount of theoretical research is going to diminish their importance.
- Symbolic and statistical methods can be combined, and that seems to be where most MT research is at the moment, although just reciting "hybrid systems" does not solve the crucial issue of exactly how they are to be combined.
- Interlingual methods remain popular, in spite of the above, at least in Japan and the US.
- Evaluation continues to drive MT, and helps keep old systems alive.
- The last ARPA evaluations showed SYSTRAN still very much in the game, but with small commercial upstarts beating the research systems, and much closer to the old, established, and more expensive ones than the latter find comfortable.
- Thanks to IBM, resource driven systems are here to stay, at least for the foreseeable future and Big-Data-Small-Program may still be a good ideal, from SYSTRAN to IBM, always to be contrasted with purely theoretically motivated systems like EUROTRA which had Big-Programs-Small-Data (Johnson et al. 1985).

An Afterword

The predictions above were not that wrong and the MT scene in 2008, to which we shall turn in the last chapter, is one where SYSTRAN has at last been superseded, though usually not in the languages where it already represented a large investment: so an effective free translator of web pages from Russian to English is till likely to be a SYSTRAN engine underneath, though for a language like Arabic or Chinese as source, the underlying engine may well be a new statistically-based system, The predictions above were not always accurate about where and in what languages corpora for training would become available – e.g. with English-Cantonese with the Hong Kong Hansards – but they were basically right that many statistically-based systems have operated by means of statistically-derived linguistic objects such as rules and lexicons. And there is no doubt whatever that quantitative models have clearly won hands down in the overall argument, and that a range of groups have come into being that have taken over the leadership in statistical machine translation from the (disbanded) IBM group: Johns Hopkins U (with Jelinek himself, David Yarowsky and others); ISI (Kevin Knight); as well as Edinburgh (with Philip Koehn) in the UK.

Chapter 8
The Revival of US Government MT Research in 1990

Prefatory paragraph in 2008: shortly after this paper was written and presented, DARPA did begin a 5 year program of support for MT, funding both the IBM CANDIDE system (described in Chapter 7 above) and PANGLOSS, a cooperative interlingual system involving CMU, USC – ISI and NMSU. In that sense only, the arguments presented here were successful in helping restart US MT after a long period when few agencies would support the subject since the ALPAC report of 1966. However, the PANGLOSS system, advocated here was not successful, although it resulted in a number of useful editorial aids for translators; by the end of the project it was clear that the methods of statistical PANGLOSS (discussed in Chapter 7) were in fact the way ahead, as has been proved since.

Machine translation remains the paradigm task for natural language processing. Unless NLP can succeed with the central task of machine translation, it cannot be considered successful as a field. We maintain that the most profitable approach to MT at the present time (1990) is an interlingual and modular one. MT is one of the few computational tasks falling broadly within artificial intelligence (AI) that combine a fundamental intellectual research challenge with enormous proven need. To establish the latter, one only has to note that in Japan alone the current MT requirement is for 20 billion pages a year (a market of some $66 billion a year, as cited in a Japanese survey).

The vulgarized version of the history of MT is as follows: In the 1950s and 1960s large funds were made available to US MT which proved to be a failure. The ALPAC report (1966) said MT was impossible and doomed all further US funding. MT work then moved to Canada and Europe where it partly succeeded, which was then followed by highly successful exploitation in Japan. The truth, of course, is not at all like that.

MT work did not stop in the US after ALPAC: the AFOSR continued to fund it in the US and there were and are enormous commercial developments subsequently (the best known commercial systems being SYSTRAN, ALPS, LOGOS, METAL and SMART).

ALPAC did not say MT was impossible nor that the work done was no good: only that at that point in history, with the cost and power of 1960s computers, human translation was cheaper.

MT work did not move to Europe, since much of it stopped there also in response to the ALPAC report. The UK believed the ALPAC report, and only in France did serious work continue, where the GETA system in Grenoble became the foundation for a range of others, including the major Japanese university system (Mu) and aspects of the Eurotra system, which was designed to be a multilingual system between the languages of the EEC.

The longevity of systems such as SYSTRAN is proof of the need of stamina and persistence in MT to achieve serious results, but also of the need for periodic redesign from scratch, since old formalisms and software reach a point where they cannot be further optimized, a point reached long ago with SYSTRAN itself. But one way in which all MT work is in SYSTRAN's debt is that it is the main existence of MT proof: it convinces doubters that there that machine translation now exists, albeit in primitive form, and can be purchased on a large scale and at a quality that many users find acceptable for their needs. A key defect in the ALPAC report was that it underestimated how large a market there was for partially accurate, low quality, MT, and SYSTRAN filled that market. The point now, of course, is to move on to the huge market for higher-quality MT.

It is certainly not the case that most major MT installations in the world are now Japanese. In the list given in the 1989 JEIDA report, only one Japanese system occurs among the list of major installed systems in the world outside Japan. All the rest are American. However, that list is becoming quickly dated, as Japanese system are being researched, developed and deployed at a much faster rate, reflecting a lopsided ten-to-one total funding skew in favor of Japan over America. A crucial difference between US and foreign strategies to date has been that the Japanese government made machine translation central to the Fifth Generation effort, and the European Community began in 1980 a $45 million investment (later grown to $70m) in the EUROTRA project as part of their overall information technology drive.

Why This is a Good Time to Get Back into MT

There is a growing need for translation in intelligence, commerce, science, government, and international organizations. This is due to factors such as the following:

- Increases in international cooperation and competition, which involve an ever-growing volume of text to be communicated.
- World-wide electronic networks have made international communication much easier.
- Reports, documentation, legal papers, and manuals are increasingly produced in one culture and exported to various other cultures, often in multiple languages.
- More emphasis is being placed on the use of national languages in documents and systems.
- The economic rise of South-East Asia and the opening of the European market in 1992 add significantly to these factors.

Strategic Reasons for an MT Effort

MT systems live and decay like natural organisms: they have natural life spans that cannot be indefinitely prolonged. The SYSTRAN system has lived long and done well but it is 30 years old and cannot be optimized above the 75% level. Later systems from the early 1970s (GETA, LOGOS, ALPS, WEIDNER, MU, etc) were better constructed but cannot rise above their current levels; the evidence for this being that the two research systems in that list (GETA & MU) have now effectively collapsed and their teams dispersed. The right thing is now to promote a new design using the enormous and transferable advances that have been made in interfaces, hardware, linguistics, AI, machine lexicons etc.

The most recent new large-scale efforts have either been badly managed and proved impractical (like EUROTRA) or set very narrow commercial goals (usually involving only Japanese and English or Asian languages) like the major Japanese systems.

Much of the MT-related research performed in the US is being applied elsewhere. No nationwide project utilizing the best research talents in NLP has been attempted in the U.S. in over two decades. Today, DARPA is probably the only institution with the resources and scope to mount a large-scale MT effort successfully. Such an effort would harness and coordinate NLP work of various kinds and would create a setting in which new innovations could be used within this country first.

A second strategic reason pertains to interproject collaborations. Currently, there is relatively little collaboration and sharing of resources and expertise among NLP research groups in the US. A new national agenda with a set of clearly focused goals could serve as an integrating agent. The development of a standard interlingua representation, a set of standardized lexicons, one or more grammars, support tools and interfaces, and additional software, can shape much future NLP research in this country by enabling researchers to make use of existing work and tools with much less effort than is currently the case. [**Afterword 2008:** the landscape has been totally changed in the US and worldwide since this was written, and wholly for the better: under DARPA pressure over a sustained period, there are now many repositories such as the Linguistic Data Consortium (LDC – paralleled by ELDA in Europe) as well as a range of DARPA (and other) competitions in aspects of NLP: TREC, SENSEVAL, SEMEVAL, ASIFAL etc. all of which rely on the production and later sharing of corpus and lexical resources.]

Technical Reasons for an MT Effort

Steady developments in various aspects of NLP make available large portions of an MT system more or less off the shelf, which greatly facilitates the construction of new MT systems. These developments are the following:

1. Clearer understanding of semantics: Recent refinements of taxonomical ontologies of representation provide an interlingua-like basis for a new, more powerful,

MT. Making maximal use of the high-level linguistic and semantic generalizations shared among languages, one can minimize or even eliminate language-to-language lexical or structural transfer rules and so increase the portability of the system across domains.
2. More complete grammars: Development of grammars is an ongoing process. There exist today grammars that cover English (and other languages such as German, Chinese, Japanese, and French) far more extensively than the most comprehensive grammars of 20 years ago did.
3. Better existing generation and parsing technology: Single-sentence parsing and generation has been studied to the point where a number of well-established paradigms and algorithms exist, each with known strengths and weaknesses, a situation which greatly facilitates the construction of a new MT system (in fact, in recent years a number of general-purpose generators have been distributed: Penman, Mumble, Frege, etc.).

An Interlingual Approach Versus Transfer or Massive Statistics

A fundamental technical notion in our cooperative plan is interlinguality: it is one of the three basic structural methods for MT, contrasted with direct and transfer approaches. The direct method was used for early systems like SYSTRAN as well as large recent ones like SHALT from IBM Japan. If one is only ever going to be interested in one language couple in one direction, as SYSTRAN originally was, there is no reason not to use it. We assume, however, that that is not our situation and multilinguality is essential. It should also be noted that some form of interlinguality is now becoming the standard position in AI-knowledge representation and our approach meshes best with that. The interlingua approach overcomes the problem of building thousands of transfer rules by using a central representation into which and from which all the languages are parsed and generated.

The aim to design an interlingua which is both specific enough to allow simple and unambiguous processing and general enough to enable different approaches with different theoretical strengths to represent the information they can extract from the text. Fortunately, none of us have ever been committed to the highly formalized representation languages and systems which have been (and still are) popular in various areas of NLP, formalisms whose logical properties have been studied extensively but whose practical utility is low.

Consider now the following example:

"Mary was in a severe accident. She lost a foot". vs. "Mary was buying cloth, but measured it incorrectly by accident. She lost a foot".

There is no statistical measure (e.g., no low-order n-grams) that will disambiguate "foot" reliably in such contexts. Languages other than English have different ambiguities that must be resolved to translate to English or to fill a database for an intelligence analyst.

The interlingua approach is far better able to exploit domain knowledge in order to produce reliable translations than the other two approaches. The massive statistical approach is inimical to any infusion of domain knowledge or any comprehension of the language. Pure statistical translation had been rejected in the early years, but has been brought back to life in the recent IBM research effort, (Mercer, Jellinek, Brown et al, see chapter 7 above). Experience has consistently shown that unaided statistical methods perform only at a low level which cannot be raised much, and only on a carefully selected materials (in the IBM project based on the copious high-quality parallel French-English Hansard texts from Canada – data not found for other language pairs) or Even the 50% success claimed may depend crucially on order similarities between English and French. Their paper claims that for 63% of tested sentences under 10 words, the most probable word order, based on trigram probabilities, was the correct one 80% of the time, which together produce the figure above.

Statistics, although not a complete translation paradigm, plays several important roles in MT, however such as selecting the most normative (frequent) rendition into words in each target language. Statistics can select collocations from large text corpora (such as the preferred use of "pitch black" rather than "asphalt black"). Given a large potential lexicon, simple frequency analysis can direct the dictionary-building work towards the most frequent words first, so as to obtain maximal utility of a system during development phases. All evaluation metrics of fluency, accuracy and cost of translation are statistically based.

Machine translation systems must be concerned with the knowledge encoding, with modular software architectures, with good engineering, with scalable and evaluable systems development, much more than with specific linguistic theories prevalent in modern transfer approaches. In practice, MT approaches motivated by theoretical-linguistic concerns, like EUROTRA, tend to be too driven by linguistic fashion (since their chief motivation is to be theoretically interesting rather than effective). This opinion is shared by the Japanese researchers. Thus, the 1989 JEIDA report concluded that linguistic theory had made no discernible contribution to the advance of MT.

Key features of the cooperative approach we advocate are:

1. The use of an interlingua instead of transfer rules or statistical co occurrences;
2. Modularity: both programs and data will be produced in a modular fashion allowing them to be assembled into a number of prototype MT systems;
3. Commitment to gradual increase in the levels of automation of the systems we create;
4. The central role of world knowledge in addition to knowledge about language;
5. The use of a representation based on commonsense semantics and pragmatics;
6. Emphasis on the large scale of the systems under construction;
7. Ensuring portability across domains by building reusable tools and information repositories such as lexicons;
8. Developing within a translator's workstation environment to facilitate the integration of the above modules to support the creation of useful machine-aided

translation systems at the earlier stages of the project, while the various automatic processing modules are being developed. Included here will be a separate, but compatible, lexicology workstation, to assist the incorporation of large-scale semantic, syntactic and collocational information from machine -readable dictionaries and text corpora.

The Modularity Assumption

Modularity is independent of interlinguality though opting for the latter requires the former. Strong modularity of language components would now be supported by most researchers and developers in MT, largely because it allows the addition of new languages with minimum dislocation. It is also essential if it is to be possible to treat different languages by different methods and to combine work at a range of sites. Agreeing on suitable interfaces is a practical not a theoretical matter, and the experience of EUROTRA has shown it is perfectly feasible (this is the main scientific contribution of EUROTRA).

In order to harness the NLP research potential in this country, we advocate a modular approach to the construction of prototype MT systems. Under this approach, various sites will build various modules which can be assembled in various ways to construct various prototype systems.

The advantages of this modular approach include the following:

- Various projects and various theoretical approaches will be able to participate.
- Projects need not have experience in all aspects of MT to participate.
- Redundant development of modules will be eliminated.
- Interproject collaboration will be stimulated throughout the U.S.

The common goal of translation will provide a more coherent focus for the various research endeavors and will facilitate the comparison of various approaches to tease out their strengths and weaknesses.

As new and promising projects are found, they can be included into the program.

The theory-neutral modules, all in a standard form, will be made available to the whole NLP community as a basic resource.

Large-scale lexicons, automatically constructed from text, can be used in parsing and generation and in interactive help.

Existing work on collocation, co occurrence, and clustering of words and phrases can be put to use (for example, to guide lexicon construction).

World Knowledge, Semantics and Pragmatics

Ours is an AI approach in that we shall, in processing expressions so as to select a particular interpretation, apply computationally expressed knowledge of the world, as well as our knowledge of language. We thus select the most sensible interpretation of ambiguous expressions, recovering the most sensible referents for pronouns and inferring information which is implicit. This knowledge of the world is general in the sense that we know a great deal about objects, actions, states, events and situations, such as the classes to which they belong and the attributes they possess. Through the application of such knowledge, we weed out incoherent interpretations as they develop and select the most appropriate interpretation from those that survive.

Another crucial component is a realistic pragmatics, bringing in the best of AI work on speech act, belief etc. phenomena. These are now tractable and usable notions in MT systems. We shall commit ourselves to commonsense semantic approaches rather than formal ones since these have not proved fruitful in MT in any language. This will also involve a commitment to algorithmic elements of AI-based semantics (such as Preference Semantics) that have already proved useful in message-understanding work, and have an intimate connection with understanding of ill-formed, metaphor-laden text that is the normal form of actual documents.

In order to produce MT of superior quality that existing systems, one of the most powerful key ideas is the use of discourse-related and pragmatic terms. Most MT systems operate on a sentence-by-sentence basis only; they take no account of the discourse structure. Given recent work on discourse structure at various centers in the U.S., structural information should be taken into account and can be used to improve the quality of the translation. Similarly, pragmatic information, such as Speech Acts, reference treatment, and perhaps even some stylistic notions (to the extent that notations have been developed to represent them) will be used to improve the quality of the translation.

We emphasize scale phenomena, both in the sense of bringing large-scale lexical material automatically via existing work on machine readable dictionaries, but also making use where possible of statistically-based work on corpora to guide lexical entry selection, corrigibility of sentences to particular syntax rules etc.

Portability

One of the well-known weaknesses of current MT systems is their limited applicability. In order to achieve an acceptable level of translation quality, the current brute-force approaches require large collections of translation rules which invariably contain increasingly domain-specific information. Porting these systems to a new domain becomes a major undertaking.

By using the newest NLP technology while focusing on the development and use of a number of very general information resources (such as a high-level concept ontology under which domain-specific ontologies are subordinated, and a general lexicon for closed-class words), this proposal is aimed at overcoming the problem of domain-dependence without compromising on translation quality.

A major factor supporting the domain-independence is the ability to acquire information – conceptual, lexical, phrasal, translational – interactively during the translation process. When the system encounters input it cannot handle, it queries the human assistant, who decides what type of information the input is and then inserts appropriate definitions into the system's information banks for future use, using the interfaces and acquisition tools provided. The proposed MT program devotes a large amount of effort on the development of interactive acquisition software and interfaces, via the notions of the Translator's and Lexicologist's workstations.

The Strengths and Weaknesses of this Interlingual Approach

The strengths of the interlingua approach have been briefly discussed above. We would like now to defend the interlingua approach against three most commonly held negative opinions.

CRITICISM 1: An interlingual Approach Forces Unneeded Processing

If a source language has, say, an expression which is three ways ambiguous and some target language has an expression which has precisely the same three-way ambiguity, unanalyzed why not simply carry the ambiguity from the source to the target and let the reader figure it out? Why disambiguate needlessly?

The response is that, on the one hand, that a third language probably has different expression for each of the possible interpretations, so that if the same representational apparatus is to be applied to translations between the source language and a third language or from the target language and a third language, such processing is necessary in any case. On the other hand, a quick inspection of bilingual dictionaries shows that cases of complete correspondence of ambiguity across languages is extremely rare, even in closely related languages such as German and Dutch.

The issue of "since we sometimes can get away with less processing, why risk doing unnecessary work?" can be compared with intelligence-gathering work, where much of the effort is routine; information often confirms expectations; and therefore much of the work is "unnecessary". With such an attitude, all unexpected, important intelligence would often be ignored, much to the detriment of the analysts and policymakers. Ignoring meaning in translation because it need not always be interpreted, is an equally flawed philosophy. The times when deeper analysis is required can be absolutely crucial to produce meaningful, rather than misleading translations.

CRITICISM 2: Interlingual Approaches are Based on a Particular Language, thus Creating Unnatural Analyses for Other Languages

This is the "cultural imperialism" argument. If, however, there exists such a thing as a universal descriptive linguistic framework, then there is no reason to assume that language imperialism must be a side-effect of the interlingual approach. Our experience in the development of an interlingual representation based on a cross-linguistic comparison of parallel texts has indicated, at least, that such a language independent framework is possible. But even if no such framework exists, then at worst, such language particular bias would simply be defect of the approach, rather than wholly invalidating it.

A standard example here would be the case of the verb wear in English and the problem of expressing the notion in Japanese or Chinese. It so happens that in Japanese the corresponding verb depends entirely on what is worn e.g. shoes (verb= hateiru), coat (verb= kiteiru), spectacles (verb= kaketeiru) and so on (and similarly for Chinese). It is thus reasonable to say that Japanese does not have a concept of wear in the way English does.

However, that observation is no kind of argument at all against an interlingual approach, merely one for intelligent generation. In an interlingual environment there will be at least one interlingual node (which may or may not correspond to wear) that links the relevant sense representations. The crucial point is that it would be the intelligent Japanese generator (since no problem arises in the Japanese to English direction) that makes the choice of output verb based simply on selection semantics (e.g. if the worn object is "koutoo" the verb is kiteiru and so on).

Chapter 9
The Role of Linguistic Knowledge Resources in MT

In this chapter we examine, largely by reference to Japanese systems, since they are still little known in the West, the issue of what knowledge sources one expects to find in modern MT systems. Later we go on to ask about the role and need of linguistic knowledge in particular.

What linguistic knowledge sources are needed to perform MT depends, at least to a limited extent, on which MT method is used. For example, some US projects (Brown et al., 1989 and Chapter 7 above) made use of very large scale statistical information from texts, while Japanese systems do not. Conversely, an experimental MT system at Kyoto University made use of large lists of sample sentences against which a sentence to be translated is matched (Nagao, 1990), whereas no US systems did this until the turn of the century (the CMU system). Most MT systems however, make use of at least some, or possibly all of the following kinds of lexical knowledge sources as distinct from corpora alone (as in Brown et al.):

- Morphology tables
- Grammar rules
- Lexicons

Representations of World Knowledge

For instance, it is possible both to analyze and to represent the English language without the use of morphology tables, since it is inflected only to a small degree; for the analysis of a highly inflected language like Russian or German, on the other hand, they are almost essential. Some analysis systems claim not to use an independent set of identifiable grammar rules, but they must somewhere contain information such as the fact that an article precedes a noun in English. Although there is room for doubt as to which of the first two categories (morphology or grammar) certain items of linguistic knowledge belong to (in Italian, for example, forms such as pronouns may stand alone but can also act as suffixes to verbs: e.g. *daglielo*), in Japanese and English this ambiguity of type is very unlikely indeed.

The third form of knowledge (lexical) appears in virtually every MT system, except for the purely statistical type of system referred to Chapter 7. But, as we shall see, only some MT systems (usually those that owe some allegiance to artificial intelligence methods) claim to contain world knowledge representations. The distinction between the last two categories of knowledge can also be tricky: (in a German lexicon, for example, *Das Fraeulein* is marked as neuter in gender but, in the real world, it must be marked female, as the word means "a young woman"). We should deduce from this that a lexicon is a rag-bag of information, containing more than just *semantic* information about meanings.

It is interesting to see, in the following figure, that Toshiba Corp., for example, chose to develop these knowledge sources in chronological order:

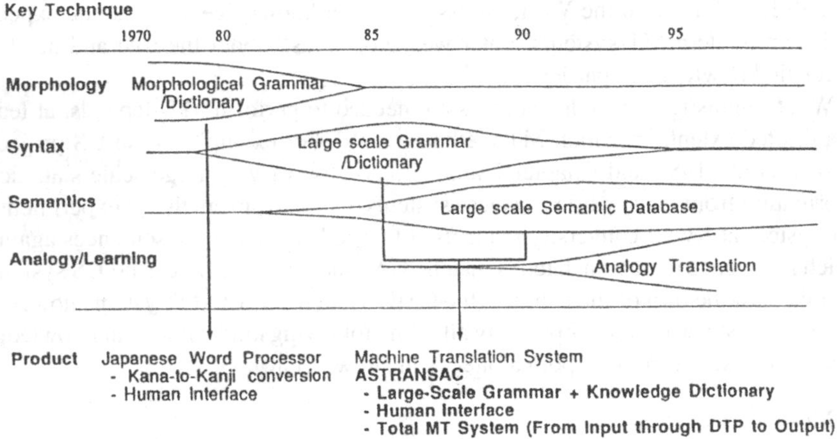

Fig. 9.1 Toshiba's development of knowledge sources

In the figure below (9.2), Toshiba indicated their system's overall translation procedure. Without committing ourselves to a specific view of what "semantic transfer" means (a topic discussed elsewhere in this report), we can infer that the bolder arrows represent the translation tasks to be performed, while the lighter arrows indicate Toshiba's view of where the knowledge forms they emphasize (a merger of our latter two items, omitting morphology) distribute across those tasks.

Much of this chapter's content could be summed up by the following table, which simply lists twenty-two systems by their major features, such as the type of MT system (direct, transfer, or interlingual), the major language directions expressed as letter pairs (e.g. JE for Japanese to English), the type of grammar (ATN's, case-frame, etc.), the number of its rules (if available), the lexicon's size and type (also if available), and any kind of knowledge representation that is used.

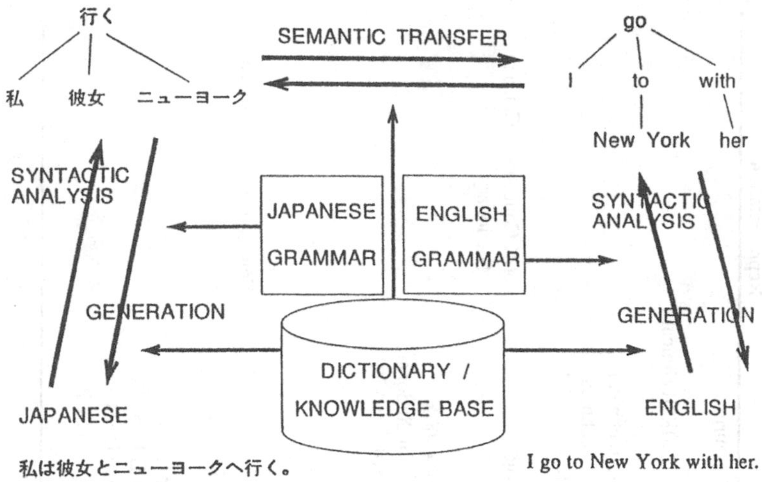

Fig. 9.2 The translation process in the Toshiba system

A noticeable feature of the table is that only one system claims to use a knowledge representation: IBM Japan's SHALT2 uses the Framekit-based system. The Japanese Electronic Dictionaries (EDR, see below) is not strictly an MT system, but a very large scale lexical and conceptual tool, as we shall see below.

It is worth noting here that what NTT describe as JJ transfer means extensive, automatic, pre-editing to (a) remove character combinations known to cause problems for analysis programs; and (b) to insert segmentation boundaries into sentences so as to break them up into sections, thereby making analysis easier. Variations of these methods exist at other sites (e.g. Sharp, NHK), and although (b) originated in earlier MT practice, these methods do constitute a genuine and practical heuristic that has almost certainly improved translation quality.

In a way, they fall under the rubric of what Bar-Hillel (wrongly believed by many to be the arch-enemy of MT) wrote (Bar-Hillel, 1971): "MT research should restrict itself, in my opinion, to the development of what I called before 'bags of tricks' and follow the general linguistic research only to such a degree as is necessary without losing itself in Utopian ideas".

More so than in the US, and much more so than European projects like EUROTRA, Japanese MT work 1n the 1980s and 1990s arrived at very much the same conclusion as Bar-Hillel. Very little Japanese work (with the possible exception of the IBM system JETS, and the ATR system) owes much to western-style linguistic theory, while the NTT system claims to be following a more indigenous, Japanese, tradition of linguistic description.

If it is accurate, this observation should cause us to re-examine our notion of "knowledge sources" for MT. Given that the list at the beginning of this chapter

Company	System Type	Grammar	Lexicon	Knowledge Representation
ATR	Semantic Transfer E/J	Lexically-Based Unification Grammar (JPSG) 130 Rules	Case-Roles Thesaurus	–
Bravice	Syntactic Transfer J/E & E/J	J/E 4K Rules E/J LFG/UNIFIC 8K Rules	J/E: 70K Basic 240K Technical E/J: 40K Basic	–
Catena STAR	Syntactic Transfer E/J	2000 Context-Free Rules	20K Basic 55K Technical	–
The Translator	Syntactic Transfer E/J	3000 Context-Free Rules	25K Basic 35K Technical	–
CICC	Interlingual (J,C,TH,IN,MAL)	–	50K Basic 25K Technical	–
CSK	Interlingual J/E & E/J	ATNS	50K	–
EDR (not an MT system)	Implicitly Interlingual	–	J: 300K E: 300K	400K Concepts in Concept Dictionary
Fujitsu ATLAS-I	Syntactic Transfer J/E	–	–	–
ATLAS-II	Interlingual J/E	5K J Rules 5K E Rules 500 Transfer Rules	70K Each Way +300K Technical in subdictionary	–
Hitachi	Semantic Transfer J/E & E/J	Case-Based J/E: 5,000 Rules E/J: 3,000 Rules	J/E: 50K E/J: 50K	–
IBM SHALT	Syntactic Transfer E/J	Phrase Structure 200 E Rules 800 Transfer Rules 900 J Rules	E/J: 90K	–
IBM SHALT2	Semantic Transfer E/J	–	LDOCE	Framekit-Based Representation
JICST	Semantic Transfer J/E	1500 J Rules 500 Transfer Rules 450 E Rules	350K J 250K E	–
Matsushita	Syntactic Transfer J/E	800 J Rules 300 Transfer Rules	31K Each Direction	–
NEC	Interlingual J/E & E/J	Case-frame Grammar	90K J/E, 70K E/J +600K Technical Lexicons	–
NTT	Syntactic Transfer J/E (J/J Transfer)	–	400K (Includes 300K Proper Nouns)	–

Fig. 9.3 Knowledge sources in Japanese systems

Company	System Type	Grammar	Lexicon	Knowledge Representation
Oki	Syntactic Transfer J/E & E/J	Context-Free Rules 1K Rules Each Direction	J/E: 90K E/J: 60K	–
Ricoh	Syntactic Transfer E/J	2500 Rules 300 Transfer Rules	55K	–
Sanyo	Syntactic Transfer J/E & E/J	Context-Free Phrase-Structure 650 Rules Each Way	50K Each J/E & E/J	–
Sharp	Semantic Transfer J/E & E/J	Augmented Context-Free and Case Frames	J/E: 70K E/J: 79K	–
Systran Japan	Transfer J/E & E/J ↔	Multi-Pass Phase Finding	E/J 200K (Interpress) J/E 50K	–
Toshiba	Semantic Transfer J/E & E/J	ATN+Lexical Rules 100K Rules Each Way	50K General <200K Technical <200K Users	–

Fig. 9.3 (continued)

.3.4 依頼

人に動作をするように頼む場合のムード。直接依頼の「下さい」「てもらう」のみ登録されている。

[接依頼形式 直接相手に動作の依頼をする。

]接依頼形式 自分の実情を述べて、相手に間接的に動作の依頼をする。

- 〜て / て下さい / てちょうだい
- 〜てくれませんか / てもらえますか / てもらえませんか
- 〜て欲しい / てもらいたい / て欲しいんだけど
- 〜てくれるといいんだが / てくれるとありがたいんだけど

「下さい」の語彙記述の例

「下さい」は、動詞テ形(「送って下さい」)、または、サ変名詞(「御参加下さい」「お送り下さい」)を下位
]化する補助動詞として記述されている。

```
([[PHON (:DLIST          kudasai
               |?X07| )]
  [SYN [[SLASH [DLIST[IN ?X04[]]
                     [OUT ?X04]]]
        [HEAD [[POS  V]
               [GRFS [[SUBJ [[SYN [[SUBCAT (:LIST  )]
                                   [HEAD [[POS  P]
                                          [FORM  が]
                                          [COMPLEMENT  +]]]]]
                             [SEM ?X02[]]]]]]
               [ASPECT  +]
               [VASP [[CHNG  +]
                      [MOME  -]
                      [ACTV  +]]]
               [SUBV  +]]]
        [WH [DLIST[IN ?X05[]]
                  [OUT ?X05]]]
        [MORPH [[CTYPE  NONC]]]]]
  [SEM [[RELN  下さい-REQUEST]
        [AGEN ?X03[]]
        [RECP ?X02]]]
  [PRAG [[RESTR (:DLIST        [[RELN  RESPECT]
                                [AGEN ?X03]
                                [RECP ?X02]]
                               [[RELN  POLITE]
                                [AGEN ?X03]
                                [RECP ?X02]]
                          |?X01| )]
         [SPEAKER ?X03]
         [HEARER ?X02]]]
  [ORTH (:DLIST            下さい
                |?X06| )]]
  ([[SYN [[MORPH [[CFORM  INFN]]]]]]) ; 連用形(「下さいますか」)
   ([[SYN [[MORPH [[CFORM  IMPR]]]]]]); 命令形(通常の用法)
  ([[SYN [[SUBCAT (:LIST         ?X11[[SYN [[SUBCAT (:LIST         ?X10[[SYN [[SUBCAT (:LIST  )]
                                                                          [HEAD [[POS  P]
                                                                                 [FORM  が]
                                                                                 [COMPLEMENT  +]]]]]
                                                                    [SEM ?X08[]]]
                                                      )]
                                            [HEAD [[POS  ADV]
                                                   [GRFS [[SUBJ ?X10]]]]]]]
                                      [SEM ?X09[]]]
                         )]
          [HEAD [[MODL [[EVID  DIRC]]]
                 [GRFS [[SUBJ [[SEM ?X08]]]
                        [COMP ?X11]]]]]]]
    [SEM [[RECP ?X08]
          [OBJE ?X09]]]
```

Fig. 9.4 An example entry from the ATR dictionary

took its categories directly from western linguistics and does not tailor itself very well to Japanese MT work (if one agrees that the most successful Japanese systems are mainly driven by the information in their lexicons, as is SYSTRAN), then our very assumptions of what knowledge sources actually drive MT should be re-assessed.

For the sake of clarity, it may be profitable to return to the general notion of a knowledge source, and to throw some additional light on it by contrasting it with MT without knowledge sources.

Earlier, we mentioned that the MT work at IBM Yorktown Heights (Brown et al. see Chapter 7 above) performed EF MT without help from any of the knowledge sources we listed above. Even its definition of what constitutes a word is derived from frequent collocation measures of other "words", and therefore is not a *priority*. What that system generates is the word strings that fit together to form statistically "natural strings. All this is done without any knowledge sources: that is, without any analytic, combinatory, or symbolic structures beyond the basic text data from which the statistics are derived.

The contrast with SYSTRAN is also instructive here, partly because the two systems aim to translate by statistical and symbolic methods, respectively; and partly because it is SYSTRAN's "sentence correct percentage" that IBM would have to beat to be successful (although it was nowhere near doing so at the time of writing this).

SYSTRAN has also been described (at least in parody) as utilizing no knowledge sources; it has been thought of by some as having, in effect, a mere sentence dictionary of source and target languages. Nor is this notion as absurd as linguists used to think: the number of English sentences under fifteen words long, for instance, is very large, but not infinite. So, on the above definition, an MT system that did MT by such a method of direct one-to-one sentence pairing would definitely not have a knowledge source. But, although part of the success of the Dayton-based SYSTRAN Russian-English system is certainly due to its roughly 350K lexicon of phrases, idioms, and semi-sentences (Wilks, 1991), SYSTRAN does not really conform to this parody of it (Toma, 1976). It is interesting to note in passing that, utterly different as they are on a symbolic-statistical spectrum, SYSTRAN and CANDIDE have earned similar opprobrium from linguists!

One might say that while US and European systems tend to fall towards the extremes of a different spectrum (running from linguistically-motivated systems at one end to those with no knowledge sources at the other), Japanese systems tend to fall in between, and to have *sui generis* knowledge sources, as does SYSTRAN itself.

Another way of thinking about knowledge sources for MT is that they are never completely pure data in the way that linguistic theory sometimes supposes. That is to say that the role and content of a knowledge source cannot really be understood without some consideration of the processes that make use of it. We shall return to this point at the end, when considering the EDR Lexicon project, which is intended to be universal, or process-free.

Lexicon Samples

The following example figure is from the ATR lexicon, and is for the verb *kudasai*.

One can immediately see that what makes it unusual is that it is a lexical entry for a strongly linguistically-motivated system; indeed, one can deduce from its feature structure that it is almost certainly intended to fit within an HPSG grammar system. This confirms the above point that such knowledge sources are not independent of the processes that apply to them.

It is important to emphasize once more the paramount role of lexicons in many Japanese systems, their substantial size (and the manpower they required to construct), and the wealth of specialized technical lexicons available in some of these systems. Here for example is the set of technical lexicons available for the Fujitsu ATLAS system.

Field	Number of Entries
Biology and Medicine	9,200 words
Industrial chemistry	14,400 words
Meteorology, Seismology, and Astronomy	13,500 words
Mechanical engineering	28,100 words
Civil engineering and Construction	14,400 words
Physics and Atomic Energy	15,000 words
Transportation	21,800 words
Plant	36,000 words
Automobile	18,000 words
Biochemistry	15,000 words
Information processing	26,000 words
Electricity and Electronics	17,100 words
Mathematics and Information	31,900 words

Fig. 9.5 Technical lexicons available for the ATLAS system and used to supplement the basic general-purpose lexicon

As we already noted, SYSTRAN is a strongly lexically-dependent MT system, and its JE and EJ modules were owned in Japan at the time of writing (by Iona) and are therefore technically speaking Japanese systems. SYSTRAN's JE and EJ modules have three types of dictionaries, and are described in the company's own words as follows (SYSTRAN, 1991):

A "word boundary" dictionary for matching words and establishing word boundaries in Japanese text, where each word is not clearly bounded by spaces (as in English and other European languages).

A "stem" dictionary containing source language words and their most frequently used target language equivalents. This dictionary also contains morphological, syntactic, and semantic information about each entry word.

A "limited semantics" (LS) dictionary of expressions, special collocations, and macro instructions for handling translation problems of low to medium complexity.

These are accessed within the main SYSTRAN framework as follows:

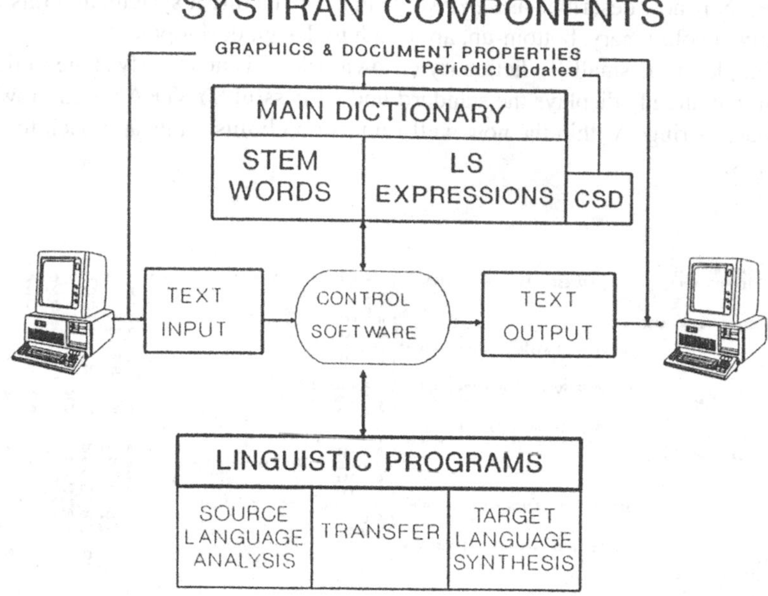

Fig. 9.6 The use of dictionaries in SYSTRAN

SYSTRAN's dictionary list for its newer multitarget systems (from information in 1992) was as follows:

E-Multitarget	Source	Target
ENGLISH SOURCE	172,056	
English-French		200,166
English-German		129,916
English-Italian		149,387
English-Portugese		42,130
English-Spanish		103,337
English-Korean		6,412
English-Arabic	162,640	150,147
English-Dutch	97,994	79,075
English-Japanese	156,866	66,384
English-Russian	19,329	34,773

Fig. 9.7 SYSTRAN dictionary size

From this we can see that the English-Japanese component (at 150K source items) is about three times the size of the corresponding JE dictionary. This newer system is called *multitarget* because SYSTRAN has now fully integrated its earlier methodology of detaching and reusing chunks of older (direct) programs for new languages.

SYSTRAN is now described as a *transfer* rather than a direct system; and this is an interesting evolutionary, bottom-up, approach to design development.

A sample of the small JE dictionary (shown below) is at an early stage of development, but already displays the standard and successful SYSTRAN trend towards long source strings, within the now well-understood limits, in its approach to other languages.

```
1NEW DICTIONARY RECORDS
1DC STEM/ID/EXPRESSION        POS  JAPANESE - ENGLISH      140     W T M MEANING     02-18-91  PAGE     1  D SYN AA GR CC WC   DATE
                              BPO                                  N G I                                   P     RN AE 22 D2   LAST
                                                                       D                                   Q      T DF 01 13  UPDATED
031  #ATAMA#WARI .BCPRT Q#DE                                       1 0 0 HEAD                              1 000 00 00     0  01-24-91
                                                                   2 0 0 PER                               0 000 00 00     0
                              N01 01-24-91 ASSIGN MNG TO 'ATAMAWARI DE'; ASK-7 (KE)
 B1  #GEN#BA Q#DE                                                  1 0 0 SITE                              1 000 00 00     0  10-29-90
                                                                   2 0 0 ON                                0 000 00 30     0
                              N01 10-29-90 GENBA DE = 'ON SITE'; J3INTEC2-88  (LG)
 41  #HAI#KA .AD Q#DE                                              1 0 0 DIRECTION                         1 000 20 00     0  09-21-83
                                                                   2 0 0 UNDER                             0 000 00 30     0
                              N01 09-21-83 JFAC3C-235 (HA)
                              N02 09-21-83 SET TR= 'UNDER THE DIRECTION OF' (HA)
 B2  #HURUI Q#TOKORO Q#DE Q#HA                                     1 0 0 $$$                               0 000 00 20     0  10-10-90
                                                                   2 0 0 LOOKING BACK INTO HISTORY         0 000 00 30     0
                                                                   3 0 0 $$$                               0 000 00 20     0
                                                                   4 0 0 $$$                               0 000 00 20     0
                              N01 10-10-90 ASSIGN MNG., TOKORO MULT MN PROJECT.  MMWDTOKO-132 (LG)
 41  #I#MI Q#DE                                                    1 0 0 SENSE                             1 004 00 00     0  06-09-89
                                                                   2 0 0 IN                                0 000 00 30     0
0                             N01 06-09-89 JABAF-42; JFIFTHC-22,46; JFIFTHB-7 (HA/LG)
 41  #I#TAKU .POS=10 .AD/MODL                                      1 0 0 REQUEST                           1 004 00 00     0  04-08-83
        .IF .B28 .$Q#YORU                                          2 0 0 AT                                1 000 00 30     0
        .OR .BCPRT Q#DE
                              N01 04-08-83 VOX79-4 (HA)
 B4  #ITI #KOU.KUTI Q#DE #IEBA                                     1 0 0 $$$                               0 000 00 20     0  10-11-89
                                                                   2 0 0 $$$                               0 000 00 20     0
                                                                   3 0 0 $$$                               0 000 00 20     0
                                                                   4 0 0 PUT SIMPLY                        0 000 00 30     0
                              N01 10-11-89 BIT1 (MC)
 41  #ITU#POU .BL+SSU .PW,CW .BR Q#DE .BR .$Q#HA                   1 0 0 OTHER HAND                        1 000 20 00     0  03-17-87
                                                                   2 0 0 ON                                0 000 00 30     0
                              N01 03-17-87 TRANSLATE EXPRESSION 'ON THE OTHER HAND' (YD/HA)
 418 #KAN#REN Q#DE .PW,CW .BMODL+BPQ=28 .PW,CW,B20,B30             1 0 0 RELATION                          1 000 00 00     0  02-22-84
        .Z-LMOD .PW,CW .Z-MODL                                           CDS-GENTO
                                                                   2 0 0 IN                                0 000 00 30     0
                              N01 02-22-84 RESET 16/26 TO 30/20 BETWEEN PW AND BPQ28 MODIFIER AND
0                             N02 02-22-84 SET ON SPMNCD GENTO (HA)
 41  #KEI.KATATI Q#DE .PW,CW                                       1 0 0 WAY                               1 004 00 00     0  01-07-91
        .IF .BANTEC+ANSUB .MID,0                                       1 FORM                              1 004 00 00     0
        .OR .ANTEC+N-LINKGVR .MID,1                                2 0 0 IN                                0 000 00 30     0
        .OR .Z-MODL .AD .MID,1                                         1 IN                                0 000 00 30     0
        .OR .B26 .POS=20 .PW,CW .MID,0
                              N01 10-29-90 ALLOW CONSISTENTLY ADVERBIAL FUNCTION OF KATATI DE (LG)
                              N02 10-29-90 CASE MARKER DE PROJECT.  (LG)
 818 #KIYOU#DOU .BR Q#DE .POS=50 .PW,CW .S-POS=30                  1 0 0 JOINTLY                           0 000 00 30     0  10-29-90
                                                                   2 0 0 $$$                               0 000 00 20     0
                              N01 10-29-90 KIYOUDOU IS ADV WHEN FLLWD BY DE.  DE IS MADE CSMKR
                              N02 10-29-90 IN HOMOR.  J3ENERGY-25 (LG)
 41  #KOU#SEI .PSV .BOBJ .BCPRT                                    1 0 0 CONSIST                           3 004 00 01     0  09-08-83
        .IFNB Q#KARA                                               2 0 0 OF                                0 000 00 30     0
        .OR Q#DE                                                   3 0 0 OF                                0 000 00 30     0
                              N01 09-08-83 XJEOBJ2-34 (HA)
                              N02 09-08-83 EXPAND TO INCL #KARA CPRT AS WELL AS Q#DE (HA)
 41  #KUTI#UTUSI .N-LINKGVR .BCPRT                                 1 0 0 MOUTH TO MOUTH                    0 000 00 00     0  04-08-83
0       .IFNB Q#NI                                                 2 0 0 $$$                               0 000 00 20     0
        .OR Q#DE                                                   3 0 0 $$$                               0 000 00 20     0
                              N01 04-08-83 SET TRANSLATE Q#NI/Q#DE WHEN PW IS NOT A PRED. NOM. (MO)
                              N02 04-08-83 SST01-136 (MO)
 B2  #SE#KAI #KI#BO Q#DE                                           1 0 0 WORLDWIDE                         2 000 80 00     0  01-02-90
                                                                   2 0 0 SCALE                             1 000 00 00     0
                                                                   3 0 0 ON                                0 000 00 30     0
                              N01 01-02-90 AGRMNT-2 (HA/MS)
 41  #SIYU#DOU .BCPRT Q#DE                                         1 0 0 HAND                              1 004 70 00     0  05-07-81
                                                                   2 0 0 BY                                0 000 00 30     0
                              N01 05-07-81 NIS4-27 (BO)
 418 #SOBA .AD Q#DE .PW,CW .Z-LOCAT+S-PROX                         1 0 0 VICINITY                          1 000 20 00     0  09-21-83
```

Fig. 9.8 A Sample from the SYSTRAN J/E dictionary

The adventurous EDR lexicon project (EDR, 1989), is one which aims to provide a formal, conceptual, description of at least 400,000 head items (roughly corresponding to word senses), along with an interface to sense definitions in English and Japanese. Here is a sample of the English interface.

```
【royal】 《00C7405》 very fine and costly
【royal】 《0d48d2》 a member of the royal family
【royal】 《03F6944》 of a person noble and refined in mind and character
【royal】 《0d48d3》 a small mast, sail, or yard, set above the topgallant
【royal】 《0d48d4》 a size of writing paper
【royal】 《0d48d5》 a size of printing paper
【royal】 《0d48d6》 any one of various coins in former times
【royal】 《0ea551》 to become holy and sacred／尊くおごそかなさまになる
【royal】 《00F7FF4》 of a condition of a thing, excellent／すぐれてよいさま
【royal】 《0fa960》 of a condition of a view, magnificent／眺めが壮大であるさま
【royal】 《1086d6》 precious things／得がたいもの
【royal】 《03BD198》 a facility built by a king or his family／国王や王族が設立した施設
【royal】 《03CE55B》 of a condition, excellent／すばらしいさま
【royal】 《03CE649》 of a condition, satisfactory／満足がいく状態であるさま
【royal】 《03CF0DA》 a state of being excellent and noble／優れて気高いさま
【royal】 《03CF119》 luxurious and magnificent／規模が大きく，りっぱで美しいさま
【royal】 《03CF2E5》 a condition of someone having a noble position／身分が高く，尊いさま
【royal】 《03CF6A7》 a state of being solemn and respectable／おごそかで立派なさま
【royal antler】 《26d6a3》 the third tine above the base of a stag's antler
【royal blue】 《03C6272》 a vivid bright indigo named royal blue／ロイヤルブルーという，あざやかな明るい藍色
【royal blue】 《03EE202》 a colour named royal blue
【royal coachman】 《026D6A5》 a fishing fly named royal coachman
【royal coachman】 《03C34FB》 a fishing fly with a mosquite-shaped feather attached to it／羽毛で蚊の形に作ったつり針
【royal commission】 《26d6a6》 a group of people commissioned by the Crown
【royal commission】 《26d6a7》 the inquiry conducted by royal commission
【royal demesne】 《26d6a8》 the private property of the Crown
【royal fern】 《026D6A9》 a fern named royal fern
【royal fern】 《03C0EBF》 a fern named osmund／ゼンマイというシダ植物
【royal flush】 《26d6aa》 a straight flush in poker, named royal flush
【royal jelly】 《026D6AB》 a nutritious secretion of the pharyngeal glands of the honeybee, named royal jelly
【royal jelly】 《03C6271》 a nutritious secretion of the honeybee named royal jelly／ロイヤルゼリーという，ミツバチの栄養になる分泌物
【royal mast】 《26d6ac》 the mast next above the topgallant
【royal moth】 《0d5293》 a moth named saturniid
【royal moth】 《03BCDB7》 an insect named io moth／山繭蛾という昆虫
【royal palm】 《26d6ae》 a palm tree named royal palm
【royal poinciana】 《26d6af》 a tree named royal poinciana
【royal purple】 《03C5BA7》 a color named royal purple／青紫という色
【royal purple】 《03EDB37》 a dark reddish purple
【royal tennis】 《26d1f2》 court tennis
【royal tern】 《26d6b2》 a tern named royal tern
【royal water】 《03C3172》 a mixture of nitric acid and hydrochloric acid／濃塩酸と濃硝酸の混合液
【royalism】 《03E9908》 the condition of adhering to monarchism
【royalist】 《0d48d8》 someone who supports a king or queen, as in a civil war, or who believes that a country should be ruled by a king or
              queen
【royalist】 《0d48d9》 typical of someone who supports a king or queen, as in a civil war, or who believes that a country should be ruled by
              a king or queen
【royalize】 《0d48da》 to make royal
【royalize】 《0d48db》 to assume royal power
【royally】 《0d48dd》 with the pomp and ceremony due a sovereign
【royally】 《0d48dc》 by the crown
【royally】 《0d48de》 with the utmost care and consideration
【royally】 《0d48e0》 on a large scale: gloriously
【royally】 《0d48df》 in a splendid manner: magnificently
【royalty】 《00D48E2》 people of the royal family
【royalty】 《00D48E3》 a payment made to an author or composer for each copy of his or her work sold, or to an inventer for each article
             sold
【reyalty】 《03F6436》 the rank of a king or queen
【royalty】 《0d48e4》 a share of the product or profit kept by the grantor of especially an oil or mining lease
【royalty】 《026BDB7》 a payment made to the mineral content of a certain area of land
【royalty】 《03C1A4A》 a payment made as a fee for a copyright／著作権の使用料
【royalty】 《03C1A4C》 authority of the king／王の威光
【royalty】 《03CEBCC》 the rank of king or queen／王としての位
【royalty】 《0d48e1》 royal power and rank
【royalty】 《03E99DC》 the condition of having regal charactor or bearing
【royster】 《00DB85E》 to swagger
【rozzer】 《03CB627》 a person whose occupation is called policeman
【rozzer】 《03F5E91》 a person who belongs to the police
【rpm】 《0d48e8》 = r.p.m.
【rps】 《0d48e9》 = r.p.s.
【rpt】 《00F0C4C》 to announce something publically／（何かを）公表する
【rpt】 《03F60F0》 to repeat: an act of repeating
【rpt.】 《03CF4EF》 to announce something publically by a paper or orally／何かを書類や口頭で公表する
【rpt.】 《00F0C4C》 to announce something publically／（何かを）公表する
```

Fig. 9.9 An example of the English interface to EDR's concept dictionary

This is an enormous enterprise, both manpower and computation-intensive. It is not yet clear how much of the conceptual coding is completed, even though both language interfaces are available.

EDR itself strives to be maximally cooperative with researchers world-wide on the project, both in terms of joint effort on the project itself (where they already have collaboration agreements with UK and French teams), and on subsequent use of the material for MT.

Funds for the project have been provided both by the government, and by major companies with MT activity (Fujitsu, Hitachi, NEC, etc.). While these companies all intend to make use of the EDR lexicon's final form, the intention is also to make the entire system available everywhere at a low cost. The lexicon is intended to be a knowledge source free of implied processes in the pure sense; although in fact, its conceptual coding scheme will most likely appeal to a lexically-driven, interlingual MT system.

Is Linguistic Knowledge Essential to MT?

In this chapter, we have used Japanese experience to survey the *kinds* of linguistic knowledge resources needed to do MT. But, the question must be asked, whether conventional linguistic knowledge is needed at all. One negative answer is that, as we saw in Chapter 7, came from the IBM statistics and corpus approach, through, as we saw, their experience in competing with SYSTRAN, led them to realize that they would have to recreate linguistic knowledge resources, albeit by empirical corpus-based methods. However, there has been another claim that knowledge is not needed for MT, from Somers and what one might call the UMIST school of thought.

Somers wrote: "All MT systems so far have been designed with the assumption that the source text contains enough information to permit translation" .And again (p. 10): "the source text alone does not carry sufficient information to ensure a good translation". This theme appears in the writings of other UMIST colleagues and clearly became an important slogan for them. Somers does not discuss the claim in any detail, yet it seems to me (to reuse the old opposition of elementary philosophy classes) plainly trivial or false. It is a triviality that an English sentence does not contain the information about French morphology that would permit it to be translated into French. No, of course not, and that was not what Somers meant at all. Then what was meant exactly? I think the conjunction of the words "contain" and "permit" in Somers' first sentence above ensures the trivial truth of the claim (in the way that "contain" followed by "yield" would have been plainly false). If "permit", however, means "permit translation when taken along with the other knowledge sources needed and which can be accessed from cues contained in the original", then that is indeed how translation is done (unless the original sentence is demonstrably defective in some way) and so his counter-claim (p.10) would be, on that interpretation, false. Roughly the same point could be made about "carry" and "ensure" in the second quoted sentence above.

If Somers actually agrees with this gloss on "permit", then what point is he making with his own claim, since the gloss seems to invalidate it? My gloss is in fact an assumption of all knowledge-based approaches (whether statistical, linguistic, lexical-semantic or AI): namely, that some additional knowledge must be stored somewhere, over and above the symbols in the source sentence, if translation is to be done. Is Somers really denying this, or just making a mystery of its obvious truth? I think we should be told. The whole point can be put monolingually, with greater clarity and so as to take in the dialogue case as well as follows. If we take the old chestnut of pragmatics, where a hearer infers from "It's sweltering hot in here" that he should open the window, which is to say he infers "I should open the window for the last speaker right now", then no one could believe for a moment that the second is contained (as an English-to-English translation) in the first. Yet, plainly, if this inference ever works, and I suppose we have to assume it does, there is enough information in the first to permit derivation of the second, given rules of speech act inference and, importantly, quite independent of the ambient temperature, since the hearer is requested to do that action even if he does not feel hot himself.

There is no mystery here: there is not enough in the sentence, true, but an intelligent organism knows enough to add in to get the required translation, given the surface cues in the source. I wish this demonstration would kill this particular line of UMIST argument stone dead. If we have no more than muddle here, and Somers does accept my gloss on "permit" (and even IBMers could accept it, so he will be very lonely if he does not) then we have to ask what that knowledge is to be. It is an odd lacuna that Somers never addresses this: he has dark mutterings about the sufficiency of linguistic knowledge, but dismisses the interlingua approach with a line and no argument on (p. 3) even though it precisely meets his translators' requirement for "structure preservation as a last resort" and embodies exactly the approach to intelligent generation that he praises in MacDonald's work, and which is essential to make the interlingual approach work at all. He makes no commitments for filling this gap between source and target, nor the intellectual gap between linguistic and statistical approaches, and it may be that Somers, deep down, thinks it is to be filled by what Bar-Hillel's "bags of tricks" mentioned earlier, and Somers' Alternative Avenues at the end suggest that that may be his position. If it is, one might reply that there is no clear distinction at all between bags of tricks and what, in AI, are called heuristics, of which the interlingual approach is just one example. He seems to believe in some firm distinction here (interlingua vs. heuristic-bags-of-tricks) just where, historically and intellectually, there is not one.

Curiously, too, much of what Somers advocates owes more to AI-heuristics that he seems to concede: the Nagao example-based approach descends precisely from Case-Based Reasoning; the menu-based document composition method descends equally from Tennant's approach to constrained NLP in his thesis (Tennant, 1981) that he later turned into a technology at Texas Instruments.

Somers' final message is something I wholeheartedly agree with: that advances are most likely to come from hybrid (rather than ideologically pure) methods and we shall return to this at the end of the book. It is interesting to note here that the IBM (see Chapter 7 above) group were far more hybrid-prone than is sometimes shown in descriptions of their work, and before they broke up they sought to augment their purely word-level statistical approach with some statistical derivation of rules to give precisely the long-range dependencies they need (Sharman et al., 1988). Though we shall have, as always, to bear in mind a principle of mine (Wilks, 1989) that Somers is kind enough to quote (p. 7) that successful MT systems rarely work with the theory they claim to. Let me add that the emphasis in that statement is on "successful".

Chapter 10
The Automatic Acquisition of Lexicons for an MT System

Introduction

For some time, researchers in Computational Linguistics and Natural Language Processing (NLP) have eyed machine-readable dictionaries with interest because they might provide a practical resource for overcoming the "lexical acquisition bottleneck". Many researchers, however, view this problem of lexical acquisition as too difficult to solve at present using a machine-readable dictionary, and the result has been that the focus of much research has shifted to identifying the kind of information needed in NLP lexicons (Atkins, 1990; Miike, 1990; McNaught, 1990; Onyshkevych and Nirenburg, 1991; Hanks, 1991; Pustejovsky, 1990; Russell et al., 1991; Kay, 1989), the goal being eventually to create a lexical data base that will allow the creation of a lexicon to be used for processing natural language. While we agree that it is unlikely that the information in machine-readable dictionaries is sufficient for this grand database of facts that will support NLP as a whole, we are optimistic about making use of the information they do provide to support the creation of lexical entries for specific natural language processing systems.

We will describe the ULTRA Machine Translation System (Farwell et al., 1993) and its lexicon in some detail (focusing on the information requirements of its lexical entries), and then discuss the lexical entry construction process: describing LDOCE and the standard format of its entries, the extraction process from LDOCE, and the process of specifying the remaining information. Finally, we offer some suggestions for fully automating the entire process. We believe this method for the automatic provision of lexical entries is original, although similar in spirit to the work of Neff and McCord, 1990.

The work we describe in this chapter was used to increase dramatically the size of the lexicons of the MT system, originally based on about 2,500 word senses, to cover just over 10,000 word senses. While the number of citation forms varies from one language to the next, the average size vocabulary size is about 6,500 words with the English vocabulary just under 6,000 words and the Spanish vocabulary just under 7,000 words. The new lexical items were chosen on the basis that they are common words which we expect to be useful in translation. However, we envision a future system which will automatically create a lexical entry for each item in the source-language text which does not already appear in the lexicon. This more ambitious task requires that for any input, the system can 1) use the linguistic context to decide the sense of each word and its corresponding interlingual concept, and 2) automatically create lexical entries for each of those senses which are not already in the lexicon. The techniques used in this work can be applied to the second part of the process and research is underway to accomplish the first.

ULTRA

ULTRA (Universal Language TRAnslator) is a multilingual, interlingual machine translation system which currently translates between five languages (Chinese, English, German, Japanese, Spanish) with vocabularies in each language based on about 10,000 word senses. It makes use of recent AI, linguistic and logic programming techniques, and the system's major design criteria are that it be robust and general in purpose, with simple-to-use utilities for customization.

Its special features include:

- a multilingual system with a language-independent system of intermediate representations (interlingual representations) for representing expressions as elements of linguistic acts;
- bidirectional Prolog grammars for each language incorporating semantic and pragmatic constraints;
- use of relaxation techniques to provide robustness by giving preferable or "near miss" translations;
- access to large machine-readable dictionaries to give rapid scaling up of size and coverage;
- multilingual text editing within Xwindows interface for easy interaction and document preparation in specific domains (e.g., business letters, proforma memoranda, telexes, parts orders).

Below is a sample screen from the ULTRA system. Each of the Spanish sentences in the SOURCE TEXT window have been translated into Japanese. In producing a translation, the user grabs a sentence from the source text using the system's "cut and paste" facilities and moves it to the bottom left SOURCE SENT window. The user then selects a target language from the choices above the TRANSLATION window (bottom right) and clicks on the TRANSLATE button at the bottom of the screen. The translation then appears in the bottom right TRANSLATION window. From there, the user moves the translated sentence to the TARGET TEXT window.

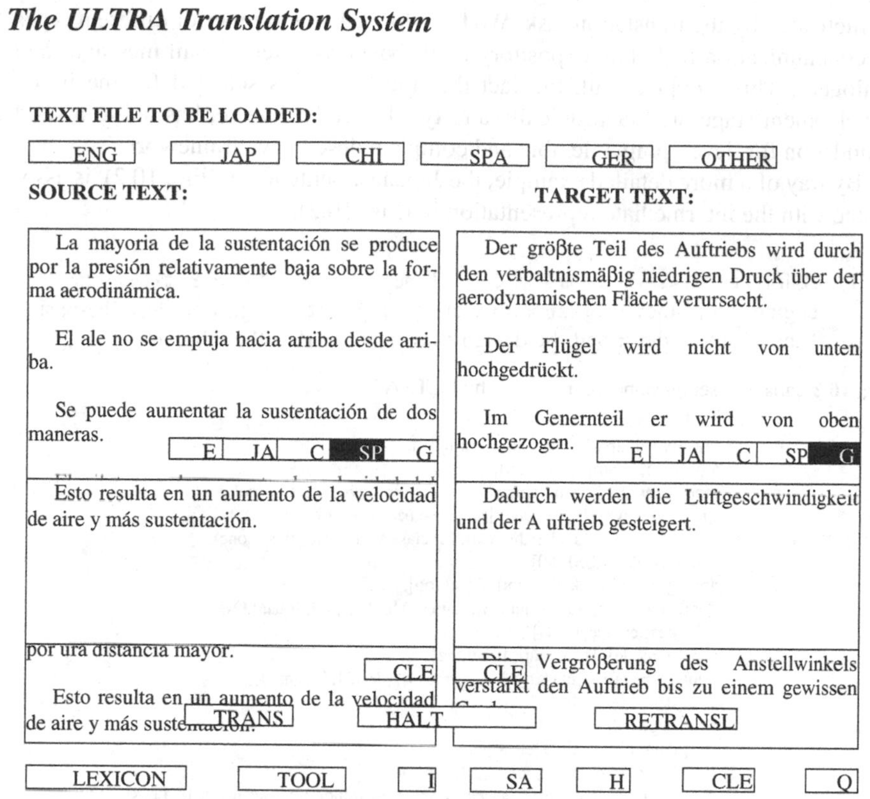

The ULTRA Translation System

TEXT FILE TO BE LOADED:

ENG | JAP | CHI | SPA | GER | OTHER

SOURCE TEXT:

La mayoria de la sustentación se produce por la presión relativamente baja sobre la forma aerodinámica.

El ale no se empuja hacia arriba desde arriba.

Se puede aumentar la sustentación de dos maneras.

E | JA | C | SP | G

Esto resulta en un aumento de la velocidad de aire y más sustentación.

por ura distancia mayor.

CLE

Esto resulta en un aumento de la velocidad de aire y más sustentación.

TRANS | HALT

TARGET TEXT:

Der größte Teil des Auftriebs wird durch den verbaltnismäßig niedrigen Druck über der aerodynamischen Fläche verursacht.

Der Flügel wird nicht von unten hochgedrückt.

Im Genernteil er wird von oben hochgezogen.

E | JA | C | SP | G

Dadurch werden die Luftgeschwindigkeit und der A uftrieb gesteigert.

CLE

Vergrößerung des Anstellwinkels verstärkt den Auftrieb bis zu einem gewissen

RETRANSL

LEXICON | TOOL | I | SA | H | CLE | Q

Fig. 10.1 The screen interface for ULTRA (Farwell et al., 1993)

The System of Intermediate Representation

The interlingual representation (IR) has been designed to reflect our assumption that what is universal about language is that it is used to perform acts of communication: asking questions, describing the world, expressing one's thoughts, getting people to do things, warning them not to do things, promising that things will get done and so on. Translation, then, can be viewed as the use of the target language to perform the same act as that which was performed using the source language. The IR serves as the basis for analyzing or for generating expressions as elements of such acts in each of the languages in the translation system.

The representation has been formulated on the basis of an on-going cross-linguistic comparative analysis of hand-generated translations with respect to the kinds of information necessary for selecting the appropriate forms of equivalent expressions in the different languages in the system. The comparison is based on a traditional informal descriptive framework which allows for extensions or revisions as motivated by the translation task. We have looked at a number of different types of communication including expository texts, business letters, email messages and dialogues. This, coupled with the fact that the languages selected for the initial development stage are diachronically and typologically diverse, has led to a solid foundation for developing a flexible and complete descriptive framework.

By way of a more detailed example, the Japanese sentence in (Fig. 10.2), is associated with the intermediate representation in (Fig. 10.3).

(1) 技術者は 彼らが 研究所で 開発した デザインを 説明した。
engineer-top they-subj laboratory-at develop-past design-obj describe-past
''the engineer described the design they developed at the laboratory*''

Fig. 10.2 Japanese sentence being translated by ULTRA

```
(2) [prdctn, [type,indpnt], [class,dcl], [form,fin],
     [prop, [type,indpnt], [class,dcl],
      [pred, [tense,pst], [aspect,simp], [mood,indic], [voice,actv], [pol,pos],
       [rel, [type,dyn], [s_case,agnt], [o_case,pat], [io_case,none],
                        [s_class,human], [o_class,a_obj], [io_class,none],
        [r_desc,describe0_1]]],
      [arg, [g_rel,subj], [k_rel,agnt], [t_rel,top],
       [ent, [type,nrm], [class,human], [agree,A], [det,spin], [quant,Q],
        [c_desc,engineer1_1]]],
      [arg, [g_rel,do], [k_rel,pat], [t_rel,foc],
       [ent, [type,nrm], [class,a_obj], [agree,A], [det,D], [quant,Q],
        [c_desc,
         design2_4,
         [c_mod, [type,rel], [class,prop],
          [prop, [type,dpnt], [class,dcl],
            [pred, [tense,pst], [aspect,simp], [mood,indic], [voice,actv], [pol,pos],
              [rel, [type,dyn], [s_case,agnt], [o_case,pat], [io_case,none],
                                 [s_class,human], [o_class,a_obj], [io_class,none],
               [r_desc,develop0_2]]],
            [arg, [g_rel,subj], [k_rel,agnt], [t_rel,top],
              [ent, [type,pro], [class,human], [agree,tp], [det,spin], [quant,unq],
               they_1]],
            [arg, [g_rel,do], [k_rel,pat], [t_rel,null], pro],
            [p_mod, [g_rel,oo], [k_rel,position], [t_rel,foc],
              [ent, [type,nrm], [class,p_obj], [agree,A], [det,D], [quant,Q],
               [c_desc,laboratory0_0]]]]]]]]]]
```

Fig. 10.3 Intermediate representation in ULTRA (Farwell et al., 1993)

Without going into the specifics of the framework, (2) is intended to represent the fact that the expression is part of a single conversational turn, prdctn, consisting of a single, complete assertion, prop . . . dcl. All assertions are communicative acts, attempts to inform the addressee that the world is thus-and-so. It is composed of three elements: a predicate, pred . . . describe1_1, a subject argument, arg . . . subj . . . engineer1_1, and an object argument, arg . . . do. That the predicate is classified as indicative, pred . . . [mood, indic] . . ., also expresses communicative information, namely, that the speaker takes the assertion as a fact. The subject and object arguments are classified as topic, arg. . . [t rel, top] . . ., and focus, arg . . . [t rel, foc] . . ., respectively, thus expressing the rhetorical organization of the speech act. The object argument is itself complex, containing an entity descriptor, e desc, design2 4, and a modifying assertion, e mod ... prop ... dcl. The modifying element, in turn, is made up of four elements: a predicate, pred ... developO_ 2, a subject argument, arg ... subj ... theyO_ 1, an object argument, arg ... do ... pro, and a proposition modifier, p mod ... position ... laboratoryO_O.

Thus, IRs are representations of the explicit information motivated by a given expression, including the referential (what is being said), rhetorical (how it is being said) and communicative (why it is said) aspects as applied to any language. Although these IRs are "language neutral", they represent linguistic events and the interrelationship of the elements of these events, rather than the conceptual contents of expressions.

The Language Components

Each individual language system is independent of all other language systems within ULTRA. Corresponding sentences in different languages must produce the same IR and any specific IR must generate corresponding sentences in the five languages. However, the particular approach to parsing or generation which is used in each of the languages may differ. Each language has its own procedures for associating the expressions of the language with the appropriate IRs. These independent systems communicate by handing each other IRs, and no actual transfer takes place.

Independence of the language-particular systems is of both theoretical and practical interest. Given the required equivalence of the input-output behavior of each of the language systems, this paradigm is excellent for comparing various approaches to parsing or generation for their coverage and efficacy.

A new language may be added to the translation system at any time without unpredictable or negative side effects on the previously developed language systems, or on the system's overall performance. The language system developers have freedom of choice as to the class of grammar, and the type of parser and generator they prefer to use, which allows for rapid extension to new translation applications as well as allowing for greater flexibility when designing supporting software.

Furthermore, the addition of any new language system will have the effect of multiplying the number of language pairs in the translation system by the number of languages already in the system (having developed an English-Japanese system, we need only develop the Spanish module to have an English-Spanish system and a Japanese-Spanish system, and so forth). This expandability is a vast improvement over most existing systems which require the same amount of development time for each direction of translation for a given language pair, and/or for each of the two directions of each new language pair even if one or more of those languages are already part of a working system.

ULTRA's Grammars and Parsers

At present, we have developed five prototype language systems for ULTRA. Each system has been implemented in PROLOG and can both analyze an expression from the language (the IR is the output), and generate an expression in the language (when the IR is the input). Through the use of logic programming techniques, we have been successful in developing symmetric or bidirectional parser/generators for all of the languages. That is to say, in a given language system, the same algorithm is used to do either the analysis or the generation of the expressions of the language.

The individual language systems for ULTRA, which translate from a source language to the intermediate representation and vice versa, have been based on a number of different grammatical approaches including Definite Clause Grammar (Pereira and Warren, 1980), Case Grammar (Nagao et al., 1985), Categorial Grammar (Uszkoreit, 1986), as well as a semantic constituent structure grammar. All of these systems utilize both semantic and syntactic constraints for dealing with ambiguity. Such grammars are "clean", allowing individual language programmers to explain their respective rule systems, and compare their approaches for dealing with particular linguistic problems, as well as for the rapid development of new grammars. It is this flexibility that distinguishes our system from others.

The Spanish component of our system, for instance, currently takes the form of a Semantic Definite Clause Grammar (Huang, 1988). This formalism is an extension of Definite Clause Grammars (Pereira and Warren, 1980) which allows the inclusion of semantic information. The grammar is essentially a context-free phrase structure grammar with complex categories. The resolution mechanism of Prolog provides a top-down, depth-first, left-to-right, unification-based parser/generator of a subset of Spanish expressions.

In every rule of the grammar, bidirectionality (or, more properly, symmetry; see Jin and Simmons, 1986) is introduced through the explicit mention of the representational schema, together with the string under analysis, and the string which is left over after the analysis. In effect, this converts each rule into an equivalence statement between structures and expressions. When the rule is used to prove one has an equivalent, it provides the other as a by-product of the proof. If used to prove a specific string and structure are in fact equivalent, it succeeds if they are and fails if they are not. If used to prove which strings are paired with which structures, it provides all of the provable structure-expression equivalence pairs. Since all the rules in system are of this format, symmetry or bidirectionality is maintained at every level.

Relaxation

While the system is capable of handling a wide range of phenomena, including compound and complex sentences, relative clauses, complex noun phrases, questions (yes-no and Wh types) and imperatives. There will always be certain classes of non-standard input (e.g. "Where station?") which fall outside the system's normal capabilities and to deal with such irregular input, we are developing a number of techniques which together we call "relaxation". Our assumption is that if a given string or IR cannot be successfully processed even though all the lexical items are available in the system, it should be reprocessed with the various constraints systematically weakened.

Three basic cases are being investigated: grammatical relaxation, semantic relaxation, and structural relaxation (thus far, only semantic relaxation has been implemented in prototype form).

Semantic relaxation copes with the following problem: suppose that an initial analysis of the expression "the man kicked the dog" failed to produce an IR because "kicking" required that a physical object be kicked, and "dog" was specified as an animate. Our technique requires access to LDOCE hierarchical relationships (Guthrie et al., 1990) which results in the introduction of a special predicate to identify two semantic classes as an acceptable (if not strict) match, that is, that would allow animate objects to be compatible with physical objects and so on. This would allow the system to recognize "dog" as compatible with the requirement for physical object at the point where unification takes place. Another class of special predicates allows for non-dominant relaxations (e.g., for forces as animate objects as in "the wind opened the door"), thus avoiding overly constraining relaxation along a strict "is-a" hierarchy.

Methods of this general sort have been investigated over a very long period, especially within Artificial Intelligence (at least since Wilks, 1979), where the problem was seen as one of accepting and representing collocations that broke preference-restrictions. More recently, there has been a range of suggestions for formal inheritance structures in the lexicon, deriving from DATR (Evans and Gazdar 1990), which are not concerned explicitly with relaxation in sentence interpretation but with the inheritance mechanisms and lexical data that make the above relationships and associated features explicit.

Grammatical relaxation systematically removes specific grammatical constraints such as agreement in number between subject and verb, agreement in gender and number between adjectives and nouns, and other feature-based syntactic constraints, and then reprocesses the string. Structural relaxation reanalyzes a string as an arbitrary sequence of lower level constituents such as an argument, a predicate, or a dependent clause, if a given input cannot be parsed as a full sentence.

If all of the above methods fail, a word-by-word translation is provided in order to present grammatical and semantic information of each lexical item in the input, if nothing more.

ULTRA's Lexicons

There are two types of entries related to the specification of a lexical item in the ULTRA system: those for intermediate representation (IR) word sense tokens (refer to the bottom INTER TOKEN box in the sample screen below in Fig. 10.4), and those for the words of the individual languages (the top five boxes in the sample screen).

Currently, there are eight IR word sense categories including entities (often corresponding to nouns), relations (often corresponding to verbs and adjectives), entity specifiers (often corresponding to determiners), relation specifiers (often corresponding to auxiliaries), case relations (often corresponding to prepositions), proposition specifiers (often corresponding to complementizers), proposition modifiers (often corresponding to sentential adverbials), and conjunctions. Each category is associated with a special set of constraints which ranges in number from one for sentential adverbs, to nine for relations. The number of lexical categories for the individual language lexicons varies from eight to fourteen. There is no simple correspondence between the language-particular lexical categories and the IR categories although the gross relationships stated above appear to hold.

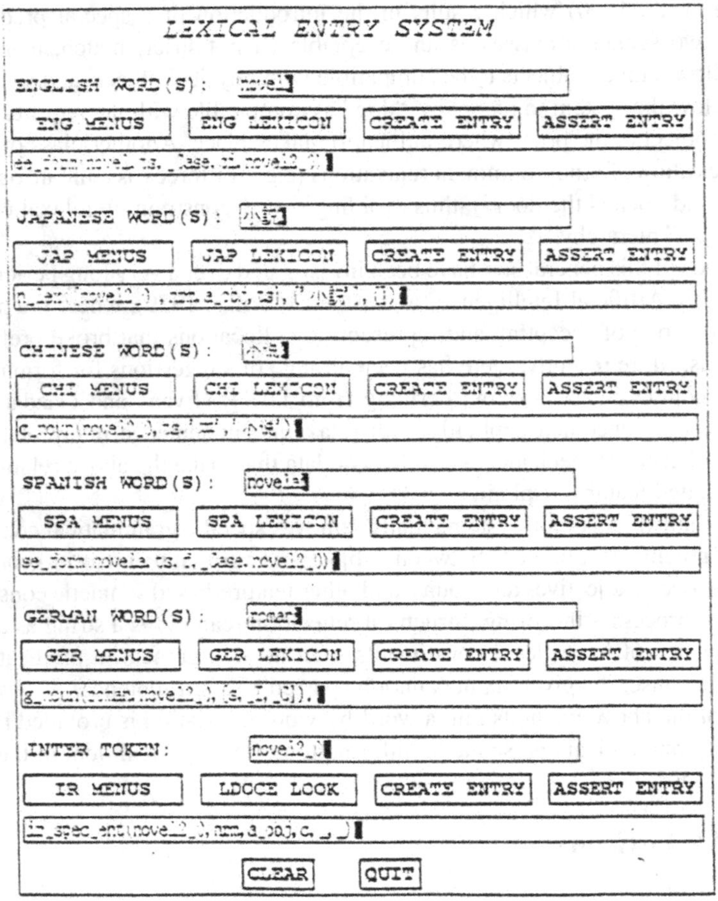

LEXICAL ENTRY SYSTEM

ENGLISH WORD(S): novel

ENG MENUS | ENG LEXICON | CREATE ENTRY | ASSERT ENTRY

ee_form(novel, ts, _, case, nl, novel2_0))

JAPANESE WORD(S): 小説

JAP MENUS | JAP LEXICON | CREATE ENTRY | ASSERT ENTRY

n_lex(novel2_0), nm, a_obj, ts), ('小説', [])

CHINESE WORD(S): 小说

CHI MENUS | CHI LEXICON | CREATE ENTRY | ASSERT ENTRY

c_noun(novel2_0), ts, '本', '小说')

SPANISH WORD(S): novela

SPA MENUS | SPA LEXICON | CREATE ENTRY | ASSERT ENTRY

se_form(novela, ts, f, _, case, novel2_0))

GERMAN WORD(S): roman

GER MENUS | GER LEXICON | CREATE ENTRY | ASSERT ENTRY

g_noun(roman, novel2_0), [s, _I, _C]).

INTER TOKEN: novel2_0

IR MENUS | LDOCE LOOK | CREATE ENTRY | ASSERT ENTRY

ir_spec_ent(novel2_0, nm, a_obj, c, _, _)

CLEAR | QUIT

Fig. 10.4 Lexical entry system for ULTRA (Farwell et al., 1993)

All entries take the general form of simple Prolog unit clauses in (3):

(3) category (Form, F1, F2, . . .).

where F1, F2 and so on, are constraints. For language-particular entries, these are generally syntactic constraints associated with an orthographic form, Form, such as the gender of a noun, whether a verb is reflexive, and so on. For example, (4) is a simplified and readable version of a Spanish entry for the noun banco.

(4) noun (banco, third_singular, masculine, bank4_1).

Similarly, (5) is an Spanish entry for the verb ingreso.

(5) verb (ingreso, third singular, finite, past, simple, indicative, active, deposit1_3).

The final argument represents the IR word sense the Spanish form is used to express. This sense token is associated with a sense definition in LDOCE and is used to index the corresponding IR entry.

For IR entries, the features F1, F2, and so on, correspond to universal semantic and pragmatic constraints on the word sense, Form, such as the classification of an entity as countable or not, the semantic case structure of a relation, and so on. For example the IR entry for bank4_1 would look something like:

(6) entity (bank4_1, class, countable, institution, abstract object, economics banking).

while the IR entry for deposit1_3 would look like:

(7) relation (deposit1_3, dynamic, placing, agent, patient, human, amount, human, abstract object, economics banking).

The classes of features associated with each of the IR word sense categories, then, are the target of the automatic extraction process that we will describe in the section The Automatic Construction of IR Lexical Items. This section will also provide more detailed descriptions of the features.

The Interface to the ULTRA System

The interface for the machine translation system has been developed using Xwindows. Editing is accomplished through a modified Athena Widget, having a subset of the editing capabilities of Gemacs. Input of Chinese and Japanese is handled in a similar manner via Nemacs which provides all of the editing capabilities of Gemacs with the additional ability of using the Japanese or Chinese character sets. Below is a sample screen for ULTRA where Chinese sentences appear on the left and translations of sentences 17 into Japanese appear on the right (Fig. 10.5). A translation is requested using the lower windows. In the cases where the translation is not unique, the retranslate button allows the user to view the alternate translations.

A lexical item can be entered into the system in several ways. Lexical items can be created off-line, independent of the MT program. This entry procedure is described in the section entitled From LDOCE to a partially specified entry. In addition, we have an on-line lexical entry procedure which allows a lexical item to be generated while the MT program is running. This will be activated whenever the system is asked to translate a word which does not appear in the lexicon. In every case, the full process of creating a lexical entry includes the specification of the IR sense token, the specification of the source language lexical item, and the specification of the target language lexical item. Having completed each specification, the user is then presented with the full specification of the item for confirmation or, possibly, correction.

During the translation process, the missing lexical items can in some cases be identified automatically, namely, through a pre-processing for unknown spelling forms, if an unknown form is found, the item is marked and translation proceeds as usual. When the analysis system reaches the point where processing begins on the marked item, processing is interrupted and the user is prompted for a specification of the new item. This allows for the use of information from the context of the item, thus reducing the amount of information that the user needs to provide. With the specification of the source language and IR items completed, a pseudo target language item is constructed with the source language spelling form temporarily standing as the target language form. Processing then continues and the translation is completed with the source language item appearing in the target language text. The user is again consulted, this time as to the appropriate target language item. In cases where the spelling form is in the lexicon but not associated with an appropriate sense, the items to be entered must be identified by the user through the observation of inappropriate target language output. Here also, we are developing an interruptive interactive technique for adding the appropriate entry to source and target languages.

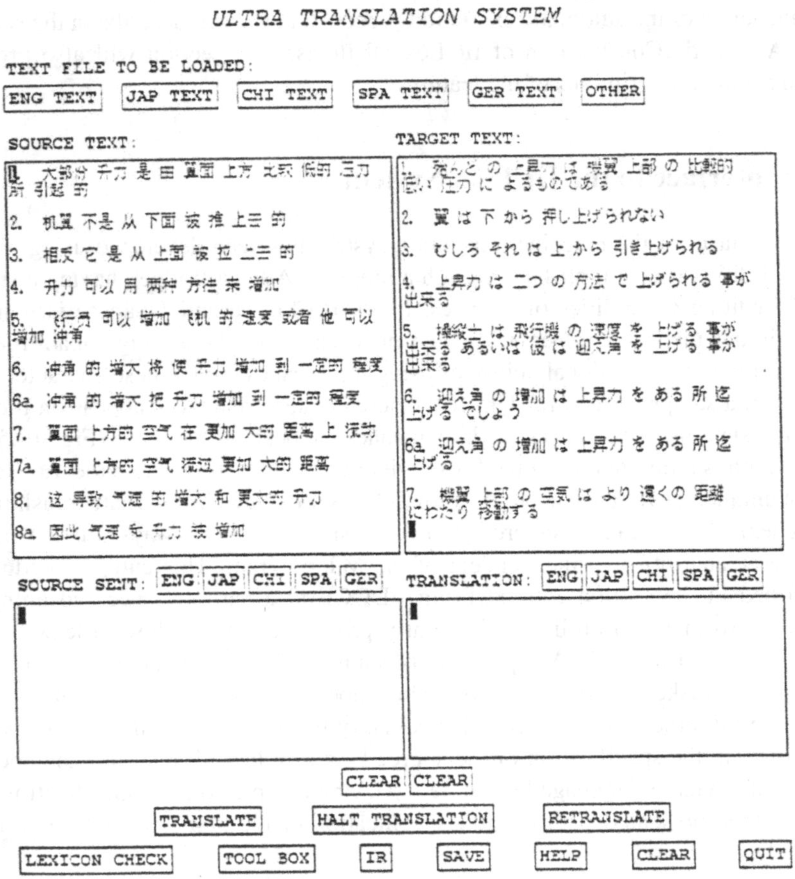

Fig. 10.5 Screen for Chinese-Japanese translation in ULTRA (Farwell et al., 1993)

The Automatic Construction of Lexical Items

The work on automating lexical entry has drawn upon extensive research at the Computing Research Laboratory in deriving semantic structures automatically from large machine-readable dictionaries (Slator, 1988; Guthrie et. al 1990; Wilks et al., 1995). Much of the core IR lexicon has been derived from the 72,000 word senses in LDOCE. Codings from the dictionary for such properties as semantic category, semantic preferences and so on have been used, either directly or indirectly, to generate partial specifications of some 10,000 IR tokens for the system. We are looking at the application of machine-readable versions of bilingual dictionaries to the automatic entry of items in individual language lexicons. Together, these two entry techniques will allow for the rapid increase in the size and coverage of the vocabularies and for tailoring them to the individual needs of the user.

The partially automated lexical entry process proceeds in three steps: I) given a sense in LDOCE, an entry is constructed by a process of automatic extraction and formatting of information in the form of a standardized data structure, 2) any remaining unspecified information in that structure is provided interactively, followed by 3) the automatic mapping from the fully specified data structure to the corresponding Prolog facts. Step 3) is very straightforward and will not be described here. Below we give a short description of LDOCE and then discuss the techniques we have used to accomplish steps 1) and 2).

LDOCE

The Longman Dictionary of Contemporary English (Procter et al., 1978) is a full-sized dictionary designed for learners of English as a second language. It contains 41,122 headword entries, defined in terms of 72,177 word senses, in machine-readable form (a typesetting tape). With few exceptions, the definitions in LDOCE are stated using a control vocabulary of approximately 2,000 words. The control vocabulary words tend to be highly ambiguous (approximately 17,000 senses are listed in LDOCE for the 2,000 spelling forms).

Both the book and tape versions of LDOCE use a system of grammatical codes of about 110 syntactic (sub)categories which vary in generality. Nouns, for example, may be assigned categories such as count-noun (e.g., a table) or count-noun-followed-by-infinitive-with-to (e.g., a need to do something), or vocative-noun-used-indirect-address (e.g., sir). The syntactic categories for verbs are particularly extensive and include categories such as verb-with-one-object-followed-by-the-infinitive-without-to (e.g., to see something do something).

In addition, the machine-readable version of LDOCE contains box and subject codes which are not found in the book. Many researchers have made use of these (e.g., Walker and Amsler, 1986; Boguraev et al., 1989) but not, we think, in the way we have, although we give no details here. There are 10 different types of box codes which represent a variety of types of dialectal and sociolinguistic information, as well as the semantic class of a noun and the selection restrictions on the complements of verbs and adjectives. The selection restrictions are chosen from a set of 34 semantic categories, 17 of which are primitives (such as abstract, concrete, and animate) and organized into a type hierarchy; the remaining categories are composites of the 17 primitive categories such as liquid-or-solid which is used to classify words such as "flask", "barrel" and "bouillabaisse".

The subject codes are used to classify meanings by the subject domains in which they commonly appear. For example, one sense of "current" is classified as common in the domain of geology-and-geography, while another sense is common in the domain of electrical-engineering. These terms also organized into a hierarchy which consists of over 100 main headings such as engineering, with over 300 subheadings like electrical.

From LDOCE to a Partially Specified Entry

The mapping process from LDOCE to ULTRA word sense entries assumes a particular linguistic context. Information contained in the LDOCE definition is automatically extracted and used in the corresponding ULTRA specification. For some parts of speech (e.g., nouns), most of the information required by the interlingual entry can be extracted automatically; for others (e.g., verbs and adjectives), only a portion of the information is available.

For this project we began with a Lisp version of LDOCE, which formats the information from the typesetting tape (Boguraev et al., 1987). A boldface headword in the dictionary, together with all of its definitions, becomes a Lisp list with sublists corresponding to various parts of the definition (such as part of speech, pronunciation, grammar code, box and subject codes, definition, derived forms, usage notes, etc.).

As mentioned earlier, there are currently eight IR sense categories, each of which is associated with a special set of constraints (see the above section on ULTRA's Lexicons). To date, we have extracted information from LDOCE nouns for specifying IR entries for entities, from verbs and adjectives for specifying IR entries for relations, and from adverbs for specifying IR entries for relation modifiers and proposition modifiers. These are the major open class categories of IR word sense tokens and constitute over 95% of the tokens defined thus far. The following is a summary of the information required by each of these categories (the information which is currently not provided automatically is marked by o).

Entities

- a word sense token which indexes a corresponding LDOCE definition,
- a classification as either a class name, a name of an individual, or an anaphoric element,

- a classification as either countable or not countable,
- a semantic class,
- a LDOCE semantic class,
- a LDOCE subject domain classification.

Below are sample screens of the interactive session for completing the IR lexical entry for one sense of "bank". The screen on the left is created automatically and the screen on the right is then produced manually.

Note that for entities (nouns) only one feature, described above as "the semantic class", is not provided automatically from LDOCE. This field corresponds to a set of some 100 semantic categories used by the five language components of the ULTRA system which were developed prior to the use of LDOCE for automatically extracting information. These semantic categories were hand crafted, based on the comparative analysis of surface linguistic phenomena in the different languages and are primarily used for implementing semantic preferences. The automatically created entries for entities contain the LDOCE semantic categories as well, but these are not currently being used by the ULTRA systems pending an evaluation of their consistency and their appropriateness as a basis for semantic preferences in the translation context. We expect that we will eventually move to a modified version of the LDOCE systems of semantics categories in which those categories are further developed to provide the finer distinctions the MT system often requires (for example, the LDOCE category "abstract" corresponds to several hand-crafted ULTRA categories).

Relations

- a word sense token which indexes a corresponding LDOCE definition,
- a classification as either stative or dynamic,
- a semantic class,
- the number of arguments,
- a case role corresponding to each argument,
- a semantic preference for the filler of each case role,
- a LDOCE semantic preference for the filler of each case role,
- a LDOCE subject domain classification.

The sample screens below show the interactive session for completing the IR lexical entry for one sense of "deposit".

As before, the screen on the left is created automatically and the screen on the right is then produced manually. Note that in the case of relations, LDOCE does not provide case roles for the arguments, a semantic class for the relation, or a direct classification of the relation as stative or dynamic. We have developed a verb hierarchy from LDOCE, based on genus (hypernym) of a verb definition, and are in the process of disambiguating the terms in this hierarchy. These, then, will be used as the verb classes for ULTRA's relations. We have been able to extract case role information in some cases (Wilks et al., 1990) from implicit information in Longman's and will include this in the lexical entries. Again the semantic preferences for the fillers of the case roles are those originally used in ULTRA. As in the case of entities above, the LDOCE semantic preferences are also included in the entry for future use.

Relation Modifiers

- a word sense token which indexes a corresponding LDOCE definition,
- a semantic class,
- a semantic preferences for the relation modified.

These lexical entries correspond to adverbs and the information kept here is not identified explicitly in LDOCE. It is still an open question how to use the implicit information in machine readable dictionaries to identify this type of information.

Proposition Modifiers

- a word sense token which indexes a corresponding LDOCE definition.

Extraction is performed by applying a sequence of flex programs (a new generation version of the UNIX lexical analyzer utility, lex) which transform information from the LDOCE LISP format into a LISP association list, the data structure used by the interactive lexical entry interface for the ULTRA system (sample screens appear in the previous section). In addition to the requirements marked as automated above, the semantic class for nouns and the semantic preferences for the fillers of the different case relations are also specified automatically through the use of a mapping function from LDOCE categories to ULTRA categories. However, since the function results in only a partial mapping, in many cases this information must be added by hand.

The word senses added to the ULTRA system using these techniques were chosen first on the basis of whether they were exemplified in the dictionary entry, and second, whether they were one of the first three senses of a given homonym (the LDOCE senses are listed in order of frequency of use). Files containing the definitions of all noun, verb, adverb and adjective senses for which there were example sentences were first automatically generated. An additional file containing example sentences tagged by the word sense being exemplified was also created. Next, association lists corresponding to IR entries for each of the word senses were generated. Finally, another procedure was applied which automatically supplied a pointer to the example context in the example sentence file.

Interactive Completion of Specification

For this particular project, we used the active-forms based lexical entry system, which is more developed. When the partially specified lexical structure is passed to the interactive entry system from the automatic extraction process, it becomes the basic data structure of the entry system. The user is presented with the sense token and the source language context, and proceeds to specify the item as usual. The primary difference is that much of the information which is normally gathered from the user has already been identified automatically. Particular forms or menus may appear completely filled out, and the user need do no more than check to see that the information presented is correct. Only the missing information is actually requested by prompts. So, for example, in specifying an entity, the only requirement is specify a semantic class compatible with the ULTRA system of semantic classification. No further information is needed since all of the information can be extracted from LDOCE. In the specification of a relation, only the semantic class of the relation, the case roles of the different argument slots, and the ULTRA semantic preferences must be filled. The semantic type of the relation, its subject domain, the number of arguments and the LDOCE semantic preferences for the fillers of the different roles need not be specified. They can be extracted from LDOCE. The previous two sample screens give examples of this interface. The result is that, even as it stands today, the rate of lexical entry creation has been greatly improved from an average of 20 to 30 entries per hour to an average of 80 to 120 entries per hour. In addition, the consistency among definitions has improved since the users (different people working at different times, on different languages) are now directly responsible for fewer decisions.

Approaches to Achieving Full Specification

It was clear at the outset of this project that a great deal of lexical acquisition could be done automatically and we have initiated projects to investigate whether the missing information can be identified automatically through further analysis of the definitions, examples, grammatical categories, etc. Currently, we are concerned with automating the construction of the IR entries such as those illustrated in (6) and (7), above. Using the Lexicon Provider of Slator (Wilks et al., 1996), we have parsed the definitions in LDOCE and from those results, extracted a taxonomy for verbs. This will be used as a basis for defining semantic classes for relations. We have had some success in defining case roles for relations and work in that area is continuing. Another project has been initiated to investigate whether we can automatically infer or identify case relations (the meanings of prepositions) and preferences on the elements related by case relations.

Eventually, we hope to investigate the use of information in dictionaries to identify preferences of adverbs on the semantic classes of the relations they can modify.

In addition, in order to automate the construction of lexical items fully on the fly during translation, procedures must be defined to select specific senses on the basis of the source language linguistic context of the item being defined. Similarly, procedures must be developed to automatically specify the different language-particular lexical entries (these procedures do exist in English to a limited extent), and these must be adapted to other languages. Finally, techniques for using bilingual dictionaries in the specific language lexical specification process must be developed.

Afterword 2008: The ULTRA system, designed at built at NMSU, was the second practical system in which I was involved as which is reported in this book: the first was the Stanford semantics-based system, built by two people (Annette Herskovits and myself), using the system I had designed for my thesis work. The second was this ULTRA system, funded in part by New York investors but never developed commercially by them. It was never properly evaluated and its only interesting feature may be that it used much of the architecture of the EUROTRA system and finally achieved better performance that that system at perhaps 1% of the cost. The third system was the multi-site PANGLOSS system, funded by DARPA in competition with IBMs CANDIDE, which proved in the end very much the way forward at that time, even though PANGLOSS led to usable machine-aided spin offs and made points about the sue of resources, linguistics and semantics that have not disappeared altogether and will be discussed the final chapters.

Part III
MT Future

Chapter 11
Senses and Texts

Introduction

Empirical, corpus-based, computational linguistics reaches by now into almost every crevice of the subject, and perhaps pragmatics will soon succumb. Semantics, if we may assume the sense-tagging task is semantic, taken broadly, has shown striking progress and, in Yarowsky's work (1995) produced very high levels of success in the 90%s, well above the key bench-mark figure of 62% correct sense assignment, achieved at an informal experiment in New Mexico about 1990, in which each word was assigned its first sense listed in LDOCE.

A crucial question in this chapter will be whether recent work in sense-tagging has in fact given us the breakthrough in scale that is now obvious with, say, part-of-speech tagging. Our conclusion will be that it has not, and that the experiments so far, however high their success rates, are not yet of a scale different from those of the previous generation of linguistic, symbolic-AI or connectionist approaches to the very same problem.

A historian of our field might glance back at this point to, say, Small et al. (1988) which covered the AI-symbolic and connectionist traditions of sense-tagging at just the moment before corpus-driven empirical methods began to revive. All the key issues still unsettled are discussed there and the collection showed no naiveté there about the problem of sense resolution with respect only to existing lexicons of senses. It was realised that that task was only meaningful against an assumption of some method for capturing new (new to the chosen lexicon, that is) senses and, most importantly, that although existing lexicons differed, they did not differ arbitrarily much. The book also demonstrated that there was also strong psychological backing for the reality of word senses and for empirical methods of locating them from corpora without any prior assumptions about their number or distribution (e.g. Plate's work in Wilks et al. 1990, and see also Jorgensen, 1990).

Our purpose in this chapter will be to argue that Kilgarriff's (1993) negative claims are simply wrong, when he argued that there really are no word senses and hence they cannot be discriminated by computer Yarowsky is largely right in arguing against this, as we shall show, although we have some queries about the details and the interpretation of his claims. Both authors however agree that this is a traditional and important task: one often cited as being, because of the inability of systems of the past to carry it out, a foundational lacuna in, say, the history of machine translation (MT). It was assumed by many, in that distant period, that if only word-sense ambiguity could be tamed, by the process we are calling sense-tagging, then MT of high quality would be relatively straightforward. Like may linguistic tasks, it became an end in itself, like syntactic parsing, and, now that it is, we would claim, firmly in sight (despite Kilgarriff) it is far less clear that its solution will automatically solve a range of traditional problems like MT. But clearly it would be a generally good tool to have and local triumph if this long-resistant bastion of NLP were to yield.

The Very Possibility of Sense-Tagging

Kilgarriff's paper (1993) is important because it has been widely cited as showing that the senses of a word, as distinguished in a dictionary such as LDOCE, do not cover the senses actually carried by most occurrences of the word as they appear in a corpus. If his paper does show that, it is very significant indeed, because that would imply that sense-tagging word occurrences in a corpus by means of any lexical data based on, or related to, a machine-readable dictionary or thesaurus is misguided. I want to show that here the paper does not demonstrate any such thing. Moreover, it proceeds by means of a straw-man it may be worth bringing back to life!

That straw-man, Kilgarriff's starting point, is the 'bank model' (BM) of lexical ambiguity resolution, which is established by assertion rather than quotation, though it is attributed to Small, Hirst, and Cottrell as well as the present author. In the BM, words have discrete meanings, and the human reader (like the ideal computer program) knows instantly and effortlessly which meaning of the word applies (Ibid. p. 367), "given that a word occurrence always refers to one or the other, but not both" of the pair of main meanings that a word like 'bank' is reputed to have. The main thrust of Kilgarriff's paper is to distinguish a number of relationships between LDOCE senses that are not discrete in that way, and then to go on to an experiment with a corpus.

But first we should breathe a little life back into the BM straw-man: those named above can look after themselves, but here is a passage from Wilks (1972, p. 12) ".it is very difficult to assign word occurrences to sense classes in any manner that is both general and determinate. In the sentences "I have a stake in this country" and "My stake on the last race was a pound" is "stake" being used in the same sense or not? If "stake" can be interpreted to mean something as vague as "Stake as any kind of investment in any enterprise" then the answer is yes. So, if a semantic dictionary contained only two senses for "stake": that vague sense together with "Stake as a post", then one would expect to assign the vague sense for both the sentences above. But if, on the other hand, the dictionary distinguished "Stake as an investment" and "Stake as an initial payment in a game or race" then the answer would be expected to be different. So, then, word sense disambiguation is relative to the dictionary of sense choices available and can have no absolute quality about it". QED.

In general, it is probably wise to believe, even if it is not always true, that authors in the past were no more naive than those now working, and were probably writing programs, however primitive and ineffective, to carry out the very same tasks as now (e.g. sense-tagging of corpus words). More importantly, the work quoted, which became an approach called preference semantics, was essentially a study of the divergence of corpus usage from lexical norms (or preferences) and developed in the Seventies into a set of processes for accommodating divergent/non-standard/metaphorical or what-you-will usage to existing lexical norms, notions that Kilgarriff seems to believe only developed in a much later and smarter group of people around 1990, which includes himself, but also, for example, Fass whose work was a direct continuation of that quoted above. Indeed, in Wilks (1972) procedures were programmed (and run over a set of newspaper editorials) to accommodate the divergent usage to that of an established sense of another word in the same text, while in Wilks (1977b) programmed procedures were specified to accommodate such usage by constructing completely new sense entries.

A much more significant omission, one that bears directly on his main claim and is not merely an issue of historical correctness, is the lack of reference to work in New Mexico and elsewhere (e.g. Cowie et al. 1992) on the large-scale sense tagging of corpora against an MRD-derived lexical data base. These were larger scale experiments whose results directly contradict the result he is believed to have proved. I shall return to this point in a moment. The best part of Kilgarriff's paper is his attempt to give an intuitive account of developmental relations between the senses of a word: there is, of course, a large scholarly literature on this. He distinguishes Generalizing Metaphors (a move from a specific case to a more general one), from Must-be-theres (the applicability of one sense requires the applicability of another, as when an act of matricide requires there to be a mother); from Domain shift (where a sense in one domain, like "mellow" of wine, is far enough from the domain of "mellow" of a personality, to constitute a sense shift).

It is not always easy to distinguish the first two types, since both rest on an implication relationship between two or more senses. Again, the details do not matter: what he has shown convincingly is that, as in the earlier quotation, the choice between senses of a given word is often not easy to make because it depends on their relationship, the nature of the definitions and how specific they are. I suspect no one has ever held a simple-minded version of the BM, except possibly Fodor and Katz, who, whatever their virtues, had no interest at all in lexicography.

The real problem with Kilgarriff's analysis of sense types is that he conflates:

1. text usage different from that shown in a whole list of stored senses for a given word e.g. in a dictionary, (which is what his later experiment will be about) with
2. text usage divergent from some "core" sense in the lexicon.

Only the second is properly in the area of metaphor/metonymy or "grinding" (Copestake and Briscoe, 1991) work of the group in which he places himself, and it is this phenomenon to which his classification of sense distinctions summarized above properly belongs. This notion requires some idea of sense development; of senses of a word extending in time in a non-random manner, and is a linguistic tradition of analysis going back to Givon (1967). However, the straw-man BM and the experiment he then does on hand-tagging of senses in text, all attach to the first, unrelated, notion which does not normally imply the presence of metonymy or metaphor at all, but simply an inadequate sense list. Of course, the two types may be historically related, in that some of the (a) list may have been derived by metaphorical/metonymic processes from a (b) word, but this is not be so in general. This confusion of targets is a weakness in the paper, since it makes it difficult to be sure what he wants us to conclude from the experiment. However, since we shall show his results are not valid, this distinction may not matter too much.

One might add here that Kilgarriff's pessimism has gone hand in hand with some very interesting surveys he has conducted over the Internet on the real need for word-sense disambiguation by NLP R&D. And one should note that there are others (e.g. Ide and Veronis, 1994) who have questioned the practical usefulness of data derived at many sites from MRDs. Our case here, of course, is that it has been useful, both in our own work on sense-tagging (Cowie et al. 1992) and in that of Yarowsky, using Roget and discussed below.

Kilgarriff's experiment, which what has been widely taken to be the main message of his paper, is not described in much detail. In a footnote, he refuses to give the reader the statistics on which his result was based even though the text quite clearly contains a claim (p. 378) that 87% of (non-monsemous) words in his text sample have at least one text occurrence that cannot be associated with one and only one LDOCE sense. Hence, he claims, poor old BM is refuted, yet again.

But that claim (about word types) is wholly consistent with, for example, 99% of text usage (of word tokens) being associated with one and only one dictionary sense! Thus the actual claim in the paper is not at all what it has been taken to show, and is highly misleading.

But much empirical evidence tells also against the claim Kilgarriff is believed to have made. Informal analyses (1989) by Georgia Green suggested that some 20% of text usage (i.e. to word tokens) could not be associated with a unique dictionary sense. Consistent with that, too, is the use of simulated annealing techniques by Cowie et al. (1992) at CRL-New Mexico to assign LDOCE senses to a corpus. In that work, it was shown that about 75%–80% of word usage could be correctly associated with LDOCE senses, as compared with hand-tagged control text. It was, and still is, hoped that that figure can be raised by additional filtering techniques.

The two considerations above show, from quite different sources and techniques, the dubious nature of Kilgarriff's claim. Wierzbicka (1989 following Antal 1963) has long argued that words have only core senses and that dictionaries/lexicons should express that single sense and leave all further sense refinement to some other process, such as real world knowledge manipulations, AI if you wish, but not a process that uses the lexicon.

Since the CRL result suggested that the automatic procedures worked very well (nearer 80%) at the homograph, rather than the sub-sense, level (the latter being where Kilgarriff's examples all lie) one possible way forward for NLP would be to go some of the way with Wierzbicka's views and restrict lexical sense distinctions to the homograph level. Then sense tagging could perhaps be done at the success level of part-of speech tagging. Such a move could be seen as changing the data to suit what you can accomplish, or as reinstating AI and pragmatics within NLP for the kind of endless, context-driven, inferences we need in real situations.

This suggestion is rather different from Kilgarriff's conclusion: which is also an empirical one. He proposes that the real basis of sense distinction be established by usage clustering techniques applied to corpora. This is an excellent idea and recent work at IBM (Brown et al. 1991) has produced striking non-seeded clusters of corpus usages, many of them displaying a similarity close to an intuitive notion of sense.

But there are serious problems in moving any kind of lexicography, traditional or computational, onto any such basis. Hanks (1994) has claimed that a dictionary could be written that consisted entirely of usages, and has investigated how those might be clustered for purely lexicographic purposes, yet it remains unclear what kind of volume could result from such a project or who would buy it and how they could use it. One way to think of such a product would be the reduction of monolingual dictionaries to thesauri, so that to look up a word becomes to look up which row or rows of context bound semi-synonyms it appears in. Thesauri have a real function both for native and non-native speakers of a language, but they rely on the reader knowing what some or all of the words in a row or class mean because they give no explanations. To reduce word sense separation to synonym classes, without explanations attached would limit a dictionary's use in a striking way.

If we then think not of dictionaries for human use but NLP lexicons, the situation might seem more welcoming for Kilgarriff's suggestion, since he could be seen as suggesting, say, a new version of WordNet (Miller, 1985) with its synsets established not a priori but by statistical corpus clustering. This is indeed a notion that has been kicked around in NLP for a while and is probably worth a try. There are still difficulties: first, that any such clustering process produces not only the clean, neat, classes like IBM's (Hindu Jew Christian Buddhist) example but inevitable monsters, produced by some quirk of a particular corpus. Those could, of course, be hand weeded but that is not an automatic process.

Secondly, as is also well known, what classes you get, or rather, the generality of the classes you get, depends on parameter settings in the clustering algorithm: those obtained at different settings may or may not correspond nicely to, say, different levels of a standard lexical hierarchy. They probably will not, since hierarchies are discrete in terms of levels and the parameters used are continuous but, even when they do, there will be none of the hierarchical terms attached, of the sort available in WordNet (e.g. ANIMAL or DOMESTIC ANIMAL). And this is only a special case of the general problem of clustering algorithms, well known in information retrieval, that the clusters so found do not come with names or features attached.

Thirdly, and this may be the most significant point for Kilgarriff's proposal, there will always be some match of such empirical clusters to any new text occurrence of a word and, to that degree, sense-tagging in text is bound to succeed by such a methodology, given the origin of the clusters and the fact that a closest match to one of a set of clusters can always be found. The problem is how you interpret that result because, in this methodology, no hand-tagged text will be available as a control since it is not clear what task the human controls could be asked to carry out. Subjects may find traditional sense-tagging (against e.g. LDOCE senses) hard but it is a comprehensible task, because of the role dictionaries and their associated senses have in our cultural world. But the new task (attach one and only one of the classes in which the word appears to its use at this point) is rather less well defined. But again, a range of original and ingenious suggestions may make this task much more tractable, and senses so tagged (against WordNet style classes, though empirically derived) could certainly assist real tasks like MT even if they did not turn out wholly original dictionaries for the book buying public.

There is, of course, no contradiction between, on the one hand, my suggestion for a compaction of lexicons towards core or homograph senses, done to optimize the sense-tagging process and, on the other, his suggestion for an empirical basis for the establishment of synsets, or clusters that constitute senses. Given that there are problems with wholly empirically-based sense clusters of the sort mentioned above, the natural move would be to suggest some form of hybrid derivation from corpus statistics, taken together with some machine-readable source of synsets: WordNet itself, standard thesauri, and even bilingual dictionaries which are also convenient reductions of a language to word sets grouped by sense (normally by reference to a word in another language, of course). As many have now realised, both the pure corpus methods and the large-scale hand-crafted sources have their virtues, and their own particular systematic errors, and the hope has to be that clever procedures can cause those to cancel, rather than reinforce, each other. But all that is future work, and beyond the scope of a critical note.

In conclusion, it may be worth noting that the BM, in some form, is probably inescapable, at least in the form of what Pustejovsky (1995) calls a "sense enumerative lexicon", and against which he inveighs for some twenty pages before going on to use one for his illustrations, as we all do, including all lexicographers. This is not hypocrisy but a confusion close to that between (a) and (b) above: we, as language users and computational modellers, must be able, now or later, to capture a usage that differs from some established sense (problem b above), but that is only loosely connected to problem (a), where senses, if they are real, seem to come in lists and it is with them we must sense-tag if the task is to be possible at al.

Recent Experiments in Sense-Tagging

We now turn to the claims in (Gale, Church, and Yarowsky 1992, abbreviated to GCY, see also Yarowsky 1992, 1993 and 1995) that:

1. That word tokens in text tend to occur with a smaller number of senses than often supposed and, most specifically,
2. In a single discourse a word will appear in one and only one sense, even if several are listed for it in a lexicon, at a level of about 94% likelihood for non-monosemous words (a figure that naturally becomes higher if the monosemous text words are added in).

These are most important claims if true for they would, at a stroke, remove a major excuse for the bad progress of MT; make redundant a whole sub-industry of NLP, namely sense resolution, and greatly simplify the currently fashionable NLP task of sense-tagging texts by any method whatever (e.g. Cowie et al. 1992, Bruce & Wiebe 1994).

GCY's claim would not make sense-tagging of text irrelevant, of course, for it would only allow one to assume that resolving any single token of a word (by any method at all) in a text would then serve for all occurrences in the text, at a high level of probability. Or, one could amalgamate all contexts for a word and resolve those taken together to some pre-established lexical sense. Naturally, these procedures would be absurd if one were not already convinced of the truth of the claim.

GCY's claims are not directly related to those of Kilgarriff, who aimed to show only that it was difficult to assign text tokens to any lexical sense at all. Indeed, Kilgarriff and GCY use quite different procedures: Kilgarriff's is one of assigning a word token in context to one of a set of lexical sense descriptions, while GCY's is one of assessing whether or not two tokens in context are the same sense or not. The procedures are incommensurable and no outcome on one would be predictive for the other: GCYs procedures do not use standard lexicons and are in terms of closeness-of-fit, which means that, unlike Kilgarriff's, they can never fail to match a text token to a sense, defined in the way they do (see below).

However, GCYs claims are incompatible with Kilgarriff's in spirit in that Kilgarriff assumes there is a lot of polysemy about and that resolving it is tricky, where GCY assume the opposite.

Both Kilgarriff and GCY have given rise to potent myths about word-sense tagging in text that I believe are wrong, or at best unproven. Kilgarriff's paper, as we saw earlier, has some subtle analysis but one crucial statistical flaw. GCY's is quite different: it is a mush of hard to interpret claims and procedures, but ones that may still, nonetheless, be basically true.

GCY's methodology is essentially impressionistic: the texts they chose are, of course, those available, which turn out to be Grolier's Encyclopaedia. There is no dispute about one-sense-per-discourse (their name for claim (2) above) for certain classes of texts: the more technical a text the more anyone, whatever their other prejudices about language, would expect the claim to be true. Announcing that the claim had been shown true for mathematical or chemical texts would surprise no one; encyclopaedias are also technical texts.

Their key fact in support of claim (1) above, based on a sense-tagging of 97 selected word types in the whole Encyclopaedia, and sense tagged by the statistical method described below, was that 7569 of the tokens associated with those types are monosemous in the corpus, while 6725 are of words with more than two senses. Curiously, they claim this shows "most words (both by token and by type) have only one sense". I have no idea whether to be surprised by this figure or not but it certainly does nothing to show that (Cowie et al. 1992) "Perhaps word sense disambiguation is not as difficult as we might have thought". It shows me that, even in fairly technical prose like that of an encyclopaedia, nearly half the words occur in more than one sense.

And that fact, of course, has no relation at all to mono- or poly-semousness in whatever base lexicon we happen to be using in an NLP system. Given a large lexicon, based on say the OED, one could safely assume that virtually all words are polysemous. As will be often the case, GCY's claim at this point is true of exactly the domain they are dealing with, and their (non-stated) assumption that any lexicon is created for the domain text they are dealing with and with no relation to any other lexicon for any other text. One claim per discourse, one might say.

This last point is fundamental because we know that distinctions of sense are lexicon—or procedure-dependent. Kilgarriff faced this explicitly, and took LDOCE as an admittedly arbitrary starting point. GCY never discuss the issue, which makes all their claims about numbers of senses totally, but inexplicitly, dependent on the procedures they have adopted in their experiments to give a canonical sense-tagging against which to test their claims.

This is a real problem for them. They admit right away that few or no extensive hand-tagged sense-resolved corpora exist for control purposes, So, they must adopt a sense-discrimination procedure to provide their data that is unsupervised. This is where the ingenuity of the paper comes in, but also its fragility. They have two methods for providing sense-tagged data against which to test their one-sense-per-discourse claim (2).

The first rests on a criterion of sense distinction provided by correspondence to differing non-English words in a parallel corpus, in their case the French-English Canadian Hansard because, as always, it is there! So, the correspondence of "duty" to an aligned sentence containing either "devoir" or "impot" (i.e. obligation or tax) is taken as an effective method of distinguishing the obligation/tax senses of the English word, which was indeed the criterion for sense argued for in (Dagon and Itai, 1994). It has well known drawbacks: most obviously that whatever we mean by sense distinction in English, it is unlikely to be criterially revealed by what the French happen to do in their language.

More relevantly to the particular case, GCY found it very hard to find plausible pairs for test, which must not of course share ambiguities across the French/English boundaries (as interest/interet do). In the end they were reduced to a test based on the six (!) pairs they found in the Hansard corpus that met their criteria for sense separation and occurrence more than 150 times in two or more senses. In GCYs defence one could argue that, since they do not expect much polysemy in texts, examples of this sort would, of course, be hard to find.

Taking this bilingual method of sense-tagging for the six word set as criterial they then run their basic word sense discrimination method over the English Hansard data. This consists, very roughly, of a training method over 100 word surrounding contexts for 60 instances of each member of a pair of senses (hand selected) i.e. for each pair $2 \times 60 \times 100 = 12{,}000$ words. Notice that this eyeballing method is not inconsistent with anything in Kilgarriff's argument: GCY selected 120 contexts in Hansard for each word that did correspond intuitively to one of the (French) selected senses. It says nothing about any tokens that may have been hard to classify in this way. The figures claimed for the discrimination method against the criterial data vary between 82 and 100% (for different word pairs) of the data for that sense correctly discriminated.

They then move on to a monolingual method that provides sense-tagged data in an unsupervised way. It rests on previous work by Yarowsky (1991) and uses the assignment of a single Roget category (from the 1042) as a sense-discrimination. Yarowsky sense-tagged some of the Grolier corpus in the following way: 100-word contexts for words like "crane" (ambiguous between bird and machinery) are taken and those words are scored by (very roughly, and given interpolation for local context) which of the 1042 Roget categories they appear under as tokens. The sense of a given token of "crane" is determined by which Roget category wins out: e.g. 348 (TOOLS/MACHINERY) for the machinery contexts, one hopes, and category 414 (ANIMALS/INSECTS) for the bird contexts. Yarowsky (1991) claimed 93% correctness for this procedure over a sample of 12 selected words, presumably checked against earlier hand-tagged data.

The interpolation for local effects is in fact very sophisticated and involves training with the 100 word contexts in Grolier of all the words that appear under a given candidate Roget head, a method that they acknowledge introduces some noise, since it adds into the training material Grolier contexts that involve senses of a category 348 word, say, that is not its machinery sense (e.g. crane as a bird). However, this method, they note, does not have the sense-defined-by-language2 problems that come with the Hansard training method.

In a broad sense, this is an old method, probably the oldest in lexical computation, and was used by Masterman (reported in Wilks 1972) in what was probably the first clear algorithm ever implemented for usage discrimination against Roget categories as sense-criterial. In the very limited computations of those days the hypothesis was deemed conclusive falsified; i.e. the hypothesis that any method overlapping the Roget categories for a word with the Roget categories of neighbouring words would determine an appropriate Roget category for that word in context.

This remains, I suspect, an open question: it may well be that Yarowsky's local interpolation statistics have made the general method viable, and that the 100-word window of context used is far more effective than a sentence. It may be the 12 words that confirm the disambiguation hypothesis at 93% would not be confirmed by 12 more words chosen at random (the early Cambridge work did at least try to Roget-resolve all the words in a sentence). But we can pass over that for now, and head on, to discuss GCY's main claim (2) given the two types of data gathered.

Two very strange things happen at this point as the GCY paper approaches its conclusion: namely, the proof of claim (2) or one-sense-per-discourse. First, the two types of sense-tagged data just gathered, especially the Roget-tagged data, should now be sufficient to test the claim, if a 93% level is deemed adequate for a preliminary test. Strangely, the data derived in the first part of the paper is never used or cited and the reader is not told whether Yarowsky's Roget data confirms or disconfirms (2).

Secondly, the testing of (2) is done purely by human judgement: a "blind" team of the three authors and two colleagues who are confronted by the OALD main senses for one of nine test words, and who then make judgements of pairs of contexts for one of the nine words drawn from a single Grolier article. The subjects are shown to have pretty consistent judgements and, of fifty-four pairs of contexts from the same article, fifty-one shared the same sense and three did not.

Notice here that the display of the OALD senses is pointless, since the subjects are not asked to decide which if any OALD sense the words appear in, and so no Kilgarriff style problems can arise. The test is simply to assign SAME or NOTSAME, and there are some control pairs added to force discrimination in some cases.

What can one say of this ingenious mini-experiment? Lexicographers traditionally distinguish "lumpers" and "splitters" among colleagues: those who tend to break up senses further and those who go for large, homonymic, senses, of which Wierzbicka would be the extreme case. Five GCY colleagues (one had to be dropped to get consistency among the team) from a "lumper" team decided that fifty-one out of fifty-four contexts for a word in a single encyclopaedia article (repeated for eight other words) are in the same sense. Is this significant? I suspect not very, and nothing at all follows to support the myth of discovery that has grown round the paper: the team and data are tiny and not disinterested. The Grolier articles are mini-texts where the hypothesis would, if true, surprise one least. Much more testing is needed before a universal hypothesis about text polysemy enters our beliefs. Of course, they may in the end be right, and all the dogma of the field so far be wrong.

More recently, Yarowsky (1993, 1995) has extended this methodology in two ways: first, he has established a separate claim he calls "one sense per collocation", which is quite independent of local discourse context (which was the separate "one-sense-per-discourse" claim) and could be expressed crudely by saying that it is highly unlikely that the following two sentences (with the "same" collocations for "plants") can both be attested in a corpus:

- Plastic plants can fool you if really well made (=organic)
- Plastic plants can contaminate whole regions (=factory)

One's first reaction may be to counter-cite examples like "Un golpe bajo" which can mean either a low blow in boxing, or a score one below par, in golf, although "golpe" could plausibly be said to have the same collocates in both cases. One can dismiss such examples (due to Jim Cowie in this case) by claiming both readings are idioms, but that should only focus our mind more on what Yarowsky does mean by collocation.

That work, although statistically impressive, gives no procedure for large-scale sense-tagging taken alone, since one has no immediate access to what cue words would, in general, constitute a collocation sufficient for disambiguation independent of discourse context. An interesting aspect of Yarowsky's paper is that he sought to show that on many definitions of sense and on many definitions of collocation (e.g. noun to the right, next verb to the left etc.) the hypothesis was still true at an interesting level, although better for some definitions of collocation than for others.

In his most recent work (1995) Yarowsky has combined this approach with an assumption that the earlier claim (2: one-sense-per-discourse) is true, so as to set up an iterative bootstrapping algorithm that both extends disambiguating collocational keys (Yarowsky 1993) and retrains against a corpus, while at the same time filtering the result iteratively by assuming (2): i.e. that tokens from the same discourse will have the same sense. The result, on selected pairs (as always) of bi-semous words is between 93 and 97% (for different word pairs again) correct against handcoded samples, which is somewhat better than he obtained with his Roget method (93% in 1991) and better than figures from Schuetze and Pederson (1995) who produce unsupervised clusterings from a corpus that have to be related by hand to intelligible, established, senses.

However, although this work has shown increasing sophistication, and has the great advantage, as he puts it, of not requiring costly hand-tagged training sets but instead "thrives on raw, unannotated, monolingual corpora—the more the merrier", it has the defect at present that it requires an extensive iterative computation for each identified bisemous word, so as to cluster its text tokens into two exclusive classes that cover almost all the identified tokens. In that sense it is still some way from a general sense-tagging procedure for full text corpora, especially one that tags with respect to some generally acceptable taxonomy of senses for a word. Paradoxically, Yarowsky was much closer to that last criterion with his 1991 work using Roget that did produce a sense-tagging for selected word pairs that had some "objectivity" predating the experiment.

Although Yarowsky compares his work favorably with that of Schuetze and Pederson in terms of percentages (96.7 to 92.2) of tokens correctly tagged, it is not clear that their lack of grounding for the classes in an established lexicon is that different from Yarowsky, since his sense distinctions in his experiments (e.g. plant as organic or factory) are intuitively fine but pretty ad hoc to the experiment in question and have no real grounding in dictionaries.

Conclusion

It will probably be clear to the reader by now that a crucial problem in assessing this area of work is the fluctuation of the notion of word sense in it, and that is a real problem outside the scope of this chapter. For example, sense as between binary oppositions of words is probably not the same as what the Roget categories discriminate, or words in French and English in aligned Hansard sentences have in common.

Another question arises here about the future development of large-scale sense-tagging: Yarowsky contrasts his work with that of efforts like (Cowie et al. 1992) that were dictionary based, as opposed to (unannotated) corpus based like his own. But a difference he does not bring out is that the Cowie et al. work, when optimized with simulated annealing, did go through substantial sentences, mini-texts if you will, and sense-tag all the words in them against LDOCE at about the 80% level. It is not clear that doing that is less useful than procedures like Yarowsky's that achieve higher levels of sense-tagging but only for carefully selected pairs of words, whose sense-distinctions are not clearly dictionary based, and which would require enormous prior computations to set up ad hoc sense oppositions for a useful number of words.

These are still early days, and the techniques now in play have probably not yet been combined or otherwise optimised to give the best results. It may not be necessary yet to oppose, as one now standardly does in MT, large-scale, less accurate, methods, though useful, with other higher-performance methods that cannot be used for practical applications. That the field of sense-tagging is still open to further development follows if one accepts the aim of this chapter which is to attack two claims, both of which are widely believed, though not at once: that sense-tagging of corpora cannot be done, and that it has been solved. As many will remember, MT lived with both these, ultimately misleading, claims for many years.

Chapter 12
Sense Projection

Afterword: this paper's origins are earlier than the last chapter, and go back to the late 1970s: its re-presentation is intended to show the antiquity (and unsolved nature in the present) of the task of locating novel senses by algorithm. The content is firmly n the tradition of AI: that understanding rests on representations of world knowledge – in this case the pseudo-text, or text-like representation of some context-dependent area of world knowledge, roughly what AI used to calla frame, in Minsky's sense. The difference here is the assumption, coming ultimately from Wittgenstein, that language is primary, even in the representation of world knowledge, and that our representations will have language-like (as opposed to logic-like and language-free, the standard AI assumption) properties. Wittgenstein sometimes expressed this by remarks like "A ruler must be in the same space as what is to be measured"; that knowledge that is to connect to language must be in some ways language-like – it cannot connect directly to the world, as he had believed in his earlier work. This chapter contains a claim that world-knowledge representations can help determine and interpret new senses of words but only by being language-like in a way logic pretends not to be.

This brief chapter sets out how one might deal with extensions of word sense in a natural language understanding system: that is to say, normal utterances that break pre-assigned selection, or preference, restrictions. The proposals here extend the knowledge representation of the preference semantics system (Wilks 1967, 1973a, 1973b, 1975, and Chapter 3 above) with pseudo-texts (PT) which are frame structures in the sense of Minsky (1975), but which are also consistent with the general assumptions of this NLUS (Natural Language Understanding System), and were described in Chapter 2 above.

It is essential to see that extended use, in the sense of preference-violating use is the norm in ordinary language use, and so cannot be relegated in an NLUS to some special realm of treatment, as "performance" is in generative linguistics, nor neglected in a general consideration of MT. The following sentence is chosen, I promise you, at random from the front page of a daily newspaper: (The Times, #5 – 2 – 76):

> Mr Wilson said that the line taken by the Shadow Cabinet, that an Assembly should be given no executive powers would lead to the break-up of the United Kingdom.

The sentence presents no understanding problems whatever to an informed reader, yet each of the four italicised entities violates the normal preference restrictions of an associated verb: "line", for example, would violate the normal physical object restriction on "take", and soon.

The process to be described in this chapter is called projection; we shall show how sense descriptions for words can be rewritten, in preference-violating texts (as in 1), with the aid of the specific knowledge in PTs: part of the PT will be projected into the sense description for a word. So, for example, in (1) some detailed political knowledge in a PT for "United Kingdom" could show that a breaking of that entity could be caused, and we would then replace the sense description of "lead to "by one equivalent to "cause", thus overcoming the preference violation in "lead to the break-up" and providing a more appropriate sense description of "lead to" for analysis of the rest of this text. It is an assumption of everything here that full MT requires not a discrimination of word senses in text, but the ability to interpret senses not encountered before.

In Chapter 2 we gave a "semantic formula" for the action drink, Fig 2.1.

It was a formal structure of semantic primitives expressing the meaning of the action (see King and Wilks, 1977): that drinking is a CAUSing to MOVE, preferably done by an ANImate SUBJect (=agent) and to a liquid (FLOW STUFF), TO a particular ANImate aperture (THRU PART), and INto the SELF (=the animate agent). For short we will write the formula as [drink]. The text structures in the system are semantic templates (together with semantic ties between them): a template is a network of formulas, containing at least an agent, action and object formula. Thus the template for "The adder drinks water" will be written the+adder drinks water for short where the whole of the formula above is in fact at the central (action) node.

The process of setting up the template allows the formulas to compete to fill nodes in templates. Thus the formula for the (snake-)adder goes to the agent node in the template above in preference to the (machine-)adder because (2) specifies, by (*ANI SUBJ), that it prefers to be accompanied in a template by an animate agent formula. However, in the sentence:

My car drinks gasoline

the available formula for the first template node, namely [car], is not for an animate entity, yet it is accepted because there is no competitor for the position. The purpose of this paper is to sketch how the system might not merely accept such a preference-violating structure for this sentence but might also interpret it.

An important later process (see Chapter 2 above) is called extraction: template-like structures are inferred and added to the text representation even though they match nothing in the surface text. They are "deeper" inferences from the case structures of formulas in some actual templates – where the case primitives are those italicised in the formula. Thus to the template for the sentence above, we would add an extraction (in double square parentheses in abbreviated form):

[[gasoline in car]]

which is an inference extracted from the containment subformula of [drink], namely (SELF IN) Analogous extractions could be made for each case primitive in each formula in the template for the sentence above.

Since the programmed version of the system, reported in Wilks (1975), a structural change (Wilks, 1978) has allowed a wider, and more specific, form of expression in formulas by allowing thesaurus items, as well as primitives, to function in them. No problems are introduced by doing this, provided that the thesaurus items are also themselves words in the dictionary and so have their formulas defined elsewhere in their turn. One advantage of this extension is to impose a thesaurus structure of the whole vocabulary, and so render its semantic expression more consistent.

A thesaurus, like Roget, is simply an organisation of a vocabulary into semi synonymous rows, which are themselves, classified hierarchically under heads, and even more generally. sections. Thus under some very general section name MOVE (=motion) we would find heads two of which might be engine and vehicle. The former might be the name of a row of actual types of engine:

525 engine: turbine, internal combustion, steam . . .

where the number simply indicates the sequence position of the head engine in the thesaurus. It is no accident that the most general section names like MOVE can be identified with the semantic primitives of the present system.

The organization is imposed by requiring inclusion relations, between the formulas for word senses, corresponding to the thesaurus relations of the words. Thus, all the words in the row above would have a common subpart to their formulas, and that common subpart would be the dictionary formula for "engine", probably expressing in primitives no more that "a thing used by humans to perform some task and self-moving in some way". If now thesaurus items can be inserted in formulas we may expect a formula for "car" at least as specific as

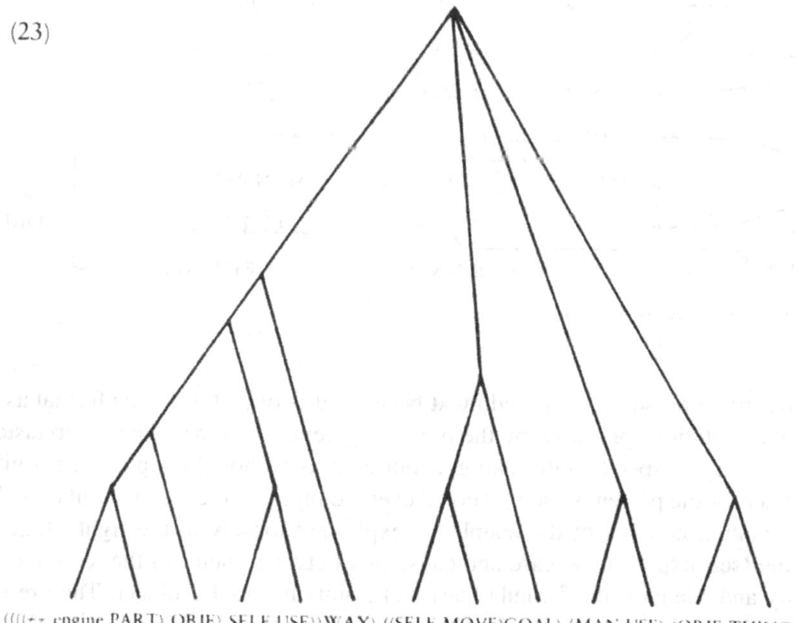

Fig. 12.1 A semantic formula for "car"

Language Boundaries and Projection

Let us return to examples like the car sentence above for which the system constructs a, template even though it contains a violated preference, and ask what should an intelligent system infer in such a situation? I would suggest that cars can be said to drink in virtue of something a system might already know about them, namely that they have a fluid (gas/petrol) injected into them, and they use that in order to run. That is to say, the program should have access to a sufficiently rich knowledge structure to express the fact that cars stand in a relation to a particular fluid, a relation that is of the "same semantic structure" as the relation in which a drinker normally stands to the thing drunk. All that may sound obvious, but how else are we to account for the naturalness of the example sentence, but the relative unnaturalness (and uninterpretability) of "My car chews gasoline", and, the more distant, 'My car carves the Sunday roast". One upshot of these proposals is to distinguish plausible (with respect to a knowledge base) preference violation from the implausible.

The procedural upshot of the above would be to replace at least one formula in the template for the sentence with another, either constructed by rule above or drawn from the relevant knowledge structure itself, to be called a pseudo-text (PT). Let us now postulate that "car" points not only to the formula [car] but that [car] in turn points to:

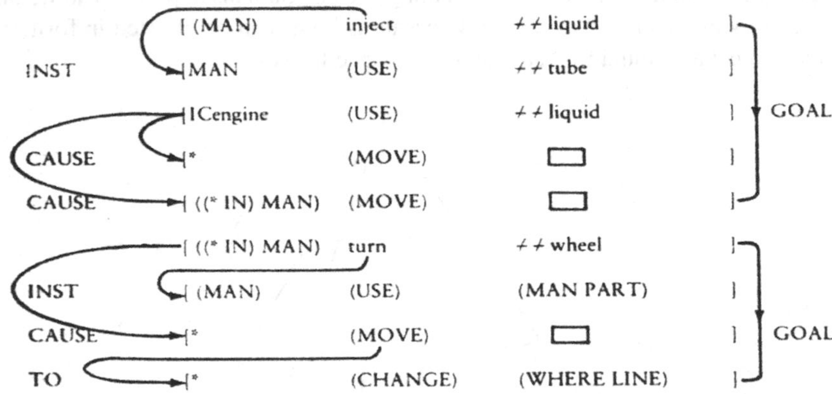

Fig. 12.2 A pseudo-text for "car"

This structure is called a pseudo-text because it is of just the same format as the text representations produced by the present system. It can be extended to taste to express as much specific information about cars as is thought appropriate – given the parser for the present system, it could even be input as a real text about cars. The representation consists of the templates (explained loosely at the right), together with the (self-explanatory) case and cause ties between them. In the templates, □ dummy and *denotes the formula [car] that points to this PT object. The prefixed items are thesaurus items, though "IC engine" is simply a specific dictionary word pointing to its own formula – specificity is thus a matter of taste. So, for example, the thesaurus head | liquid could be replaced by the more explicit "gasoline". Items in round parentheses remain in primitive form. It will be clear that the same information can be expressed in a number of different ways, and at different levels of generality; though the spirit of Minsky (1975) suggests that they should be as specific as possible. The intention here is that processes that operate on such entities as a PT shall be identical with those that manipulate representations derived from imput texts. The approach is thus the reverse of the conventional one: we seek to assimilate knowledge structures to text structures, rather than the reverse, on the grounds that the representation of language is the difficult task, and that the representation of knowledge as such makes no sense apart from that.

We should note, too, that just as the thesaurus structure imposes a containment relation on the formulas of co-row-member words, so it also imposes a hierarchical relationship on PTs: that for vehicle, for example, will be a less specific version of the PT. Further up the thesaurus would be PTs for high-level sections: that for MAN would be highly complex, for example. But note there is no "inheritance of property" problem in this system: the formula for "amputee" would have headMAN and would specify the loss of limbs. Any inherited pseudo-text from MAN – asserting "two legs" – would be modified by [amputee].

The system now uses the PT to make a projection, so as to derive an interpretation for the preference-breaking car example, by seeking, in the PT templates matching the source template [my+cardrinks gasoline]: namely the first and fourth lines of the PT. The first match is in virtue of the similarity of [drink] and [inject] – based on the expression in primitives, as in (2), of causing a liquid to be in an entity of the same type as the agent. This would allow us to confirm by projection, the "humanness of the drinker", that has already been noted by earlier extraction routines, extracting out from the drink formula independently of the PT. However, no projection is made at this stage onto [car]. (Though it might be later in the face of a sentence after the car example such as "His thirst is never slaked", that confirms the humanness projection) because in the case of violations of the preferences of actions, like "drink", the system *always prefers to make a projection onto the action itself if it can*. The strong match detected is between the above template and the fourth line of the PT in virtue of the containment of [engine] in [car], and by [liquid] of [gasoline], which is evident in the formulas themselves.

This results in the projection of the action node of the fourth line of the PT, namely use], onto [drink] in the template. This projection is taken to be strongly confirmed by the match with the first line of the PT, and is considered to carry over more sense than any alternative projection. The confirmation (of the match of the fourth line of the PT by the first line) is necessary here, because [my+car leaks gasoline] would also match the fourth line, but no such projection would be appropriate. Conversely, no projection could be made for "My car drinks mud" from the fourth line, even with the confirmation of the first. The general rule of action projection then is: *Seek a pseudo-text, for agent or object, with a template matching on agent and object nodes. Project this generally if there is also a pseudo-text template match to the action itself for another template in the same pseudo-text.*

We may note in passing three interesting developments of the above suggestion. First consider the more complex example presented by a headline:

Britain tries to escape Common Market.

Clearly, some projection would be appropriate here, of humanness onto the country, and perhaps even "prison likeness" onto the formula for the Common Market. These might be drawn from the formula for "escape" alone, by extraction and without recourse to the pseudo-texts for either of the entities. Even if we did consult those entities, we would find a historical account of Britain joining, but not of leaving. In such circumstances mere facts are not enough, even when highly structured. We might conceivably be able to project some notion [disassociate] onto [escape], from the "Britain pseudo-text". given some new matching criterion that placed relevance above negation in such cases (i.e. would match [escape] with[associate] or [join].).

Secondly, we might consider the problems presented by an example like:

I see what you mean.

Here the last clause breaks the preference expressed in [see] for a physical object. A system procedure will present the actual object of this sentence to the top-level template simply as the primitive SIGN (the primitive for symbols and intentional representations of them) which has been obtained, by extraction, from the preferred object in [mean]. Thus the system is effectively dealing with the template sequence [I see (SIGN)] [you mean (SIGN)]. But what could we expect as a pseudo-text for something as general as SIGN, so as to use the above procedures to project on to [see]? If we take advantage of the hierarchical nature of the thesaurus, we might expect pseudo-texts at the very top level, associated with the section names (i.e. pure primitives like SIGN) just as specific pseudo-texts are associated with the lowest level items in the thesaurus – row members like "car". The pseudo text for a primitive like SIGN would be wholly "core structural": it would consist of no more than primitive concatenations. In template form, like MAN THINK SIGN, the most general thing that can be said about what is normally done in signs. However, even something as general as this might suffice to project THINK correctly onto [see]. The interesting generality would come from using exactly the same projection procedures on the most general pseudo-texts like this, as on the most specific, like the car PT.

Thirdly, and this is treated at length in (Wilks, 1978), we can consider a quite different type of projection for phrases like:

a toy lion.

This comes from a much discussed class of examples ("plastic flower", "stone horse" etc.), where an obvious projection mechanism is to replace the head of the formula for the noun (BEAST in [lion]) by the preferred object of prediction in the qualifier, here ∗PHYSOB in [toy]. This would be a very limited and general class of projections, not requiring access to PT's, but which might still provide a "projected formula" appropriate for examples like:

The cat walked round the toy lion. Then he came back and sniffed it.

where we might be helped to refer "he" and "it" correctly by the new, projected formula [lion] whose head was no longer BEAST, and which could therefore no longer be the reference of "he" as a real lion would be.

A more radical and interesting development would be construction of "PT repacking functions" specific to certain qualifiers. Thus, for example, such a function for "toy", if faced with the phrase "toy car" might repack the car PT using a general rule to delete all constituent templates based on the action USE, as well as all those that are at end of a GOAL tie, since toy cars cannot, normally, serve human needs, uses and purposes.

The above suggestions are themselves primitive, as should be clear, and were only implemented (in New Mexico in 1986) in a simple manner. What I have tried to suggest here is that AI language programs do bear upon the traditional difficulties of MT, and often do so more directly than conventional linguistic theories, with their preoccupation with well-formedness, and with delimiting the class of all utterances of a language.

I may have given the impression perhaps that all AI programs are concerned with what could be called stratospheric considerations: the solution of the most general problems of language and understanding. That would be unfair: there is a number of more task-oriented projects under construction, attempting to limit vocabulary and world knowledge to very limited domains, such as plumbing repair, say, so as to produce concrete results while at the same time appealing to very general philosophical principles (see Levin and Moore, 1976).

What all AI projects, of whatever level, have in common is an appeal to very general knowledge and principles, coupled to the claim that MT work must take account of these if it is ever to achieve generality and reliability. The reply to this claim, from experience with projects like SYSTRAN, is that the AI examples that make these points are artificial and/or rare, and they can be ignored for practical purposes. This is clearly an empirical dispute and open to test, which is what makes the present situation interesting as I remarked at the beginning of the book.

That much does depend on one's choice of examples can be seen by returning to those of the beginning: Bar-Hillel's "slow neutrons and protons" should be amenable to treatment by an expert "atomic physics frame", one no more open to the charge of "ad hoc ness" than is human knowledge of physics itself. But with the old favourite "Time flies like an arrow", things are not so clear. In terms of what I called preferences, it may well be that the desired reading (where time does the flying) satisfies no more semantic preferences than, say, the reading where the flies like certain objects. Moreover, it is hard to imagine that any topic-determining frame could help here; one would hardly expect this slogan in any frame about time, except as an arbitrary addition. Nothing that has come from recent "speech act" theorists in linguistics and philosophy seems likely to help either. Perhaps, the only explanation of our competence with this sentence is that we read it off a list of cliches for which we have the assigned readings: a sad conclusion for all theoretically-motivated work, and an awful fate for a long cherished example.

Chapter 13
Lexical Tuning

Introduction

The principal aim of this chapter is to discuss what Lexical Tuning (LT) is, broadly defined and selectively practised, and to discuss its relationship to word sense disambiguation (WSD), with the aim of making it, too, quantitatively evaluable as WSD now is within the SENSEVAL regime (Kilgarriff 1998). Like the last chapter, this one assumes that MT must deal with word-sense ambiguity, including the wide class of cases where words in context have novel senses not in the dictionary.

Automatic word-sense disambiguation (WSD) is now an established modular task within empirically-based computational linguistics and has been approached by a range of methods (Ide and Veronis, 1998) sometimes used in combination (Wilks and Stevenson, 1998a,b). These experiments are already showing success rates at, or close to, the target ninety-five-per-cent levels attained by established modules like part of speech tagging in the mid-Nineties. Over a few text words Yarowsky has claimed success in the mid-Nineties (1995), and with systems that claim to deal with all text words, Sheffield (Wilks and Stevenson 1998b) and NMSU-CRL now also claim similar figures (Nirenburg et al., 1996).

These methods have included some, such as the use of the agent, object etc. preferences of verbs, that go back to those used in the earliest toy AI systems for WSD, such as (Wilks, 1972, 1978). Yet even those toy systems were set up with an explicit recognition that WSD was different in a key respect from tasks like part-of-speech tagging (POS): namely, that lexicons need to adapt dynamically in the face of new corpus input.

The contrast here is in fact quite subtle, as can be seen from the interesting intermediate case of semantic tagging: attaching semantic, rather than POS, tags to words automatically, a task which can then be used to do more of the WSD task (as in Dini et al., 1998) than POS tagging can, since the ANIMAL or BIRD versus MACHINE tags can then separate the main senses of "crane". In this case, as with POS, one need not assume any novelty in the tag set, in the sense of finding in the middle of the task that one needs additional tags. But one must also allow for novel assignments from the tag set to corpus words, for example, when a word like "dog" or "pig" was first used in a human sense. It is just this sense of novelty that POS tagging also has, of course, since a POS tag like VERB can be applied to what was once only a noun, like "ticket". This kind of assignment novelty, in POS and semantic tagging, can be premarked up with a fixed tag inventory, hence both these techniques differ from genuine sense novelty which, we shall argue, cannot be premarked in any simple way.

This latter aspect, which we shall call Lexical Tuning, can take a number of forms, including:

1. adding a sense to the lexical entry for a word
2. adding an entry for a word not already in the lexicon
3. adding a subcategorization or preference pattern etc. to an existing sense entry

and to do any or all of these on the basis of inductive (corpus) evidence. (a) was simulated in the early work just referred to, and (b) was first attempted in Granger (1977). (c) is at first sight more problematical in that it could be argued that it cannot be defined in a theory-free way, since what can be added automatically to a lexical entry on the basis of corpus evidence necessarily depends on the structure of the lexicon to be augmented, e.g. the nature of the features the lexicon contains. This is undoubtedly correct, but the general notion of what lexical tuning is can still be captured in a non-trivial theory-free way by means of the "etc." above: the general notion proposed being one of a very general function mapping an existing lexicon and a corpus to a new (tuned) lexicon.

In practice, the three types above are neither exclusive nor exhaustive, although task (b) may be quite different in nature in that it excludes straightforward use of a well-known technique that appears under many names, such as "lexical rules" (Copestake and Briscoe 1991; Buitelaar 1997), and which strictly falls outside the function, described above, by which new senses of a word are induced from knowing not only a corpus but an existing lexical entry. This tradition of extending dictionary entries independently of corpus context can be seen as a direct inheritor of the generative linguistics tradition, in the sense in which that is now often contrasted with the corpus linguistics tradition. We shall argue below that this is not altogether fair, since LR researchers do often refer to and call upon corpora, but always that special set of corpora that should more properly be described as meta-corpora, namely the resources of facts about usage, such as (machine readable) dictionaries, thesauri and wordnets. Note that these are all machine readable and the difference here is not about computation, only about where one seeks one's evidence and to what extent all corpus forms can be accounted for in advance, and within lexical constructions.

Combining these three types of potential LT is also a source of potential confusion: if a word is unknown to a lexicon, then any computational system can see that immediately, but many would say (clinging firmly to the force of the word "homonymy") that the three main senses of "post" (post1 = mail; post2 = stake; post3 = job) are, in effect, different words, arbitrarily linked by English spelling. So, some would say that inferring a new sense of "post" (if using a lexicon from which one of the three above senses was missing) is identical to task (b) above that of interpreting new words, and not properly task (a), since one could not expect to induce a new, major, sense of "post" from its existing senses, by any system that could so extend senses in cases of so-called "regular polysemy" (Copestake and Briscoe, 1991).

This problem is independent of a more general one affecting tasks (a) and (c): namely, when does a new context for a word give rise to a description that should be deemed a new feature or new pattern, rather than a `relaxed' version of an existing one. This is, like all forms of the problem, general learning problem and a matter in the end of arbitrary choice or parameter setting within an algorithm. In this part, we shall not always distinguish clearly between accommodating or interpreting a novel use, which might be unique and one-off, and covering a new sense, already well established, but not already in the lexicon in use. Obviously, the latter always start as the former, and the difference is only a quantitative one. A recent example in English that would repay corpus investigation, would be the verb target, as in:

The bomber targeted the city
and:
The Government targeted the poor
The Government targeted poverty.

The principal use, we are sure, is now the third, not the first, and this has been achieved by a form of meaning reversal, of "seeking out, to help", although the first sense probably persists, paradoxically, in the second example. Somehow, a new sense has been established for the third, not on the basis of semantics (poverty/the poor) but if we suggest, knowledge structures to do with the ideology of modern politics.

To summarise: this formulation of LT assumes we already have a human-created resource we shall call structure1, i.e. the lexicon we started with, perhaps together with an associated knowledge base or ontology. LT is thus the process or mapping function:

$$\text{I: structure1} + \text{corpus} \rightarrow \text{structure2}$$

which indicates that an earlier state of the structure itself plays a role in the acquisition, of which structure2 is then a proper extension (capturing new concepts, senses etc). This is a different model from the wholly automatic model of lexicon acquisition often used in, say, TIPSTER related work (Lehnert et al., 1990), which can be written:

$$\text{II: corpus} \rightarrow \text{structure}$$

Here one does not update or "tune" an existing lexicon but derives one directly and automatically from a corpus. There is no doubt process II. can be an effective tool, certainly in the case of unknown languages or domains, but the assumption made here about the quite different function I. is that we cannot understand the nature of the representation of meaning in lexicons, or elsewhere, unless we can see how to extend lexicons in the presence of incoming data that does not fit the lexicon we started with. The extension of representations, one might say, is part of an adequate theory of representation.

Evaluating WSD and its Relationship to Lexical Tuning

A central issue in any application of empirical methods to computational linguistics is the evaluation procedure used, which is normally taken to consist in some form of experiment using premarked-up text divided into training and (unseen) test portions. Standard supervised learning for WSD involves an algorithm that selects tags to each text word (or more often each content, or open-class, word) corresponding to senses from a lexicon. Ideally, this process would result in one, and only one, tag per word, but it should at least reduce the set from what is in the lexicon.

Apart from the well-known problem of the difference between sense-sets (if we can continue to use that phrase unexamined, for the moment) for a given word in different lexicons – although they are not arbitrarily different, and that is a vital fact – there are problems concerned with subjects having difficulty assigning a corpus word occurrence to one and only one sense tag during the markup phase.

Kilgarriff (1993) has described such problems, though his figures suggest the difficulties are probably not as serious as he claims (see (Wilks, 1997 and Chapter 11 above)). However, we have to ask what it means to evaluate the process of Lexical Tuning as defined above. It seems to require annotating in advance a new sense in a corpus that does not occur in the reference lexicon. The clear answer is that, on the description of WSD markup given above, the sense extension (task (1) above: tuning to a newsense) *cannot* be pre-tagged and so no success rate for WSD can possibly exceed 100% MINUS the percentage of extended sense occurrences.

One question about Lexical Tuning that is not often discussed is made explicit by the last expression: what is the percentage of senses needing tuning in normal text? One anecdotal fact sometimes used is that, in any randomly chosen newspaper paragraph, each sentence will be likely to have an extended sense of at least one word, usually a verb, which is to say a use that breaks conventional preferences (Wilks 1972) and which might therefore be considered extended or metaphorical use, and which may or may not be in a standard lexicon. This is a claim that can be easily tested by anyone with a newspaper and a standard dictionary.

That, even if true, does not give us any firm figure to work with. However, it could suggest that any figure for basic WSD for general text of over 95% must be examined with great care, because it almost certainly cannot have been done by any method using pre-tagging (to a set of existing senses). The onus on anyone making a very high claim is to show what the alternative explanation of his high success figures is. Subsequent examination of machine WSD output for a posteriori "satisfactoriness" can never be a plausible measure: i.e. anything along the lines of "this is what our system gave as new sense contents for this corpus and we liked what we got"!

Another possibility, that will be considered in more detail later, is that novel sense might be detected by an occurrence that cannot be identified by the human tagger with any of the list of senses for the word. The problem here may be just an inadequate dictionary list, though novelty is always with respect to the state of a lexical structure. Also, this procedure will conflate regular novelty, that could have been produced by LR, with any other kind. However, none of these objections are insuperable and, indeed, (Kilgarriff, 2000) used such a measure in an attempt to evaluate the Generative Lexicon (Pustejovsky, 1995) approach to lexical novelty. On a small sample, Kilgarriff estimated the occurrence of novel senses at 2\% over and above anything due to regular polysemy.

How then to Evaluate Lexical Tuning Claims?

If Lexical Tuning (alias LT) is a real phenomenon, it must be possible to evaluate it in some reasonable way. To make headway here, let us first set out possible basic paradigms or methods for sense extension and seek for clues as to how to evaluate them. One such early paradigm was set out in (Wilks, 1978) under the title "Making preferences more active", and which was implemented at the "toy" levels of that period, though it may still be false as to the relationship of new senses to existing ones. Let us call that historical example:

Method A: It was based on thc notion of:

1. The cuing function (for LT) of the preference failure of a word W1 in a text (e.g. a verb used with an unexpected agent or object class);
2. The location of another word (sense) W2 in a knowledge structure, that defines how the world for that word sense normally is, and which has the right lexical preferences;
3. The substitution in the text representation of the "failed" word by a new, more satisfactory word sense W2 (in the lexicon);
4. The claim that W1 should have its lexicon extended by the structure for the appropriate sense of W2.

where such appropriate structure may mean its preferences, subcategorization patterns, semantic or other links, explanatory gloss etc.

The main 1978 example was "My car drinks gasoline", which has a failed [human] agent preference, which is then (criterion i above) the trigger to locate a fact representable as

[cars use gasoline]

in a knowledge base about cars (ii and iii above), so that "use" can provide a plausible new sense of "drink" (iv above). However, this heuristic not wholly satisfactory, since it does not capture the idiomatic force of "drink" → "use a lot of" implicature of this usage. Moreover, the process must not just locate any action or process of cars associated with gasoline, for that will include "leak", as in

[cars leak gasoline].

We can suppose this is achieved either (or both) by assuming leaking gasoline is not described in a stereotypical car function knowledge base or that drink/use are linked by some underlying semantic structure (such as a shared type primitive or some degree of closeness, however defined, in a synonym/WordNet list classification) and in a way that drink/leak are not.

This location of a preference-satisfying KB entity to substitute for a failing semantic structure was called *projection* in 1978, and is the kind of inference that has played a substantial role in the later work of Pustejovsky and others under names like "coercion". The method illustrated above based on "preference failure" would apply only to verbs and adjectives, which were the grammatical types coded with preferences in that system, although another possibility set out in the 1978 paper was that either participant of the failed preference link could be substituted by something better fitting (i.e. the verb or its agent): the sense extension proposed above is of the action because of what was in the knowledge base (KB), and within the standard AI assumption of knowledge-based processing, but one could also take the same example as ascribing a human quality to cars. However, the KB does not support any substitution based on the agent, because one would expect to locate in the car-KB forms like [person drive cars], but not any KB form like like [person drink gasoline], which is what would be needed to support an alternative, competing, tuning of "car".

Method A2: However, this last sort of possibility is the one that underlies a metonymic preference failure like

THE CHAIR opened the meeting.

Again we have agent-action failure, but now there is no KB support for any form with a value for ACTION satisfying [chair ACTION meeting) of the kind we saw for drink/use. However, in a standard KB, there would be support for

[person open meeting]

as part of a general knowledge structure for the conduct of meetings, which satisfy the preferences of the corresponding sense of "open". So, in this class of case as well, we might expect the same procedures to tune to a new sense of "chair" as "person" (who opens meetings).

Now let us contrast the above paradigm for sense extension with that used in recent CRL work (Mahesh et al., 1997), one intended as more fine grained than the "consumer driven" (Sergei Nirenburg's term) approach, or that of "final task" driven projects, such as the ECRAN project, namely that of carrying out a "final task" such as Information Extraction, before and after tuning a lexicon against a domain corpus and then seeing if Information Extraction results are improved. "Final task" here is to be contrasted with "intermediate tasks", such as WSD, which are often evaluated directly in competitions but which have no real NLP function outside some final task, one that serves a purpose for a language understander or consumer.

The CRL basic methodology (using the Mikrokosmos KB, which we shall call MK for short, (Nirenburg and Raskin 1996) is quite different from A above. Let us (at the inevitable risk of error in summarizing someone else's work) describe its two proposals as follows:

Method B1: Locate preference failure of an occurrence of word W1 in the corpus

Seek the closest *existing* sense of W1 in the MK lexicon by relaxing the preference constraints of W1.

Consider later how to subdivide the expanded-relaxed occurrences of W1 to create a new sense if and when necessary, perhaps when the "expanded" occurrences

form a new cluster, based on related relaxations, so that a new sense of W1 can be separated off in terms of a new set of constraints in the MK lexicon.
or

Method B2: Locate preference failure of an occurrence of word W1 in the corpus

Seek in the MK KB for a word sense W2 hierarchically below W1, but whose preferences are satisfied in the example.

Take W2 to be the sense of W1 in the given context.

It is not wholly clear in the context of the paper referred to whether B1 and B2 result in adaptations to the lexicon, which is what we are asking as the minimal, necessary, condition for anything to be called LT, so as to avoid including in LT all hapax occurrences of unusual conjunctions. However, these heuristics are of interest whether or not the lexicon is permanently adapted, as opposed to deriving a new sense representation for a word for immediate use. These methods make less radical use of world knowledge than A, but one which runs far less chance of making wrong extensions. The key notion in B1 is the search for a *closest existing sense* of the same word, which may well represent a core aspect of meaning extension missing from the earlier approach, and which will in any case be essential to task (c) (though it cannot, by definition, be used for task (b) which is that of the "unknown word"). It also cannot help in true homograph/homonym cases, like "post", where the approach A might stand a chance, but we proposed at the beginning to exclude consideration of such extension for now, or rather to accommodate it to task (b) and not (a).

Method B2 shows an interesting notion of preference breaking somewhat different from that of A: a canonical CRL example is:

He PREPARED the bread.

where the declared aim of the adaptation is to tune the sense of "prepare", for this occurrence, to the appropriate sense of "bake", which is the verb in the Mikrokosmos KB for the preparation of bread and whose preferences fit a BREAD object as those of "prepare" do not. The process here is close to Method A in that a stored item in a KB licenses the tuning and, again like Method A, the result is the substitution of one word sense by the sense of another word. As with method A, this will only count as LT (on the strict definition used in this paper) if the lexicon is changed by this process so as to install "bake" as a sense of "prepare" and it seems this is not done in the CRL system.

However, the most interesting feature of the B method, is that the constraint satisfaction of "bake" is not passed up the hierarchy of actions and sub-actions. This is an idea going back to Grice (as a failure of the quantity maxim, Grice 1989), but one possibly original in lexical semantics: that a too general concept is semantically ill-fitting, just as a complete misfitting of a concept is. In preference terms, it means that the overly general is also a preference failure, quite contrary to the way that notion has usually been used to include subclasses of fillers, e.g. that to prefer a FOOD object is normally to accept a BREAD object, given that bread is a kind of food. The current suggestion is equivalent to: if a concept prefers BREAD, then FOOD would be ill-fitting.

As we noted, Method B2 is not LT if the lexical entry for "prepare" is not altered by the acceptance of "He prepared the bread", but this is mere definition. Relaxation to "higher classes" can, however, be explicitly marked in a lexicon, and is therefore LT, as would be the case with "The Chair opened the meeting" example, if viewed as relaxation to accept PHYSOBJ agents and not just HUMAN ones. There is always a price to pay in relaxation accounts of tuning because once a preference is relaxed it cannot subsequently be used to select as a constraint.

Consider the following two sentences:

- The whole office waited for the boss to arrive
- The two men cleaned the offices as ?they waited for the janitor to arrive.

One cannot both relax the lexical entry for "wait" so as to accommodate its agent in the first sentence and use the standard preferences of "wait" for [human] agents to resolve ?they in the second. This point is an argument not only against relaxation but against any method for deriving preferences by corpus analysis (Grishman 1986, Resnik, 1993) in any simple manner since both sentences could well be attested in the same corpus.

There will naturally be disputes about how widely this kind of quantity restriction can be enforced: one might also say that preparing bread is a sequence of subactions, including mixing and leaving-to-rise (rather like Schank scripts of old, Schank and Abelson, 1977); in which case the type BREAD is the proper object for all of them including "prepare", so that the B methods can never be called in because there is no preference failure to trigger them.

Method B1 should lead to a quite different interpretation of this example: on B1 "prepare bread" (if deemed preference breaking as CRL claim) should lead to a relaxation to an *existing* sense of "prepare" (and not "bake" at all), yet what is that existing sense?

Is the car/drink example (Method A) one of lexical extension when compared to the B methods; which is to say, do we want to deem "use" a sense of "drink" in the context of a car's consumption of gasoline and retain that modification in a lexicon, or is it simply a one off metaphor? Identifying this as a possible extension is a necessary but not sufficient condition for a full LT lexicon modification which requires further confirming instances of entities of a machine type drinking fuel-like liquids, e.g. steam engines drinking water, aeroengines drinking kerosene and so on. This is a different type of extension from the B-type examples involving possible relaxations of agents and objects of verbs already fixed in hierarchies. Both A and B type extensions, if real, are different from what others are calling regular polysemy, in that they cannot be precoded in lexical entries by rules or any similar method.

Closest Sense Heuristics and Text Markup

The CRL approach measures success, at least initially, by human mark up to the closest existing lexical sense (though see below on "Chateaubriand"). This may make it possible to achieve a generally acceptable type of evaluation procedure for lexical tuning (whether or not one adapts the lexicon, in the face of any particular example, need not affect the use of the procedure here) if there can be inter-subjective agreement on what is a lexically closest sense in a training text. That would then be the phenomenon being tested, along with the general (and attested) ability to assign a sense to a text word when the sense in the lexicon is used, though the human marker should also obviously have the choice of declining to mark a closest sense, given a particular state of the lexicon, if he believes it inappropriate in the context. If LT is to be evaluated in such a way, a marker will have to be able to indicate closest sense separately from appropriate sense.

Examples can be produced (due in this case to Steve Helmreich) within the well-known Restaurant Metonymy example paradigm to suggest that the extended sense to be constructed by this Method B1, leading to the closest existing sense, may not always be appropriate.

Consider:

The Chateaubriand wants a drink

where "Chateaubriand" is lexically coded both as a steak (what the diner ordered) and an Eighteenth Century French politician of that name. The latter may well be chosen (by an algorithm, though not by a human marker, of course) as the closest sense (since it satisfies the [human] agent constraint on "want") but the extended or relaxed sense should actually be related to steak, the first sense.

Restaurant Metonymies (RMs), though attested, have perhaps played too strong a role in the field, given their infrequency in real life. Proper name RMs could perhaps be dismissed as a tiny subclass of a tiny subclass and a proper subject only for AI. Perhaps the closest sense heuristic can be saved by some careful analysis of "the" in the last example; it is always the cue for a Restaurant Metonymy, but rarely in politics, and we shall assume in what remains that the heuristic can be saved in some such way. After all, there need be no similar problem here with "standard" RMs that are not proper names, as in:

The lasagna wants a drink.

Pustejovsky's Position on Lexical Expansion

In The Generative Lexicon (1995, TGL for short) Pustejovsky (JP for short) sets out a position that has features in common with work already described, but offers a distinctive view of the lexicon and in particular its underspecification in crucial respects; and the aspect that will concern us in this paper is whether or not that underspecification is any form of LT as described here, as implying the augmentation of the lexicon in the face of sense novelty in a corpus. It seems JPs position is that his key class of examples does not imply the creation of a new sense from an existing one in the face of corpus evidence, but is rather the incorporation of a prestored ambivalence within a lexical entry. That this can be misunderstood can be seen from an attack on JPs TGL by Fodor and LePore (FL for short, Fodor and

Lepore, 2000) in which they attribute to him a sense ambiguity for such examples, and indeed an unresolvable one.

They claim that JP's:

He baked a cake.

is in fact ambiguous between JP's "create" and "warm up" aspects of "bake", where baking a cake yields the first, but baking a potato the second. JP does not want to claim this is a sense ambiguity, but a systematic difference in interpretation given by inferences cued by features of the two objects, which could be labels such as ARTIFACT in the case of the cake but not the potato:

But in fact, "bake a cake" is ambiguous. To be sure, you can make a cake by baking it; but also you can do to a (pre-existent) cake just what you can do to a (pre-existent) potato: viz. put it in the oven and (non creatively) bake it. (FL. p.7)

From this FL conclude that "bake" must be ambiguous, since "cake" is not. But all this is absurd and untrue to the simplest facts about cakes, cookery and English. Of course, warming up a (pre-existent) cake is not baking it; who ever could think it was? That activity would be referred to as warming a cake up, or through, never as baking. You can no more bake a cake again, with the other (warm up) interpretation, than you can bake a potato again and turn it into a different artifact. The only obvious exception here might be "biscuit", whose etymology is, precisely, "twice cooked", though not baked.

JP has resisted augmentation of the lexicon, though other researchers would probably accept it and this difference may come down to no more than the leaving of traces in a lexicon and what use is made of them later, and where augmentation of the lexicon would be appropriate if such cases became statistically significant. However, we can still ask whether underspecification is just language-specific lexical gaps?

Let us look at the key Pustejovsky example in a new way: the bake cake/bread/ potato examples may not draw their power from anything special to do with baking but with lexical gaps and surplus in English connected with cake and bread. Suppose we adopt, just for a moment, a more Wierzbickian approach to baking and assume as a working hypothesis that there is only one, non-disjunctive, sense of bake and it is something like:

"to cook a food-substance X in a heated enclosed space so as to produce food-substance Y"

Thus we have, for X and Y for our standard food substances in English:

potato [potato, baked potato]
bread [dough, bread]
cake [cake mixture, cake]
pie [pie, pie]

as well as:

fish [fish, (baked) fish]
ham [ham, baked ham]

There is no mystery here, but looking at a range of well-known substances can take us out of the rather airless zone where we discuss the relationship of "bake" and "prepare" away from all data, and without considering in parallel "roast", "boil", "grill" etc. We would argue that there is no pressing need to gloss the implicit structure here as a disjunction of senses or aspects of "bake". It is simply that the lexical repertory of English varies from food to food, thus

- We bake ham and get baked ham
- We bake dough and get bread
- We bake cake mixture and get cake
- We bake (a) potato and get a (baked) potato

There is no reason to believe that these cases fall into two classes, the creative and non-creative at all: it simply that we have words in English for baked dough (bread) and baked cake mixture (cake) but not a word for a baked potato. If we did have such a word, baking a potato would seem more creative than it does. Contrast Kiswahili (or Japanese), which has a word for uncooked rice (mchele) and a word for cooked rice (wali). In English

We cooked rice

does not seem creative but rather matter of mere heating since there is only the same word for the object when transformed. But, on an underspecification approach to Kiswahili:

We cooked wali/mchele

are two sentences (if all in Kiswahili) bearing two differing interpretations of "cook", only one of them TELIC, and hence

We cooked rice

should also be ambiguous, underspecified and disjoined in interpretation in English. But this is surely not true, indeed absurd, and a language cannot have its verb semantics driven by its lexical gaps for nouns! If this analysis is plausible there is no disjunction present at all in baking cakes and potatoes either, and if by chance "dough" meant dough or bread in English (as is surely the case in some language) this whole issue could never have arisen.

We should not exaggerate the differences between the main approaches discussed so far: all subscribe to

1. sense is resolvable by context we can create/extend sense in context by various procedures
2. we can create/extend sense in context by various procedures
3. but not all to
4. the methods of (ii) are close to WSD and lead naturally to lexical adaptation/tuning
5. The adaptation produced by (ii) leaves some record in the lexicon.

Generalising the Contrast of LT Approaches with Lexical Rules (LR)

Lexical Tuning (LT) is closely related to, but rather different from, a group of related theories that are associated with phrases like "lexical rules" (LR); all of the latter seek to compress lexicons by means of generalisations, and we take that to include DATR (Evans and Gazdar 1996), methods developed under AQUILEX (Copestake and Briscoe 1991), as well as Pustejovsky's TGL discussed above and Buitelaar's more recent research on underspecified lexicons (1997). LR we take to be any approach, such as Pustejovsky or Briscoe, in the tradition of Givon that seeks to extend lexical entries independently of corpora.

To take a classic example, lexical entries for animals that can be eaten can be contracted and marked only ANIMAL, given a rule that extends on demand to a new sense of the word marked MEAT. This is an oversimplification of course, and problems arise when distinguishing between eatable and uneatable animals (by convention if not in strict biology). Very few want to extend "aardvark" with MEAT though there is no logical reason why not, and an ethnographic survey might be needed for completeness in this area; foods are simply not universal.

All this work can be traced back to early work by Givon (1967) on lexical regularities, done, interestingly to those who think corpus and MRD research began in the 1980s, in connection with the first computational version of Websters Third at SDC in Santa Monica under John Olney in 1966. It can also be brought under the heading "lexical compression" whether or not that motive is made explicit. Givon became interested in what is now called "systematic polysemy", as distinguished from homonymy which is assumed to be unsystematic: his key examples were "grain" which is normally given a count noun or PHYOBJ sense in a (diachronic) dictionary and cited earlier than the mass noun sense of "grain in the mass". This particular lexical extension can be found in many nouns, and resurfaced in Briscoe and Copestake's "grinding rule" (1991) that added a mass substance sense for all animals, as in their "rabbit all over the road" example. The argument was that, if such extensions were systematic, they need not be stored individually but could be developed when needed unless explicitly overridden. The paradigm for this was the old AI paradigm of default reasoning: Clyde is an elephant and all elephants have four legs BUT Clyde has three legs, and the latter fact must take precedence over the former inference. It has been some thing of a mystery why this foundational cliche of AI was greeted later within computational linguistics as remarkable and profound.

Gazdar's DATR (Evans and Gazdar, 1996) is the system that makes lexical compression the most explicit, drawing as it does on fundamental notions of science as a compression of the data of the world. The problem has been that language is one of the most recalcitrant aspects of the world and it has proved hard to find generalisations above the level of morphology in DATR; those to do with meaning have proved especially elusive. Most recently, there has been an attempt to generalise DATR to cross-language generalisations which has exacerbated the problem. One can see that, in English, Dutch and German, respectively, "house", "huis" and "Haus" are the "same word", a primitive concept DATR seems to require. But, whereas "house" has a regular plural, "Haus" ("Haueser") does not, so even at this low level, significant generalisations are very hard to find.

Most crucially, there can be no appeals to meaning from the concept of "same word": "town" (Eng.) and "tuin" (Dut.) are plainly the same word in some sense, at least etymologically and phonetically, and may well obey morphological generalisations although now, unlike the "house" cases above, they have no relation of meaning at all, as "tuin" now means garden in Dutch, unless one is prepared to move to some complex historical fable about towns and gardens being related "spaces surrounded by a fence". There has been no attempt to link DATR to established quantitative notions of data compression in linguistics, like Minimum Description Length (Risannen 1984), which gives a precise measure of the compaction of a lexicon, even where significant generalisations may be hard to spot by eye or mind. The systems which seek lexical compression by means of rules, in one form or another, can be discussed with particular attention to Buitelaar, since Briscoe and Pustejovsky differ in matters of detail and rule format but not in principle. Buitelaar continues Pustejovsky's campaign against the "unstructured list" view of lexicons: viewing the senses of a word merely as a list as dictionaries are said to do, in favour of a clustered approach, one which distinguishes "systematic polysemy" from mere homonymy (like the ever present senses of "bank").

Clustering a word's senses in an optimally revealing way is something no one could possibly object to, and the problem here is the examples Buitelaar produces, and in particular his related attack on WSD programs (including the present authors) as assuming a list-view of sense, is misguided. As Nirenburg and Raskin (1997) have pointed out in relation to Pustejovksy, those who criticise list views of sense then normally go on in their papers to describe and work with the senses of a word as a list, and Buitelaar continues this tradition. Moreover, it must be pointed out that opening any modern English dictionary, especially one for learners like LDOCE, shows quite a complex grouping of the senses it contains and not a list at all.

Buitelaar's opening argument against standard WSD activities rests on his counter-example where multiple senses of "book" must be kept in play and so WSD cannot be done: the example is:

A long book heavily weighted with military technicalities, in this edition it is neither so long nor so technical as it was originally.

Leaving aside the question of whether this is a sentence, let us accept that Buitelaar's list of possible senses (and glosses) of "book" is a reasonable starting point (with our numbering added):

1. the information content of a book (military technicalities);
2. its physical appearance (heavily weighted),
3. and the events involved in its construction (long) (Ibid. p. 25).

The issue, he says, is to which sense of "book" does the "it" refer, and his conclusion is that it cannot be disambiguated between the three.

This seems to us quite wrong, as a matter of the exegesis of the English text: "heavily weighted" is plainly metaphorical and refers to content (i) not the physical appearance (ii) of the book. We have no trouble taking "long" as referring to the content (i) since not all long books are physically large; it depends on the print size etc. On our reading, the "it" is univocal (to sense (i)) between the senses of "book". However, nothing depends on an example, well or ill-chosen, and it may well be that there are indeed cases where more than one sense must remain in play in a word's deployment; poetry is often cited, but there may well be others, less peripheral to the real world of the *Wall Street Journal*.

The main point in any answer to Buitelaar must be that, whatever is the case about the above example, WSD programs have no trouble capturing it: many programs, and certainly that of (Stevenson and Wilks, 2001) that he cites and its later developments, work by casting out senses and are perfectly able to report results with more than one sense still attaching to a word, just as many part-of-speech taggers result in more than one tag per word in the output. Historians of the AI approach to NLP will also remember that Mellish (1983), Hirst (1987) and Small (in Small et al., 1988) all proposed methods by which polysemy might be computationally reduced by degree and not in an all or nothing manner. Or, as one might put it, underspecification, Buitelaar's key term, is no more than an implementation detail in any effective tagger!

Let us turn to the heart of Buitelaar's position: the issue of systematicity (one within which other closely related authors' claims about lexical rules can be taken together). Buitelaar lists clusters of nouns (e.g. blend, competition, flux, transformation) that share the same top semantic nodes in some structure like a modified WordNet (which would be act/evt/rel in the case of the list just given).

Such structures, he claims, are manifestations of systematic polysemy. But what is one to take that to mean, say by contrast with Levin's (1993) verb classes where, she claims, the members of a class share certain syntactic and semantic properties and, on that basis, one could in principle predict additional members? That is simply not the case here: one does not have to be a firm believer in natural kinds to see that the members of the cluster above (i.e. blend etc.) have nothing systematic in common, but are just arbitrarily linked by the same "upper nodes" in Wordnet. Some such classes are natural classes, as with the one Buitelaar gives linked by being both animate and food (all of which, unsurprisingly, are animals and are edible, at least on some dietary principles), but there is no systemic relationship here of any kind. Or, to coin a phrase, one might say that the list above is just a list and nothing more!

In all this, we intend no criticism of his useful device, derived from Pustejovsky, for showing disjunctions and conjunctions of semantic types attached to lexical entries, as when one might mark something as (act AND relation), or an animal sense as (animate OR food). This is close to older devices in artificial intelligence such as multiple perspectives on structures (in Bobrow and Winograd's KRL 1977), and so on. Showing these situations as conjunctions and disjunctions of types may well be a superior notation, though it is quite proper to continue to point out that the members of conjuncts and disjuncts are, and remain, in lists!

Finally, Buitelaar's (1998) proposal to use these methods (via CoreLex) to acquire a lexicon from a corpus may also be an excellent approach, and one of the first efforts to link the LR movement to a corpus. It would probably fall under type II acquisition (as defined earlier), and therefore not be LT, which rests essentially on structural modification by new data. Our point here is that that method (capturing the content of e.g. adjective-noun instances in a corpus) has no particular relationship to the theoretical machinery described above, and is not different in kind from the standard NLP type II. projects of the 1980s like Autoslog (Lehnert et al. 1990), to take just one of many possible examples. In a small but suggestive experiment, Kilgarriff (2000) found it possible to accommodate Generative Lexicon structures, to dictionary senses for which there had not been precoded, for only some of the cases required it.

Vagueness

The critique of the broadly positive position on WSD in this paper, and its relationship to LT, comes not only from those who argue (a) for the inadequacy of lexical sense sets over productive lexical rules (as above) but also from proponents of (b) the inherently *vague* quality of the difference between senses of a given word. We believe both these approaches are muddled *if* their proponents conclude that WSD is therefore fatally flawed as a task.

The vagueness issue is an old one, one that, if taken seriously, must surely result in a statistical or fuzzy-logic approach to sense discrimination, since only probabilistic (or at least quantitative) methods can capture real vagueness. That, surely, is the point of the Sorites paradox: there can be no rational or qualitative criterion (which would include any quantitative system with clear limits: e.g. tall = over 6 feet) for demarcating "tall", "green" or any inherently vague concept.

If, however, sense sets/lists/inventories are to continue to play a role in language processing and understanding, vagueness can mean no more than highlighting what all systems of WSD must have, namely some parameter or threshold for the assignment to one of a list of senses versus another, or setting up a new sense in the list. Talk of vagueness adds nothing specific to help that process for those who want to assign words, on some quantitative basis, to one sense rather than another; sense tuning means seeing what works and fits our intuitions.

Vagueness would be a serious concept only if the whole sense list for a word (in rule form or not) was abandoned in favour of statistically-based clusters of usages or contexts. There have been just such approaches to WSD in recent years (e.g. Bruce and Wiebe, 1994, Pedersen and Bruce, 1997, Schuetze and Pederson, 1995) and the essence of the idea goes back to Sparck Jones 1964/1986) but such an approach would find it impossible to take part in any competition like SENSEVAL (Kilgarriff, 1998) because it would inevitably deal in nameless entities which cannot be marked up for.

Vague and Lexical Rule based approaches also have the consequence that all lexicographic practice is, in some sense, misguided: on that view, dictionaries for such theories are fraudulent documents that could not help users whom they systematically mislead by listing senses. Fortunately, the market decides this issue, and it is a false claim. Vagueness in WSD is either false (the last position) or trivial, and known and utilised within all quantitative methodologies.

Lexical Rules and Pre-Markup

Can the lexical rules approach to some of the phenomena discussed here be made evaluable, using some conventional form of pre-markup, in the way that we saw is difficult for straightforward LT of new senses, but which may be possible if LT makes use of some form of the "closest sense" heuristic? The relevance of this to the general WSD and tuning discussion is that the very idea of pre-markup would presumably require that all lexical rules are run, so that the human marker can see the full range of senses available, which some might feel inconsistent with the "data compression" motivation behind lexical rules. However, this situation is no different in principle from POS tagging where a language, say English, may well have a tag meta-rule that any word with N in its tag-lexicon could also have the tag ADJ (but not vice versa). Clearly, any such rule would have to be run before pre-markup of text could be done, and the situation with senses is no different, though psychologically for the marker it may seem so, since the POS tag inventory can usually be kept in memory, whereas a sense inventory for a vocabulary cannot.

Conclusion: Which of these Methods Lead to Evaluation?

What is the conclusion here on the relationship of lexical extension, in whatever form, to the task of WSD, given that the thrust of the paper has been to see if new evaluable methods of WSD apply to LT, and can be adapted to make it evaluable too? It is clear that the LR approach, at least as represented by Buitelaar, sees no connection and believes WSD to be a misleading task. And this is not a shocking result, for it only brings out in a new way the division that underlies this paper, and which is as old as the generative vs. corpus linguistics divide, one that has existed for decades but was effectively disguised by the denial by the dominant Chomskyan generative paradigm that anything akin to corpus linguistics existed.

Our reply to this is that Buitelaar's examples do not support his attack on WSD, since underspecification is largely a misnomer. Corpora could be premarked for the senses coded in such a lexicon, if treated as real disjunctions, but there is no way of knowing which of these are attested or attestable in data, and we argued that aspects of the key example "bake" are not in fact related to sense distinction or polysemy phenomena at all.

On the other hand, the method A (1978) phenomena are impossible to premark and therefore could be tested only within a final task like IE, IR or MT. The relaxation phenomena of method B (1997), on the other hand, could possibly be premarked for (and then tested as part of a WSD program) but by doing so do not constitute extended sense phenomena, in the full sense of LT, at all, since by relaxing to an existing sense one denies a new sense is in operation. In the B2 type cases, with data like that of the LR researchers, the extension of "prepare" to "bake" (of bread) should result in the representation of "bake" being added as possible sense of "prepare" (by analogy with Method A) whether or not this effects a one-off or permanent (LT) adaptation.

A further empirical possibility would be to remove a principal sense from a lexicon for a set of words, and investigate "negative markup" (along the lines of (Kilgarriff 2000)) to see whether and when markers were unwilling to assign a sense, although a problem here might be their unconscious knowledge of the missing sense. In parallel, it would be possible to deploy a large general, WSD program (like Wilks and Stevenson 1998b) to see if, with a pruned lexicon, it was unable to assign a sense in the same set of cases. An alternative might be to apply a number of independent WSD programs for such cases and see if the missing senses correspond to significant disagreement in the programs' output.

There is some evidence for the positive evaluation of tasks like WSD and LT within what we have called "final" (as opposed to intermediate) tasks: within the SPARKLE project Grefenstette (1998) produced a form of lexical augmentation that improved overall information retrieval precision and recall by a measurable amount. It is most important to keep some outcome like this in mind as an active research goal if the markup paradigm is seen to be impossible for LT, because our aim here is to separate clearly evaluable approaches from weaker notions of computer-related lexical work.

Chapter 14
What Would Pragmatics-Based Machine Translation be Like?

Introduction

The main theoretical goal of his chapter is to specify a pragmatic notion of "translation equivalence" based on modeling the author's/speaker's (source language) view of world, the author's view of the addressee's (source language) view of the world, and the author's goals and plans. This apparatus is applied to analyzing the author's/speaker's utterance in order to arrive at a representation of its content (intended meaning), form, and purpose. The representation then acts as a basis for generating a target language utterance which is again dependent on the modeling the author's/speaker's (target language) view of the world, the author's/speaker's view of the addressee's (target language) view of the world, and a possibly (target-language dependent) revised set of goals and revised plan.

The technical objective was to extend the CRL's multi-lingual machine translation system ULTRA (Farwell & Wilks, 1989 and Chapter 10 above) by utilizing aspects of Preference Semantics (Wilks, 1973a, 1978 and Chapters 3 and 12 above), Semantic Definite Clause Grammars, (Huang, 1988) and Collative Semantics (Fass, 1988) and embedding this system within the ViewGen model of belief ascription developed by Wilks and Ballim (Wilks, 1983, 1987, Ballim, 1988, Ballim and Wilks, 1990, Wilks and Ballim, 1988, 1989, Ballim et al., 1988). The work would use a large-scale semantic structure as an ontology and knowledge base, drawn automatically from the LDOCE dictionary (Wilks et al., 1996, Guthrie et al 1990). ULTRA itself could be considered as no more than one possible platform for these more theoretical developments. ULTRA's state (in 1992) was a reversible translation system between five languages (English, German, Chinese, Japanese, Spanish) with a vocabulary of about 6000 words in each language, and programmed in Prolog, and based on an interlingual representation between the language modules. We shall not discuss in detail here the syntax platform but concentrate on the pragmatic, lexical and ontological issues.

Two Recent Approaches

We turn briefly to two important approaches on the contemporary research scene (formal linguistic methods and statistical methods) and argue briefly why they will be less effective for MT than the modular and interlingual approach we propose here.

It is common to hear in formal linguistic circles that parsing by computer is now solved and we should all direct our attention to language generation. This remark is only comprehensible if taken as being about the current concerns of English-speaking linguists rather than about the processing of substantial quantities of text of the kind required for general machine translation. There is still no evidence at all that the new grammar formalisms that came to the fore in the last decades of the 20C (e.g. those in the tradition of Generalised Phrase Structure Grammar, Gazdar et al. 1985), and their associated claims about extensive coverage of linguistic phenomena, have actually resulted in large volumes of machine translation (MT) using those techniques we would be entitled to expect that if the claims were true.

This regrettable fact may be due only to shortage of time, but the argument has now been used by all leading linguistic theories for over twenty years, and progress in MT since 1990 has been almost entirely from statistically-based methods. The cause is that such recent grammatical developments remain as fragile as all their predecessors, while the real advances in MT lie elsewhere. There are also, as in much computer science, social, organizational and engineering issues in play as well as strictly intellectual ones. Here another piece of MT background will be instructive: the EUROTRA system (King 1982), was developed at a cost of some US$45 million over 10 years by the EEC, and has during that period recapitulated much of the history of modern linguistics (as ontogeny is said to recapitulate phylogeny in biology). Its changing representational base, sometimes every year or so, was the source of many of its problems. The obvious conclusion here is that linguistically-motivated MT systems, like EUROTRA, tend to be too driven by linguistic fashion (since their chief motivation is to be theoretically interesting rather than effective). It is an extraordinary fact that the five-language ULTRA platform developed at CRL and which has essentially the EUROTRA modular architecture, outperformed it (on the only measures available) at a microscopic percentage of the cost.

A Sample Interlingual Representation

In designing the ULTRA machine translation system, along the lines of Chapter 10, we began with the additional assumption that what is universal about language is that it is used to perform acts of communication: asking questions, providing information, describing the world, expressing one's thoughts, getting people to do things, warning them not to do things, promising that things will get done, and so on. These are tasks that people perform and which they use language in performing. Following Morgan (Morgan, TINLAP-2, 109), we have analyzed such tasks as having three general aspects:

- referential information content constituting what is said,
- stylistic information content constituting how it is said,
- communicative information content constituting why it is said,

and an intermediate representation (IR) has been explicitly designed to represent all three aspects without regard to any particular language. Translation, then, can be viewed as the use of the target language to perform the same act as that which has been performed using the source language and the IR serves as the basis for analyzing or for generating expressions as elements of such acts in each of the languages in the translation system (currently English, Spanish, German, Chinese and Japanese in ULTRA at CRL).

The representation was formulated on the basis of an on-going cross-linguistic comparative analysis of hand-generated translations with respect to the kinds of information necessary for selecting the appropriate forms of equivalent expressions in the different languages of the system. We examined a number of different types of communication including continuous texts, business letters, and telex messages as well as dialogues in the contexts of second language learning and foreign travel. This, coupled with the fact that the languages selected for this initial development stage were of extremely different historical and typological nature, led to a solid foundation for developing a flexible and complete descriptive framework in which explicit accounts of the great variation in the structure and lexical content of equivalent natural language texts may be formulated. What follows is merely a UL Sample_of_an_IR: and would be only one contribution to the interface to be finally selected.

By way of example, the Spanish sentence in (0), is associated with the following intermediate representation as:

(0) El ingeniero describio el deseno que habian desa2rrollado en el laboratorio.
The engineer described the design that they-had developed at the laboratory.

```
[prdctn, [type,assert], [class,A], [form,fin],
        [prop, [type,indpnt], [class,dcl],
     [pred, (1) [tense,pst], (2) [aspect,simp], (3) [mood,indic],
   (4) [voice,actv], (5) [pol,pos],
      [rel, (6) [type,dyn],
            (7) [s_case,agnt], (8) [o_case,pat],[io_case,none],
[s_class,human],[o_class,a_obj],[io_class,none],
       [r_desc,describe_1]]],
     [arg,[g_rel,subj],[k_rel,agnt],[t_rel,top],
       [ent,[type,nrm],[class,human],[agree,ts],[det,spin],[quant,unq],
         [e_desc,engineer1_1]]],
     [arg,[g_rel,do],[k_rel,pat],[t_rel,foc],
       [ent,[type,nrm],[class,a_obj],[agree,ts],[det,spin],[quant,unq],
                   [e_desc,
         design2_4,
         [e_mod,[type,rel],[class,B],
[prop,[type,dpnt],[class,dcl],
         [pred,[tense,pst],[aspect,perf],[mood,indic],[voice,actv],[pol,pos],
[rel,[type,dyn],
       [s_case,agnt],[o_case,pat],[io_case,none],
       [s_class,human],[o_class,a_obj],[io_class,none],
[r_desc,develop_2]]],
         [arg,[g_rel,subj],[k_rel,agnt],[t_rel,top],
[ent,[type,pro],[class,C],[agree,tp],[det,spin],[quant,unq],
   D]],
         [arg,[g_rel,do],[k\_yrel,pat],[t\_yrel,none],
           pro],
       [p\_ymod,[g\_yrel,oo],[k_rel,position],[t_rel,foc],
        [ent,[type,nrm],[class,p_obj],[agree,ts],[det,spin],[quant,unq],
          [e_desc,laboratory_0]]]]]]]]]]
```

This predication, "prdctn", consists of a single assertion "assert" of a state of affairs (or proposition, "prop") with specific time and place "fin". The state of affairs consists of a description of a relation (or predicate, "pred") which holds between two entities (or arguments, "arg"), the second of which is being picked out through the use of a complex description. The predicate is specified for (1) a time of occurrence, "tense", which is prior ("pst") to the time of utterance, (2) a qualitative temporal reference, "aspect", which indicates a complete time span "simp", (3) the speaker perspective with respect to the proposition, "mood", indicating the the speaker takes the proposition for a fact "indic", (4) an indication of the "ergativity" of the the relation, "voice", indicating there was an instigator "actv", and (5) the presence or absence of the relation, "pol", which is present "pos". The relation is itself a "describing" event which is classified as an action, (6) "dyn", relating two entities, an instigator, "agnt", which should be human, "human", and a object described, "pat", which should be an abstract object "a_obj". The first argument represented is the grammatical subject of the Spanish expression, "subj", acts as the required instigator, "agnt", and is the topic of the discourse. It consists of a single descriptionof an entity having a general descriptor, "nrm", which is human, "human", neither speaker nor addressee and singular, "ts", specific in the sense that the speaker could identify the individual, identifiable in the sense that the speaker implies at the addressee can identify the individual, and neither near nor far from the speaker or hearer in either a spatial, temporal or communicative sense, "spin", and unique, "unq", in the sense that there is one and only one such individual.

The individual, itself, is described as an engineer. The description of the representation of the second argument follows along the same lines, although the descriptor is complex, consisting of a general descriptor, "design2_4", such that the individual referred to plays a role in yet another state of affairs, a "developing", the representation of which could, again, be described, along the lines of the description thus far presented.

It is important to note that an IR is a representation of the explicit information in the context of the expression being processed. This includes the referential, stylistic and communicative aspects of an utterance in any language in so far as these are reflected by the form of the expression uttered, and not the information inferrable from such explicit information. Beyond the information content of the expression per se, the IR represents the way in which what has been expressed has been expressed – how the elements in the situation are viewed and which elements are related to which and by what relations. IRs, then, may be "language neutral" but they are representations of linguistic events rather than representations of the conceptual contents of expressions.

The multilingual machine translation system ULTRA developed at the Computing Research Laboratory (Farwell & Wilks, 1989) took an interlingual approach (using the IR above) and assumed here for further expostion. The representations passed from one system to the next are intended to represent linguistic utterances or acts in clear declarative form. They represent what is said, how it is said and, in gross form, why it is said.

Thus, the primary focus of the research is on two general but interrelated issues. First, to develop a sophisticated apparatus for exploiting a common ontology and knowledge of the world in the translation process. Secondly, to develop a mechanism for individualizing contexts through the construction of pragmatic belief spaces which introduce context-particular idiosyncratic assumptions which are relevant to translation. We will now present, in turn, a discussion of the application of common knowledge to dealing with interpretation and generation, a discussion of the application of belief ascription to individualizing contexts, and a discussion of applying beliefs ascription to evaluating cross-linguistic or cross-cultural equivalence.

Knowledge of the World and Lexical Semantic Coherence

In processing expressions so as to select a particular interpretation, a hearer/reader applies knowledge of the world, as well as knowledge of language. He thus selects the most sensible interpretation of ambiguous expressions, recovering the most sensible referents for pronouns and inferring information which is implicit. This knowledge of the world is general in the sense that people know a great deal about objects, actions, states, events and situations, such as the classes to which they belong and the attributes they possess. Through the application of such knowledge, the hearer/reader weeds out incoherent interpretations as they develop and select the most appropriate interpretation from those that survive. The general assumption here is, in effect, the artificial intelligence approach to language understanding and the coherence assumption is the guiding principle of Preference Semantics (Wilks, 1975, 1978).

For instance, consider the problems of lexical and structural disambiguation, a standard issue addressed in natural language systems that are based on Preference Semantics. The English sentence in (1),

(1) The speaker reached the central point of his paper.

contains five ambiguous lexical items, “speaker”, “reach”, “central”, “point” and “paper” (in fact, “the”, “of” and “his” are ambiguous as well but more on that below). Obviously these ambiguities must be resolved in order to provide an interpretation of the speaker’s intended meaning and they will also need to be resolved for the purposes of translation. The fact is that “speaker” may be translated, say, in Spanish, as “altavoz”, “parlante” or “interlocutor”, “reach” as “alcanzar” or as “llegar a”, “central” as “central” or “principal”, “point” as “posicion, “valor” or “idea” and “paper” as “papel” or “ponencia”. Spanish, of course, is not a special case. The same is true of all of the other languages in our system (Chinese, Japanese, German) although each presents a different range of lexical choices for each of the words indicated.

Choosing the right reading is impossible through syntactic mechanisms; since all the alternatives in each case are of the same category. The task is semantic in the sense that it is based on what we know about the objects, properties and actions referred to and how they normally can relate to one another in our predictable world. For instance, consider the two possible interpretations of "reach", "extend" and "get to". Generally we would assume that "loud speakers" extend while "presenters" and, less obviously, "language users" get to things. So we are immediately beginning to build two different coherent scenarios, loud speakers extending somewhere and presentors (or less likely language speakers) getting to something. Next consider the properties of "significance" and "middleness", the possible readings of "central".

It is possible for "locations" to be in the middle of things, while "(numerical) values" can either be in the middle of things or significant and "ideas" can be significant. When related to the previously established potential scenarios, we now can begin to order likelihoods of what the sentence is about. Either we are referring to "presenters getting to principal ideas" or "loud speakers extending to middle positions" or, maybe even, "loud speakers getting to middle values" but, while there may be other readings, they are becoming too remote to consider.

Finally, we arrive at "paper" which might either be some "material" or a "written report". Under the interpretation of "paper" as report, the entire expression is about a presenter's getting to the main idea in a report, a perfectly coherent and commonplace event. Under the interpretation of "paper" as some material, the entire expression is about a loud speaker's extending to the middle place of some material, a rather more peculiar situation. But it is only the first interpretation that is readily compatible with the fact that the determiner is a possessive pronoun which refers to a human male in the context of the utterance. The only explicitly mentioned element of the context is the "speaker" but it can serve as the anaphor of the pronoun only under the "presenter" reading since presenters are human and possibly male. Under the "loud speaker" reading, the pronoun would have to refer to someone else who is not mentioned.

Thus at this point we can feel fairly confident of translating (1), say, in Spanish, as in (2),

(2) El interlocutor llego al idea principal de la ponencia.

It is not that this is the only interpretation or that it is even the only coherent interpretation. It simply the most sensible interpretation given our knowledge of the world.

This description of the interpretive process, in the previous paragraph, is essentially a description of the Preference Semantics model of interpretation. To varying degrees of sophistication, the CRL had three implementations of the approach, the English analysis system of the XTRA/ULTRA English-Chinese Machine Translation System (Huang, 1988), the Meta5 English analysis system which focuses on the interpretation of Metonyny and Metaphor (Fass, 1987a, 1988), and the PREMO Preference Machine parser for robust parsing of unrestricted texts (Slator in Wilks et al., 1996).

Lexical Semantic Resolution and Ill-Formedness

The ULTRA system, at the lexical level was based on a set of semantic "senses" for lexical items derived from the definition distinctions provided by the Longman Dictionary of Contemporary English (LDOCE). So, the intermediate lexicon might contain, for example, three senses of "product" corresponding to:

1. product in the sense of agricultural/manufacturing product
   "Chiles are one of the main products of New Mexico"
2. product in the sense of the result of thought or reasoning
   "He was the product of his times".
3. product in the mathematical sense of the result of multiplying two numbers
   "The product of six times two is twelve".

For the purposes of translation, these senses need to be distinguished as they may well be represented by different lexical items in languages other than English. In ULTRA, these semantic senses will be labelled by their LDOCE senses 1,2, and 3: product0_1, product0_2, product0_3. Each of these senses will be associated with the English word "product", as well as possible synonyms. In addition, each sense should be associated with at least one lexical item in each of the remaining languages of the system.

When ULTRA processes an English sentence with the word "product" in it, each of these three senses is a possible intermediate representation of that word. Currently each sense has a small amount of semantic information attached to it. For instance, product0_1 is a type of physical object, while sense three is abstract. Using a greatly simplified version of Preference Semantics (Wilks, 1975, 1978), some disambiguation can be done. Each verb (relation) is also coded with the preference class of its arguments. Thus, a crude form of selectional restriction is imposed. The semantic type of the preferred argument and the actual argument must match. Meta5 in contrast, took a fairly sophisticated approach to Preference Semantics, using the work of Fass (1987), which he termed Collative Semantics. It did not claim that certain readings are wrong or right, but only better or worse given the level of world and language knowledge contained in the system. Meta5 was a research development at CRL that we expect to incorporate fall in the lexical semantics component of the system under design.

The program collects the possible senses for lexical items in a sentence, identifies the semantic dependencies between them, and chooses a "best" reading for the sentence. This facility allows the readings produced by a parser to be ordered in a "best-first" manner.

It should be noted that this procedure would work not just for translation of sentences out of English. Given the grammar and lexicon of any language, the (usually) ambiguous lexical items in that language are also connected to a SET of intermediate senses. The only difference from English is that instead of being tagged with numeric variants of the original word (product0_1, etc.) they would be tagged with different intermediate sense representations. For instance, the French word "queue" would be associated with tail0_2 and handle1_3. In addition, in processing the sentence, it allows for metonymical and metaphorical sentences (or what can be thought of as the ambiguous ill-formedness in all natural language use). Such readings occur frequently, but would be ruled out by the simple selectional restrictions of ULTRA.

For example, in such a simple sentence as "The ship ploughed the waves", neither "ship " nor "waves" meet the typical selectional restrictions ("human" and "soil") for "plough". Nor in the sentence, "John drank two full glasses" does the word "glass" meet the selectional restriction for drink (a liquid). In the plough case, we have an analogical reading, (the ship ploughing the waves is like a man ploughing a field), which is commonly called metaphor, while in the drink case, the word glass is used as a substitute for the contents of the glass (a metonymy). If the semantic dependencies identified by the ULTRA parse, along with the collection of possible intermediate senses for the source language lexical items can be sent directly to Ultra, the possible sense combinations can be organized in a "best-first" order, rather than in the rather inelegant manner that is encoded in the normal Prolog backtracking procedure. The range of allowable readings would also be fine-tuned to include these metaphorical and metonymical readings not possible under Ultra.

Prepositional Phrase Attachment and the Use of Belief Environment Pragmatics

Similar common sense knowledge of the world also contributes to the resolution of so-called structural ambiguity as exemplified by the prepositional phrase in (3).

(3) She described the design they had developed at the conference.

The question is what does the phrase "at the conference" modify, the describing event or the developing event? We must answer this question in order to choose between the two unambiguous Japanese translations below in (4).

(4) a. kanojo ha kaigi nioite kanojora ga kaihatsushita dezain nitsuite nobeta.
she conference at they developed design about described

b. kanojo ha kanojora ga kaigi de kaihatsusareta dezain nitsuite nobeta.
she they conference at developed design about described

Note that the resolution of the question is again not based on syntactic requirements, since under either interpretation the prepositional phrase follows the direct object slot. Nor is this a case of disambiguation on the basis of semantic class since both classes of action, describing and developing, can be located at places. Rather, the task is to select the most likely interpretation whereby "at the conference" locates the describing event, expressed in Japanese by using (4a), one for which we need to call upon our common sense knowledge about describing actions, developing actions and the things that happen at conference. The fact is that people generally attend conference for the purpose of exchanging information and describing things is one of the common tasks one needs to do in such cases. Developing things is not.

This can be made more obvious by contrasting the above example with the sentence in (5),

(5) She described the design they had developed at their research lab.

where, again, disambiguation is necessary in order to select between the two possible Japanese translations in (6).

(6) a. kano ha kanojora no kenkyuujo de kanojora ga kaihatsushita dezain nitsuite nobeta.
she their research-lab at they developed design about described
b. kanojo ha kanojora ga kanojora no kenkyuujo de kaihatsusareta dezain nitsuite nobeta.
she in contrast they their research-lab at developed design about described.

Here, to the earlier case, research labs are places where people work together for the express purpose of developing designs and not describing them so that is the preferred reading as expressed by the Japanese translation in (6b).

It is not that other readings are impossible or even incoherent. It would not be difficult to construct larger situations around these sentences that would increase the likelihood of the opposite member of each pair over the one chosen in this "neutral" context. But this is because in such contexts the relevant information is around to introduce contextually general considerations or rule out contextually neutral generalizations in those particular contexts.

The question of how to represent and reason about propositional attitudes is central to the study of discourse and text. This question is really about the beliefs, and so forth, that the system *ascribes* to the agents mentioned in a text, on the evidence presented by the discourse itself and by context and prior information, since persons have no direct access to each others' mental states. We view the ascription problem as being a fundamental one for text pragmatics.

Ascriptional reasoning is profoundly dependent on the communicative context, general information that the system has about the world, and special information the system has about the agents at hand. Moreover, there are major pragmatic features of discourse, such as *speech acts*, *metaphor* (in the general and ubiquitous sense of semantic illformed-ness), and the determination of the *intentional entities* in play in a discourse, that any system for ascribing beliefs to agents must address. We would go further, and assert that even the most apparently superficial aspects of natural language understanding, such as prepositional phrase attachment, depend on belief ascription. Anyone hearing a sentence with the all-too-familiar structure:

He told his mother about the murder in the park.

will interpret it differently according to whether he believes the speaker believes there was a murder in a park and that the speaker believes the hearer believes that too as opposed to a situation where the speaker knows the site of a "telling. The function of our basic program Viewgen (see Wilks & Ballim, 1993) is to create, or as we shall call it, *ascribe*, environments into which appropriate beliefs can be segregated so that parsing and reasoning can be done in that limited environment.

We have described the basic algorithm in Viewgen in the publication above, and we address the issue of basic parsing issues seen a belief phenomena elsewhere (see Wilks and Ballim, 1989). Here our purpose is simply to set out the claim that a belief ascription algorithm, like that embodied in ViewGen, can be a foundational part of a general account of pragmatic phenomena in translation, ranging from reference and intentional identification, down to metaphor and ill-formedness. And, in a range of cases, that must be carefully demarcated such pragmatic considerations are needed even to fix "low-level" phenomena like prepositional phrase attachment. We set out our general case on the extension of belief computation to these wider pragmatic phenomena in (Ballim et al., 1988).

In interpreting an utterance by an agent (including general texts), an understanding system must ascribe a speech act to that agent; and doing that is a matter of ascribing specific intentions, beliefs, desires, expectations and so on to the agent. Thus, speech act ascription is an important special case of ascriptional reasoning. That speech-act considerations make reasoning about prepositional attitudes essential for the computational modelling of discourse has been established at least since the work of Perrault and his colleagues (e.g. Perrault & Allen, 1980).

As for metaphor, (which we take to be any of a range of boundary-breaking semantic phenomena: a type of ill-formedness found in every "correct" newspaper paragraph) to consider it at all in a study of propositional attitudes might initially seem unmotivated or over-ambitious. However, we are amongst those who hold that metaphor is central, not peripheral, to language use, and indeed cognition in general (for related positions see, e.g.: Lakoff & Johnson, 1980).

Many, if not most, beliefs arising in ordinary discourse and reasoning are at least partly metaphorical in nature. Consider for instance the beliefs that *Terrorism is creeping across the globe, Sally's theory is threatened by the experiment*, and *Prussia invaded France in 1871*, all of which are, in a broad sense, metaphorical. As an example of the difficulties that such beliefs raise, notice that the last one cannot in general be adequately represented by any literal sense representation for *Prussia*, since it may be important to take into account exactly how the believer may be viewing the invasion:

- as a matter of the army of Prussia doing something,
- of the Prussian government doing something,
- or of the Prussian people as a whole doing something, and so on.

The simple predicate notations commonly used in belief research lead us to overlook such basic representational issues. Our work has been based on the use of *explicit belief environments*. Each of these is a group of propositions, manipulable as an explicit entity in the system, and which can, in ways we shall show, be thought of as *nested* inside other such entities. The relation of nesting or containment represents the intuitive notion of a believer (an outer proposition group) having beliefs about another entity (the inner group). Our belief environments are akin to the belief spaces and other types of cluster or partition discussed more recently by authors such as (Fauconnier 1985).

Our work has been closer in spirit to that of Perrault and his colleagues (e.g., Perrault and Allen, 1980, though without their (then) commitment to the language of speech act theory and, most importantly, without their key assumption that the partitions among beliefs are all present at the beginning of the speech act reasoning procedures. Our work makes no such assumption: for us, nested beliefs are not merely accessed but constructed and maintained in real time, a position we find both computationally and psychologically more plausible. The Gedankenexperiment here is to ask yourself if you already know what Mr Gorbachev believes the US President believes about Col. Gaddafi.

Of course you can work it out, but how plausible is it that you already have pre-computed such nested viewpoints, in advance of any such consideration?

Our work has been, since that of Wilks and Bien (1979, 1983), to construct a formalism and programs that capture the heuristic belief ascriptions that individuals actually perform in the process of understanding and participating in dialogue: that is to say, concrete beliefs and not merely meta-beliefs about the reasoning architecture of others, activities we suspect are rarely, if ever, undertaken. Thus our concern has been less with the general expressive powers of particular notations and demonstrations of their adequacy (as has been the central feature of most work on propositional attitude representation) than it has with the development of practical applications of these pragmatic considerations.

Belief Systems and the Pragmatics of Anaphora and Reference

Common sense knowledge of the world also contributes to the resolution of anaphora and the recovery of elided (or contextually implied) information. We have seen two cases of this in examples above already. The "his" of "his paper" in (1) must refer to some male human other than the speaker(s) and the addressee(s) in the context of the utterance. In this case we exploited that fact in a neutral context to increase the likelihood of the reading of "speaker" as presenter as, under that interpretation, we would have a potential anaphor in the context of the utterance and, therefore, pronominalization was sanctioned. Similarly, the resolution of the reference of "their" in "their lab" in (5) contributes to the reading where "at their lab" is part of the developing event rather than the describing event. There must be some "they" in the context of the utterance, otherwise pronominalization cannot be sanctioned in the case of the subject of "develop". Since that "they" is present, the "their" can be understood as referring to whoever this is quite sensibly.

Developing things takes place in labs and specific developings by specific people take place at the specific labs where those people work. This is all very sensible and there is no obvious reason to suppose that the generalization is incorrect in this instance.

But to make the point even more clearly, consider the sentences in (7),

(7) a. He picked the book up from the table and began to read it.
b. He picked the book up from the table and began to wax it.

We need to know what "it" refers to in order to get the translations of these sentences right in those languages that show syntactic gender (Spanish, French and German in our system). Note that the correct translations of "it" in French are "le" and "la" as shown in the translations in (8a) and (8b).

(8) a. Il a pris le livre sur la table et a commence a le lire
He lifted book on table and began to it read
Il a pris le livre sur la table et a commence a la cirer.
He lifted book on table and began to it wax

Now both the book and the table are in the context of the utterance so a priori "it" could potentially refer to either. In the French translations, however, the corresponding pronoun must reflect the syntactic gender of the anaphor so one or the other must be chosen. By applying our common sense knowledge of the actions referred to by "read" and "wax, we can infer the anaphor of "it" in (8a) is the book since one normally reads books but does not usually read tables (if that's possible at all) while the anaphor for "it" in (8b) is the table since waxing tables is common enough but waxing books less so. Thus we can feel fairly confident about the translations offered in (8). In either case, these interpretations could be wrong and once again it would not be difficult to construct situations in which the opposite readings were preferable. But such contexts would still be relying on a common knowledge of the objects and actions being talked about all be it a common knowledge of particular instances of those objects and actions, or, we maintain for a range of cases on the individual beliefs of the hearer/reader.

There is nothing particularly radical in the discussion up to this point. It is essentially Bar-Hillel's "box in the pen" point. That we wish to address it through the application of Preference Semantics is not new either, but the particular implementation of PS within a multi-lingual MT system would be novel. In the discussion that follows, which is intended to motivate the need for taking into account the author's/speaker's belief's about the world and the author's assumptions about the addressee's beliefs about the world, we are indeed taking a radically different approach to processing texts and discourse.

It is a commonplace to point out that sentence level translation is also inadequate for processing continuous texts since there is no access to information in or implied by previous text nor procedures for using that information in the processing of the current input. For instance, in the second sentence of the text in (9),

(9) I have sent you another pack of model paper for your manuscript under separate post. We would appreciate it if you could submit it to us by September 16.

the second "it" refers to the manuscript mentioned in the first sentence. Without access to the information in the text situation related to what has been discussed previously, we cannot resolve the obvious anaphoric reference and, as a consequence, select an appropriate pronoun in those languages (e.g. German, and Spanish) where gender is relevant.

But it is the information in the prior text, not the prior text itself that is relevant. What is said contributes to building up a context, but so do other assumptions that are made about the author and the addressee's beliefs.

Approaches to the Transformation of Machine Readable Dictionaries

We have pursued two approaches to the automatic translation of the information in *The Longman Dictionary of Contemporary English* (Procter et al 1978) into a machine tractable dictionary (MTD) and so to provide large scale syntactic and semantic dictionary data for machine translation. LDOCE is a full-sized dictionary designed for learners of English as a second language that contains over 55,000 entries in book form and 41,100 entries in machine-readable form (a type-setting tape). The preparers of LDOCE claim that entries are defined using a "controlled" vocabulary of about 2,000 words and that the entries have a simple and regular syntax. We have analysed the machine-readable tape of LDOCE and found that about 2,219 words are commonly used. We are also applying the same methodologies to the more recent COBUILD dictionary.

The two CRL approaches are all extensions of fairly well established lines of research and are consistent with a certain position on computational semantics (see Wilks et al., 1987). The main assumptions of this position are two-fold.

First, the problem of the **word sense** is inescapable: lexical ambiguity is pervasive in most forms of language text, including dictionary definitions, hence the words used in dictionary definitions of words and their senses are themselves lexically ambiguous and must be disambiguated.

Second, **knowledge and language** are inseparable, i.e., that the semantic structure of language text and of knowledge representations share common organising principles, and that some kinds of language text structures are a model for knowledge structures (Wilks 1978).

Examples of such knowledge structures include the planes of Quillian's Memory Model (1969), pseudo-texts from Preference Semantics and sense-frames from Collative Semantics. Supporting evidence comes from comparisons between the semantic structure of dictionaries and the underlying organisation of knowledge representations, which have observed similarities between them (Amsler 1980; Chodorow et al., 1985).

The main differences between the three CRL approaches are over what we call **bootstrapping**, i.e., over what knowledge, if any, needs to be hand-coded into an initial analysis program for extracting semantic information from a MRD, and the kinds of knowledge they produce for a MTD. Both the approaches begin with a degree of hand-coding of initial information but are largely automatic. In each case, moreover, the degree of hand-coding is related to the source and nature of semantic information sought by the approach.

Approach I, a statistically based approach, uses the least hand-coding but then the co-occurrence data it generates is the simplest form of semantic information produced by any of the approaches.

Approach II requires the hand-coding of a grammar and semantic patterns used by its parser, but not the hand-coding of any lexical material. This is because the approach builds up lexical material from sources wholly within LDOCE.

Automatically Generating Lexical Entries

Previous work at CRL, in converting an MRD to an MTD provided us with a range of techniques to transfer information from MRD's to interlingual structures and ontological structures. Our goal is to automate the process of the construction of these structures so that the proposed MT system can be tested in a somewhat more realistic environment than one constructed by hand.

One can think of this as a first step toward the construction of a common lexicon or a "poly-theoretical" lexicon. We are proposing to build a lexicography workbench, based initially on one dictionary, which will allow the automatic construction of large concept lexicons for the MT work described in this document.

In particular, our goal is to define a database of lexical facts, together with a set of procedures to access these facts, which will allow the necessary lexical items to be constructed automatically. Our initial work will be based on Longman's Dictionary of Contemporary English (LDOCE), but we believe that the techniques will be applicable to other machine readable sources. We view the construction of a lexicographers workbench as a two stage process. The first stage is to construct a Lexical DataBase, and the second is to define an interface which will allow the automatic construction of lexical structures.

Extensive research has been done on the kind of information needed by natural language programs, especially for machine translation (Nirenburg, 1987). Our claim is that a lot of what is put into NLP lexicons can be found either explicitly or implicitly in a dictionary and empirical evidence suggests that this information gives rise to a sufficiently interlingual ontology for machine translation. Techniques for extracting explicit information has been developed by many researchers (e.g. Boguraev et al., 1987), and are well understood.

Boguraev et al. and the CRL work described elsewhere (Wilks et. al., 1990), have made explicit some kinds of implicit information. Specifically, we divide the initial tasks as follows:

Extract Explicit Information

Explicit in dictionaries are cross-references, part of speech, etc., and in the LDOCE case, the pragmatic and semantic categories which are available in the MRD version. CRL developed a variety of techniques for doing manipulating these (see Chapter 11 above).

Extract implicit information:

The text of dictionary definitions contains implicit information. For example, consider the definition of the word "viaduct".

viaduct – a long high bridge which carries a road or railway line across a valley

The meaning of the definition above is obvious to a human reader, but not to a machine. For example, a natural language program might want to discover from this string that a "viaduct is a bridge", so that viaduct could inherit any properties of bridge. However, this requires resolving resolving the lexical ambiguity of "bridge" (bridge on a ship? bridge of someone's nose? bridge of a pair of glasses? bridge the card game?)

A crucial element here is the identification of semantic relations such as the one above (a viaduct IS-A bridge) and also to disambiguate any polysemous words in the definition string given in LDOCE. This information is stored as part of the Lexical Data base, so that problems such as the one above are resolved. The specific goals are:

1. Obtaining a parse of the definition text in LDOCE. We have implemented a syntactic parser (Slator 1988) for the LDOCE definitions.
2. Identify the genus word – For nouns and verbs, identify the genus word (IS-A relation to the headword), if one exists. We also propose to identify words which have a special relation to the headword (such as part of, member of, set of etc.) whenever possible. This is discussed in more detail in (Guthrie et al. 1990), and has been suggested in other research (Nagao, 1989), [Markowitz] and (Amsler and White, 1979). This work was begun as part of the Lexicon Provider system of Slator (Slator, 1988) and is being augmented to recognize new semantic relations.
3. Disambiguate the genus words – (Amsler and White, 1980) demonstrated the tangled hierarchy of word senses implicit in the Merriam-Webster Pocket Dictionary. Their work required a great deal of human intervention. We propose to construct the LDOCE tangled hierarchy automatically. We have begun this work, and have completed it for the most part in the case of nouns using a system that we have developed at CRL called the genus disambiguator (Guthrie et al., 1990). This system both identifies and disambiguates the genus word in noun definitions based on pragmatic coherence and semantic distance. Several refinements of this system are presently underway and empirical evidence suggests that these refinements will give us a very high success rate (more than 90%) on identification of the correct sense of the genus word. Another module is under development to display the derived ontology in a windowed, hypertext-type environment.
4. Disambiguate the definition words – Although [3] above discusses the resolution of any lexical ambiguity of the genus word in definitions, we also are interested

in resolving any lexical ambiguities that arise in other words of the definition string. We are currently experimenting with a range of techniques to do this. We initially pursued variations of the co-occurrence work of MacDonald and Plate mentioned in the previous section, but using co-occurrence information within LDOCE pragmatic categories. Comparisons will be made between related word sets created with the general co-occurrence matrix and those which are pragmatically motivated. We will refine the co-occurrence techniques by experimentation and then investigate combining these techniques with syntactic parsing and selection restrictions to achieve better results.

5. Eventually we will to be able to parse and disambiguate the text used in the example phrases and sentences. This is a much harder task, since we would need a parser for general text. Examples in LDOCE do not necessarily use only words from the control vocabulary. This can now be considered achieved by the work described in Chapter 11 above.
6. Several of the NLP systems at CRL identify case relations in their lexicons, and one can determine heuristics to recover this information from LDOCE.

- identify categories of verbs (like motion etc.) by operating over the genera of verb definitions;
- identify the categories of prepositions by clustering analysis over the argument structure of example sentences;
- identify case relations for nouns (purpose, substance, etc.) by pattern matching on the parse trees of definitions.

The goal here is to develop an interface for the poly-theoretical lexicon that will allow the automatic construction of lexicons for NLP systems. This interface would allow the lexicon builder to specify the format of his lexical entries to, be used as prototypes by the system. We now wish to establish the point that empirical investigations of lexicons can also be support for interlingual ontologies.

Translation Equivalence and Basic Ontologies

In describing events, we refer to central actions and states. With respect to some given situation, all languages provide alternative expressions for doing this and those alternatives may reflect different classifications of the action referred to. For instance, we might describe the same situation in English by using (10a) or (10b):

(10) a. As lift increases, the aircraft goes up.
b. As lift increases, the aircraft rises.

We represent the two expressions, “goes up” and “rises”, by different constructs in the interlingual, or intermediate representation (IR), since, among other reasons, they consistently reflect a lexico-syntactic distinction across languages, but also because they constitute different views of the situation referred to. Nevertheless, it is not surprising that in some languages the distinction is irrelevant, in this context if not generally, and so both sentences are translated using the same construction. In the Spanish equivalent of (10a) and (10b) in (11), for instance,

(11) En cuanto se incrementa la sustentacion, sube el avion.
as gets-increased lift rises aircraft

both "goes up" and "rises" correspond to a single lexical item, "sube". In order to arrive at (11) from (10a), we need to have some mechanism that identifies the IR of "goes up" as referentially if not stylistically equivalent to the IR of "rises" in the appropriate contexts.

At a structural level, the choice of equivalents for English passives presents problems. Again, the English expressions in (12a) and (12b) can be used to describe the same situation as can the expressions in (13a) and (13b).

(12) a. The lift is caused by the lower pressure above the airfoil.
b. The lift results from the lower pressure above the airfoil.

(13) a. The aircraft is given its horizontal stability by the elevators.
b. The aircraft gets its horizontal stability from the elevators.

There are lexical correspondences for both "cause" and "result" in Spanish and yet syntactic passivization of the stative "causar" in (14a) is stylistically awkward if not incorrect while reflexivization in (14b) is simply wrong.

(14) a. ?La sustentacion es causada por la presion baja sobre la forma aerodinamica.
lift is caused by pressure low above airfoil
b. *La sustentacion se causa por la presion baja sobre la forma aerodinamica.
lift gets-caused by pressure low above airfoil

In order to translate the expression in (12a), then, we might either choose a lexical item which is used to refer to the relation as active and then reflexivize as in (17a) or select a lexical item which is used to refers to the same class of situations but which is about the result rather than the cause as in (15b).

(15) a. La sustentacion se produce por la presion baja sobre la forma aerodinamica.
lift gets-produced by pressure low above airfoil
b. La sustentacion resulta de la presion baja sobre la forma aerodinamica
lift results from pressure low above airfoil

With respect to the predicate in (13a), neither Spanish nor Japanese allows the passivization of indirect objects. Thus, the possible translations either reflect the topicalization of the indirect object while maintaining a lexical correspondence at the level of the predicate as in (16),

(16) a. Al avion, se le proporciona la estabilidad horizontal por los timones.
to aircraft gets-to-it-given stability by elevators
b. koukuuki ha shoukouda niyotte suihei antei ga erareru
aircraft elevator by horizontal stability give-pasv

or they reflect a lexical substitution at the level of the predicate by an item which refers to the same class of relation but which is about the recipient as in (17).

(17) a. El avion recibe la estabilidad horizontal de los timones.
aircraft receives stability from elevators
b. koukuuki ha shoukouda kara suihei antei wo eru.
aircraft elevator from horizontal stability get

In all these cases, we need some way of evaluating the referential and stylistic content of the IR's concerned so as to have access to alternative equivalent IR's to carry through the translation.

There are several points about the data in the examples that we have looked at that have implication for the IR. Among them, a given IR may not be directly expressible in a specific language. However, there must (since translation is possible) be some "equivalent" IR to the original for which there is a direct expression in that language. Here, we have the essence of the argument for a.UL sufficiently universal, or cross-linguistic, ontology for MT whose development, we claim, will be empirically derivable from the explicit and implicit hierarchies of MRD's.

Combining Statistical Results and Symbolic Structures

Statistical studies of large texts can be used in a variety of ways to derived useful information for translation systems. Indeed, statistical information alone can be used as the basis of a somewhat effective translation system (see above, Brown, et al 1989 and Chapter 7 above), or as a method to generate lists of the specialized vocabulary found in a text (Brown, personal communications). Mutual information as derived from statistical studies of free text has been used as the basis of a parser which marks the constituent boundaries in English text (Magerman and Marcus, 1990). In addition, statistical studies of structured text such as machine readable dictionaries or computer manuals can yield information that is not directly present (Wilks et al. 1990). There are a number of features of such structured texts which yield information difficult to extract from free text. In addition, the analysis of bilingual corpora can provide information on the relationship between two languages. As a simple example, determination of words which are most similar in usage can be done by maximising the decrease in entropy of the produced language when the words are merged. This method tends to choose words the distinction between which cannot be recovered by contextual clues.

The creation and use of a statistical language model would allow us to develop automatic methods to reason from examples of usage back to partial lexical entries. In addition, a probabilistic language model can be used to prioritize the backtracking in a non-deterministic parser or generator with very large potential improvements in execution time.

Conclusion

In conclusion we must make clear one important assumption underlying our position: that practical MT implementations such as we advocate, may lead to quite different choices from theoretical MT. The ultimate goal of machine translation is undoubtedly to implement a program on an architecture which takes as input an utterance (in the form of text or speech) in one natural language and produce as output an equivalent utterance in a second (distinct) natural language. This is clearly a problem of software and hardware engineering. At one level, then, the goal of theoretical MT should be to identify the inherently limiting computational characteristics of the proposed approaches and provide alternative approaches which overcome those limitations. However, identifying such limitations and working out alternative approaches is dependent on assumptions about natural languages, and natural language processing in general, such as what the nature of natural language is, what the nature of natural language understanding is, what the nature of natural language production is, and, in the case of machine translation, what the nature of natural language translation is.

Afterword (2008): the chapter above began life as one of the first of overviews trying to accommodate statistical methodology to one (non-standard) symbolic MT system. It remains relevant if only because there are undoubtedly sense semantic and belief pragmatic phenomena that full MT, like full translation by any method, will require and yet which have not yet been performed by any system based on data and statistical algorithms. The work described here bringing together belief and metaphor phenomena has been developed since quite independently by John Barnden and his colleagues (as ATT_META)(see: Barnden 2001; Barnden et al., 2002).

Chapter 15
Where was MT at the End of the Century: What Works and What Doesn't?

Modalities of International Cross-Language Cooperation

Cooperation is now crucial to MT because resource creation demands it, and resources are now considered crucial to MT by all except those still firmly committed to formal linguistic methods, and who have therefore effectively withdrawn from empirical and evaluation-driven MT.

Obvious types of cooperation are:

- between monolingual groups within states (usually monolingual)
- between monolingual groups within the (multilingual) EU
- between groups or state organisations within blocs (US, EU, Japan), where one of those blocs is monolingual, one multilingual, and one (The US) with aspects of both.

The next question is: what should be the basis of that cooperation if it is across languages and cultures (e.g. in writing the analysis, generation and transfer modules of a conventionally structured MT system)?

Should it be on the basis of:

- each partner doing what they do best (as opposed to everyone doing and redoing everything)?
- each partner doing their own language (as opposed to "I'll help you with yours")?
- each partner doing their own interlinguas (as opposed to "I'll believe more in mine if you can use it too")?
- each partner doing their own evaluation of their own modules (as opposed to "I'll evaluate yours and you mine"

But, historically not all insight is from inside a language: one has only to think of the early keyboards for Chinese, which came from the West, and the fact that Jespersen, a Dane, produced the first full descriptive linguistic grammar for English. A morpholympics competition was won by a Finnish analyser of German which beat all the groups from Germany.

Genuine cooperation, on the other hand, can include offers such as the free availability of JUMAN, the Japanese segmenter from Kyoto University, which is of the

"I'll help you do my language" type, and which is quite different from "I'll do mine and you do yours", and attitude which drastically limits possible forms of cooperation. On the other hand, the Finnish constraint parser for English (initially as Karlsson, 1990) is "I'll help you do yours". If one doubts the need for this kind of thing, I can cite from personal experience the project at CRL-NMSU which built a Spanish lexicon from an English one largely because we could not find a Spanish machine-readable lexicon at all.

Consider, as part of this issue, the problem of the mutual perceptions of Japanese and English speakers: each group sees their own language as mysterious and hard to specify by rules. The proof of this, for English speakers, is that vast numbers of foreigners speak English but find it so hard to get the language exactly right, as opposed to communicate adequately with it. Yet, and as a way of reaching the same conclusion from the opposite evidence, the Japanese sometimes infer from the fact that few foreigners speak Japanese at all, let alone perfectly, that they cannot do it, because of some inherent property of Japanese! One imagines that this attitude will change, as foreigners speaking Japanese, at least adequately, becomes commonplace. This situation creates a paradox for English speakers because it is so widely used; with the result that native speakers often implicitly divide the language into two forms: where one is the "International English" they understand but cannot speak, and native speakers now get the experience of being somewhat isolated in conversations where everyone else is speaking "International".

A side-effect of the IBM statistical methods for MT was that they showed the surprising degree to which you do not have to understand anything of the language you are processing. Most workers in the language industries find this conclusion intuitively unacceptable, even if they do not subscribe to what one might call the "meaning and knowledge" analysis, still popular within many Japanese systems, as it used to be for English during the "artificial intelligence" period in the 1970s. Its basis in both languages was what is usually called paucity of structural information, or some such phrase, which opposes the two languages to, say, Spanish or German, whose speakers tend to believe their language rule governed. Most commentators on recent MT developments contrast as radically opposed the IBM statistical methods to those earlier AI methods explored in the US. But that contrast can disguise the closeness of Meaning-Knowledge systems to statistical systems: both rest on quantifiable notions of information or knowledge. AI systems for MT like "preference semantics" (e.g. Wilks, 1978) can be seen as quantitative systems that, at the time, lacked the necessary empirical data, since provided by more approaches like (Grishman and Sterling, 1989), and other quantifications of preference by Lehnert, Resnik and many others.

Systems that emphasise the core role of verb meaning (all those going back to Fillmore and case concepts in AI and computational linguistics generally, and beyond him to the verb centred tradition of classical logic) have to deal, in the end, with the vacuity of much verb meaning ("Kakeru" in Japanese or "Make" in English are classic examples), especially frequently used verbs, and the reliance for understanding their use on the types of things you can do with, say, keys and locks, or scrolls and branches (in the case of Kakeru). Similar situations for English arise when only the object (bed, versus book, versus point etc.) of the verb give any content at all to the meaning of "make" when used with each of them.

Like "do", "be" and "have" in English, those verbs are almost entirely redundant and the verb name is no more than a pointer to constrain abnormal uses: you could delete such verbs from a text and still guess rightly what was going on; or at least you could with Kakeru if you could distinguish open and close (e.g. by the mention of a lock versus a key) from the wider context available. To say this is no more, in the case of the vacuous verbs above, than recapitulating the basics of information theory, in that these verbs carry little or no information. Text statistics, of the IBM type, reflect this and so should our analysis.

My point here is that, with these phenomena, symbolic and statistical analyses are saying the same thing in different ways, though the symbolic tradition inherits various prejudices – like the structural primacy of verbs in English, so that we tend to think of verbs having valencies, cases and preferring their neighbours, rather than vice versa – where statistical methods are simply unprejudiced.

The Relationship of Cooperation to MT Evaluation

Certain issues to do with MT evaluation follow from the discussion of the last section, particularly in connection with international cooperation in MT, particularly projects that require modules of a single system to be built in different countries, as is standard in European R&D. Let us consider module interfaces (which may or may not be considered as interlinguas, which raise other, special, issues) and ask:

How can you evaluate an international/intermodule project properly?

The EU MT project EUROTRA (Johnson et al. 1985) was designed on the assumption that national/language groups built modules for their own language(s) and the system was held together by a strong structure of software design and, above all, agreed interfaces. But how could one assign blame for error (if any) inside an overall project designed like this after a bad evaluation of overall performance. In fact, no serious evaluations of that project based on quantitative assessment of output were ever done, but that is beside the point for this discussion.

EUROTRA was not, in its final form an interlingual system, but imagine a two-module interlingual system. Some have certainly written about the possibility of evaluating the modules:

Source Language → INTERLINGUA
and
INTERLINGUA → Target Language

separately. But could his method for assignment of error be of more than internal team interest if this were an international cooperative project? Or, more precisely, for a given bad translation, how could one know for certain which of those modules was at fault, if each chose, chauvinistically, to blame the other. Clearly, that would only be possible if they had a clear way of deciding for a given sentence what was its correct interlingual representation. If one could do that it would be clear whether or not the first module produced that representation: if it did, the error must be in module two, and if not it would be in module one.

Although not interlingua based, the participating EUROTRA groups had to agree on module interfaces that were, in effect, interlinguas in the sense of this discussion; it was just there was more than one of them, because there were more than two modules required for a translation. In any case the groups there shared similar language-family assumptions so the interface was not too hard to define. But could Japanese and English speakers agree on a joint interlingua without an indefinite number of arbitrary decisions, such as what are the base meanings of kakeru?

One possible way out of the problem of agreeing on an interlingua between two very different languages, and assuming one did not take a "third way" out by selecting another existing language as an interlingua, might it be possible to define two interlinguas (one J-orientated; one E-orientated) and use both, perhaps comparing translations achieved by the two routes from source to target? That would at least have the virtue of having to have an interlingua based only on one of the two languages and which might therefore not be comprehensible to the other team.

But we will always have the residual problem, rarely mentioned, that one cannot program the module Source → INTERLINGUA unless one is a "native speaker" of that interlingua (i.e. a native speaker of the language on which it is based), but then the other team will not be able to program the module INTERLINGUA → Target. A moment's reflection should show that the "two directions" solution is not a solution at all, because both teams can only program one module for each route, so there is no translation produced. In practice, this would just become a blame shifting mechanism: "our part was fine, so the problem must be in your generation!".

Suppose we retain the earlier assumption that everyone does analysis and generation of their own native language, and see what the possible models would be if we did have both a J-based interlingua (JINT) and an E-based one (EINT):

i. J source → (J group) → JINT – (E group) → E target
ii. J source → (J group) → EINT – (E group) → E target
iii. E source → (E group) → EINT → (J group) → J target
iv. E source → (E group) → JINT → (J group) → J target

The question we raised above was whether, say, an English-speaking group could do task (iv). It is crucial to recall at this point that some Japanese-speaking groups do perform tasks like (ii): the NEC MT group has used an English-like interlingua, and the EDR lexical group in Tokyo has certainly produced large numbers of codings in an E-based interlingua for Japanese word sense, which is effectively task (ii) without any generation to follow.

The solution may then be that we should learn enough of each other's languages to use each others interlinguas, and then compare the effectiveness of the routes above?

And we would probably want to add a safety clause that the evaluation of any module into or out of an interlingua based on language X should be done by the speakers of language Y.

If there are also to be rules going between the interlinguas we shall have what some Japanese groups call "semantic transfe"r. Whatever that is, it is quite distinct from syntactic transfer, which is right or wrong and capable of extraction from data, as in the work of Matsumoto and colleagues (e.g. Utsuro et al. 1994). This relativist notion of an interlingua, explicitly dependent on actual natural languages, is one quite separate from the classical notion, of the sort once advocated by Schank (1973) where there could not be more than one interlingua, almost by definition. The tradition being explored in this paper (cf. Wilks et al. 1995) is that if interlinguas in fact have characteristics of natural languages, then the relativist tradition may be the only one with a future.

Relativism and Interlinguas in MT

I would suggest that one can no longer continue to say, as many still do with a straight face, that items in an interlingua look like words but are in fact "just labels". This ignores the degree to which they are used as a language along with assumptions brought in from languages. They always look like languages, like particular languages, as we saw above, so maybe they are languages.

Ogden's Basic English (Ogden 1942) was a reduced primitive language of some thousand words, about the size of the inventory of head notions in a thesaurus like Roget, and about half the size of the LDOCE defining vocabulary (Procter et al., 1978). The words of Basic English were also highly ambiguous because of the small size of the set, as is the LDOCE defining vocabulary, a task Guo set out to rectify by a hand-tagging of the LDOCE defining vocabulary, to produce what he called Mini-LDOCE (Guo 1992). Interlingual items are ambiguous in exactly the same way, though this fact is rarely discussed or tackled. It did surface briefly during discussion at a 1992 Pennsylvania seminar on the EDR dictionary, when EDR colleagues explained how hard they sometimes found it to understand the EINT structures they had created in the conceptual part of EDR, and this was in part because the EINT words has senses they did not know. This may be a paradoxical advantage, as I shall discuss in a moment.

If this point of view has merit, then many empirical possibilities arise immediately: one would be to adapt to this task some of the systems for producing and checking controlled languages (e.g. Carnegie Group's CLE). These could be adapted to check not only the well-formedness of formulas in an interlingua, but the distribution and usage of the primitive terms. Again, a range of techniques has been developed to sense-tag texts against some given division of the lexical senses of words; so that each word in a text is tagged with one and only one sense tag that resolves its lexical ambiguity (e.g. Bruce et al. 1993, Edmonds and Kilgarriff, 2003). This technique could probably be extended in principle to interlinguas, if their formulas were viewed as texts, so as to control the non-ambiguity of the interlingual forms. As we noted above, Guo has already performed this task for the prose definitions of LDOCE, and that task is not different in principle from what we are discussing here.

The motivation for all this, remember, is so that interlingual expressions can be controlled so that they are understood by native speakers of the language from which the interlingual was drawn and by others, where the latter group are far more important for assessability of interlingual MT as a technique.

None of this is an argument against interlinguas, but a suggestion for treating them seriously, making them more tractable, in the way MRD-based research has made lexicons more serious and consistent than the old, purely a priori, ones.

Another possible way of dealing with the difficulty we diagnosed is Hovy and Nirenburg's (1992) argument that an interlingua could be extended by the union of primitives from the classifying ontologies for the relevant languages under definition. This would abolish at a stroke the difficulty of an interlingua as a whole being based upon a single natural language, but would not help any user understand the parts not in their language. The gain would be in equity: all users would now be in the same position of not believing they understood all the symbols in the interlingua, but the basic problem would not be resolved.

It is vital to remember here that none of the above makes any sense if you cling firmly to the belief that interlinguas are not using natural language symbols at all, but only manipulating words as "labels for concepts". If you believe that, then all the above is, for you, unnecessary and irrelevant, and some of my closes colleagues are in that position. (see discussion of this in Nirenburg and Wilks, 2000) I appeal to them, however, to look again and see that the position is sheer self deception: and we have no access at all to concepts other than through their language names which are, irreducibly, in some language. Because of the convenience that computers, say, are object to which we can all point, we may persuade ourselves that w e all have the concept of computer and the name doesn't matter. This, consolation, however does not last once one notices that of the words used to define other words (e.g. the 2000 words of the LDOCE defining vocabulary – the very words that appear in interlinguas, of course) virtually none are the least like "computer": state, person, type, argument, form are not open to simple ostensive definition and their translations are matters of much dispute and complexity. I rest my case.

Evaluation as Hegemony

I want now to move from one undiscussible subject to another, but at shorter length. We neglect at or peril the international aspects of evaluation systems and the way in which they become, or are perceived to be "hegemonic": in the sense of attempts to assert control over the R&D of another culture. There has been strong resistance in the European Commission to any general regime for the evaluation of MT based on open competitions between entrants of the kind that has developed research so rapidly, at least in its initial stages, in the DARPA community in the US. There is a belief in the Commission that such competitions are wasteful and divisive, waste resources in duplication of systems that compete, and that belief clearly helped to keep some substandard research in Europe alive and well for many years.

Protracted negotiations on sharing linguistic resources (lexicons and corpora) between the US and the EU did not progress well when they began in the early 1990s largely because of this issue of evaluation, and because the US side wanted to tie exchange of resources to the idea of common evaluation. The US side stressed the value of competitive evaluations between groups that accepted the same regime (usually imposed by the funding agency). The EU side stressed cooperative R&D and downplayed evaluation, pointing out the incestuous effects of groups that compete and cooperate too intensely.

Evidence of the latter was the unexpected successes of EU groups that entered ARPA MUC and Speech competitions (Sussex, Siemens, Philips, LIMSI, later on Cambridge, Edinburgh and Sheffield): one could indeed say they opened up a gene pool that had become too incestuous.

The Commission side saw the US position as hegemonic in the sense defined here: the US saw the European position as wanting to be shielded from open competition and ungrateful in that it expected to get US resources (chiefly speech data at the time) for no return. I retail this history, in which I was present at the initial meetings, not to show a right and wrong side – it is not so simple – but to note that international cooperation is a complex cultural matter, in MT as anywhere else, and we should be aware of the complex links between evaluation and resources as well as the more technical issues to do with representations and interfaces we noted above.

Resource Sharing in the Future

Nonetheless, resources will be essential to the future of MT and resources for MT, almost by definition, come from diverse languages and so states and cultures. Ways round these difficulties must be found, and in a range of areas:

Resources: corpora, lexicons, dictionaries
Standards: (markup (e.g. SGML)), tag sets, for lexicon interchange
Software modules: alignment, taggers etc.

In all of these areas there is progress: the EU actively encouraged the spread of the first type, and the inhibitions tend to come far more from the commercial concerns of publishers that from governments. Resource and software distribution centres have sprung up e.g. first the Consortium for Lexical Research, finally shut down in 2006, then the much better funded and successful Linguistic Data Consortium in the US, then Saarbruecken in the EU, then the official and EU-funded European Linguistic Resources Association. Software modules like taggers from the US and segmenters like Kyoto University's JUMAN became widely available through individual acts of corporate and individual good citizenship, and started a culture of sharing. The EDR in Japan and Cambridge University Press (with its new lexicon) in the EU announced plans to make lexical data far more available that was normally the case. The EU has a crucial role to play in future resource provision for MT, not only because, with its (in 2008) twenty languages; not only because its need for MT is so great but because it has already funded such substantial resource projects (and tool projects to use resource) already: NERC, ELRA, MULTEXT, GENELEX, AQUILEX, PAROLE, EAGLES before the Century's end; the names are legion.

These are still early days, even though so much as been spent, in that it is still hard to actually get hold of genuinely reusable resources and tools: interface and format problems still bedevil real reuse. Nonetheless there is no doubt that, by the Century's end, the reluctance about sharing had been firmly settled on terms close to those the US side had already laid out. But the EU is also haunted still by the spectre of English: it is more than one of the EU languages: it is now the superlanguage, that provokes both greater utilization and fear of takeover, and all tied in with the mixed attitudes to US culture that we noticed in connection with evaluation. This complex attitude worked against the EU funding of specifically English resources, on the grounds that they are available from the US and that the UK has already put such great efforts into its learner's dictionaries (LDOCE, OALD, COBUILD, the new Cambridge Dictionary etc.) and its national corpora (The Bank of English, the British National Corpus etc.). Were it not for these last, English could easily be in the extraordinary position of being the only EU language, all of whose resources were from or controlled by sources outside the EU. Sometimes this asymmetry is inevitable: when the EU funded the EUROWORDNET project in the 1990s, to build European language wordnets linked by a single spine of core English words, there was no possibility of funding an English Wordnet from scratch because it already existed (i.e. Miller (1985) and the whole Wordnet Bibliography is at http://lit.csci.unt.edu/~wordnet/). The position of that (English) Wordnet at the spine or interlingual core of the plural wordnet systems is further entrenchment of the role of English within resource systems.

All this effort and activity has tended to downplay the need to build resource in major languages (e.g. Russian, Chinese, Arabic) that are neither one's own nor, at the moment of writing, seem inclined to build or locate their own electronic resources. Russia has such resources but they see to have deteriorated in the short term with the economy itself. The issue of who builds such resources is also, of course, and in the real world tied up with perceived threats, commercial and military.

In spite of all this, we can be sure the resource issue will not now go away from MT, and that commercial and government interests will ensure that greater resources are built and maintained. What we, as researchers, need to work for is maximum availability and the way that such resources can serve international communication, politically, of course, but, crucially, within interlingual aspects of the R&D process itself.

Afterword 2008: what was not foreseen in the 1990s was the way that the Web/Internet would transform the resource issue by simply becoming THE monolingual language resource, at least for alphabetic languages, so that researchers began to talk of billions of words in corpora and The Web as Corpus. Sharing has much improved with the entrenchment of the resource associations mentioned above and the growth of additional competitions tied to annotated resources for specific linguistic functions: SENSEVAL, PARSEVAL etc. These have now grown out of the direct control of the US military authorities to civil society and to groups associated with language families e.g. ROMANSEVAL. The spread of not just statistical but machine learning techniques has led to a huge upsurge in annotations for supervised machine learning techniques and these become further resources to be shared e.g. the "Red Badge of Courage" novel, annotated with Wordnet senses. Speech researchers and corporations like AT&T led the way in this, yet again, by making available vast speech databases. But even now it is difficult to get resources for NP areas like dialogue processing because both the speech recognition and NLP processing in dialogue tends to be tied tightly to application domains and so classic existing resources do not always help researchers much if they are not in the right domain. The availability of parallel language resources, specifically for MT, has improved with the availability of corpora from international banks and the documentation of the EU itself, but the greatest source of resources for quantitative MT (see next chapter) has been the growing data provided by translation bureaux themselves.

Chapter 16
The Future of MT in the New Millennium

Methodological and Theoretical Issues in MT

As we noted at the beginning of this book, MT is having a revival in the US and to a lesser extent in Europe drive – n like so much else by the World Wide Web – and to be somewhat depressed in Japan compared with ten years ago. Ways forward from here seem to come down to either a better attempt at matching the existing technology to market needs, which are real and expanding, and in improving the basic technology by getting above the 65–70% level that customers, of the best systems on a good day, will now accept.

What does this latter mean in concrete terms and how does it relate to the arguments about principle that have raged through MT's past, and have represented in most chapters of this book? There are some things everyone, from every research school can agree with, whether one still advocates knowledge-based methods, is a believer in linguistic purity, in interlinguas, in statistical methods or (more sceptically) in no more than vastly improving editing tools and interfaces for users. There are now much better decomposable modules for linguistic analysis available: part of speech taggers, automatically and semi-automatically derived lexicons and concordances, effective grammars and parsers far closer to corpora than before. Yet their effect is not apparent in systems in the market – researchers who help build marketable systems still often throw away all their theoretical beliefs and their successes when going to market, as if they themselves do not believe in effectiveness of their own published work.

We noted at the beginning of the book that Martin Kay once argued that, even if all the problems of syntax, morphology, computational semantics had been individually solved, it might not improve MT. One may not be quite sure what he meant but it is an important thought; if one asks what he thought might still be missing one might list research in

- the gist, meaning or information content of what a text was about.
- a high enough level theory of the rhetorical structure of texts.
- a computationally accessible representation of common sense knowledge down to excruciating levels of detail.

- a model of generation that gives priority not to rules but always to the smoothest collocational choices.
- a model of the vagueness and indefiniteness of boundary of much of the categorical knowledge underlying language and thought.

Some, a few, researchers have attempted to tackle these notions directly over the years, but no one can honestly say they have yet proved that their structures when fully operational will lift the magic MT success figures much, though there is now general acceptance that data-based collocational models of generation must be the way to go.

Let us stay at this high level of abstraction and ask if the classic theoretical disputes in the history of MT have been solved or at least put to rest, and if their solution has impacted the current situation much. The following is a fairly simple first list of the crucial issues of the last twenty years with some comment on which remain current research issues:

Representations for MT: The Role of Knowledge

Bar Hillel argued this was essential for MT but unachievable with computers. AI researchers in MT accepted the premise but believed the task was achievable, yet most proprietary MT systems still do not attempt to encode anything resembling a knowledge component beyond technical vocabulary. It is unclear that this issue, so clear when stated, has yet been settled because it has had little impact on working commercial systems. The goal of a Semantic Web first described by Berners-Lee and others (Berners-Lee et al., 2000) might at first seem far from the concerns of MT, but one of that research effort's unintended consequences has been a new interest in semantic content on the Web expressed in ways quite different from the traditional logic methods of Knowledge Representation (e.g. McCarthy and Hayes, 1969) as deployed in AI and much closer both to interlingual representations and to linguistic annotations that have played such a major role in quantitative linguistics since Jelinek's MT system CANDIDE. (Wilks 2008) discusses ways in which the Semantic Web research program, one funded at very high levels in the EU since 2000, may bear on ways to represent knowledge more plausibly for NLP tasks including MT.

Representations for MT: The Argument for no Representation at Any Level

Data-driven approaches to MT – at least in extreme forms like IBMs statistical model of MT, CANDIDE – deny that any separate representation at all is required: at the knowledge level nor any linguistic level, although even the earlier CANDIDE system had some representation of (language-specific) French morphology! That approach seems to have retreated for the in extreme forms while remaining the principal opposition to representational orthodoxy, even though with little influence on commercial systems. Jelinek's own work after CANDIDE (e.g. Jelinek, 2004) discussed at length the building of some conventional linguistic resources by statistical methods, and that is now almost certainly the majority position.

Representations for MT: Language Specific or Not?

This is the interlingual argument, versus transfer and direct methods – although no one now seems to defend direct coupling methods much since SYSTRAN declared itself to be a transfer system some years ago. There is in fact little support for true interlinguas (which would, by definition, exclude language specific resources like bilingual lexicons). The remaining argument is really about interlinguas + bilingual lexicons, since renouncing a bilingual lexicon to restrict generation choices seems hobbling oneself unnecessarily. After that, interlingualism may be a matter of degree, shading into controlled language inputs used as pivot languages and so on.

Representations for MT: "High Level non-AI Theory"

Does MT need "the best linguistics": this is a hard question as there is no agreement as to what the best linguistic theory is at any given moment. Certainly there was far more contact in the 1990s between front-line linguistic systems (FUG, LFG, HPSG, GPSG type grammars, Berwick principles etc.) than in the decades before, where linguistically-motivated MT meant only IBM's early transformation based system, then McCord's (1989) system at IBM, a Dutch research system based on Montague semantics and, as always, EUROTRA. One cannot identify any linguistic theory in most MT systems under serious evaluation at the present time.

MT as a Directional Task – Analysis or Generation Driven

There has been a substantial shift in ideas here towards the role of generation as an "intelligent" task and one pre-eminent in the practice of actual translators. Generation seems to have the most successful part of Jelinek's data-driven statistical system CANDIDE. There seems general agreement on this though again it is hard to locate this fact within commercial MT systems except perhaps in the few example driven systems in operation. since these could be said to be driven entirely by past generation activities.

The Scope of a Language: the Sublanguage Issue

There is some realisation now that this has become a non-issue since all MT systems define the scope of what they cover and hence a sublanguage.

The Scope of a Language: Must Dialogue be Treated Quite Differently in MT than Running Prose?

This is an important distinction and masked by the fact that prose MT and speech-to-speech MT now seem to develop in quite different environments; this hides the fact that the role of pragmatics and the nature of the parsers required are probably utterly different in the two situations. The lack of a production speech-to-speech system, though there are many prose systems, is not entirely due to the weakness of speech front ends alone, but to the problem, mentioned earlier, of deriving project-specific, because domain-specific, speech corpora. The VERBMOBIL speech-to-speech MT system (and its EU-funded successors SMART. http://www.dfki.de/pas/f2w.cgi?iuic/verbmobil-e) which presented its second phase prototype in 2000 was a successful German effort at Speech-to-Speech MT which triggered a renaissance in mobile dialogue mT in Europe, now with its own evaluation regime (TC-STAR: http://www.tc-star.org) in which up to a dozen systems compete (in 2007).

MAT as a Distinct and Inevitable Form of MT

If one accepted Bar Hillel's argument on impossibility then MAT is really all there is – computers can certainly provide editing tools and, when Kay proposed MAT as a survivable form of MT, he probably did believe Bar Hillel and underestimated the survival potential of low quality MT. However, MAT has (with the PC revolution) proved a productive gradualist path towards MT: indeed, in a sense much MT is now for translators, and they are an identifiable market.

The Problem of Extensible or Metaphoric Lexical Meaning

This has been a major independent area of lexical research (see Chapter 13 above), which has received a new boost from the clear limitations built into the "machine readable dictionary" movement which attempted to extract lexicons for MT from existing dictionary sources and did to some extent succeed (see Wilks et al., 1996). But those limitations only highlight how much word sense coverage is not covered by existing dictionaries and which is not simply the product of aninadequate terminology coverage: i.e. the extension of sense specific to certain domains, text types, etc. There has been substantial research into whether there are lexical rules for regular, non-domain specific, extensions of sense (e.g. Briscoe and Copestake, 1996) or whether there are patterns of metaphor that endlessly repeat (as Lakoff and Martin have both claimed), but again there has been no input to systems now available.

Advances in MT Evaluation Techniques?

There has certainly been a change in techniques: most importantly the use of the BLEU technique (Papieni et al., 2002) and its variants (NIST, ROUGE, METEOR etc.) have virtually replaced all the earlier techniques mentioned earlier such as

Cloze tests etc. Their advantage is seen as being lessened of human involvement while giving clear quantitative results. Basically, all such tests rest on comparison of ngrams (up to trigrams) between the translations to be rated and a canonical translation. It is unclear at this time whether such tests have a long term future; certainly many are unhappy with them (see Callison-Burch et al., 2006), in part because they might rest on unknown features of the canonical translation – if several translations are used to avoid this, the human cost rises – and since the test works by methods close to those that produced the translation, assuming it statistical, (and that is a wholly new feature in MT evaluations) there is a risk, not wholly understood, of over fitting to the test itself. Indeed, many translation system now seem to build the test into their MT algorithm. This led in 2005 to a situation in a NIST comparative test where BLEU rated (non-statistical) SYSTRAN results way below where human judges did – 6th rather than 1st!. The jury might be said to be still out on BLEU but there is little doubt the future will be some form of automated evaluation scheme.

In summary one might say that there is progress, and this budget of MT issues does not stay unchanged over long periods of R&D. What is less clear is the ways in which, and the time scale by which, high-quality research reaches products; it is far more mysterious in MT than in most areas of computer-based R&D, such as VLSI or even closer areas like information retrieval and extraction where there seems a reasonably well understood route from tested research to fielded systems.

Where should one Look for Advance

A distinguished colleague said to me recently that parsing by computer was now solved and we should all direct our attention to language generation. I realized I could only understand, or accept, this remark if I took it to be about the current concerns of English-speaking linguists rather than about the processing of substantial quantities of text of the kind required for general machine translation. I can still see no evidence at all that new grammar formalisms that came to the fore in the last decades (e.g. fromGeneralised Phrase Structure Grammar, Gazdar et al. 1985 onwards), and associated claims about extensive coverage of linguistic phenomena, have actually resulted in large volumes of parsing or machine translation (MT) using those formalisms. We would be entitled to expect that if the claims were true. What advance there has been in parsing has been from corpus statistics-based systems like Charniak's (2001), but there relative success has been achieved in part by "moving the goal-posts". That is to say that the success of such systems is not measured by reaching a final "S symbol" as evidence of a single parse of a complete sentence, but rather by quantitative success in inserting brackets into the word string in a way that approximates the segmentation of the "gold standard parsing" of that sentence, usually taken from a tree-bank. This has proved a useful technique but is not the way parsing used to be defined; indeed, it may be that, as with MT itself, and the proven usefulness of mediocre MT, the goal-post shifting was the correct thing to do, and the earlier perfectionism was the self-imposed error.

This failure of grammar-based systems may be due only to shortage of time, but that the argument has now been used by all leading linguistic theories for over thirty years. The true cause is, I believe, that such developments remain as fragile as all their predecessors, while the real advances in MT lie elsewhere and are hard to discern. They are, like much in computer science, social, organisational and engineering matters rather than strictly intellectual ones. The EUROTRA system (King, 1982), developed at a cost of some $50 million by the EU, has during that period recapitulated much of the history of modern linguistics (as ontogeny is said to recapitulate phylogeny in biology). Its changing representational base, sometimes every year or so, was the source of many of its problems. What undoubted success there has been in symbolic MT seems to have come from choosing a representation and sticking to it for at least a decade, which suggests that MT is to a large extent a social and organisational, possibly even a management, issue. This is not a new phenomenon in the history of MT: the American ALPAC report (ALPAC 1966) was itself a devastating socio-political instrument, one that halted MT research in the West for a generation, but which said something very different from what many now believe it to have said: it certainly did not say MT was impossible, but only that, with the MT programs then available, human translation was cheaper and would remain so for the foreseeable future (a phase that has now definitely passed).

There is no doubt whatever that machine translation now exists and can be purchased on a large scale and at a quality that many users find acceptable for their needs. The proportion of internal EC documentation translation done by machine is still rapidly growing, still using a specially modified version of the SYSTRAN system. It is interesting that one still has to state this existence claim so firmly; it is because very many, otherwise well informed, people still have difficulty in accepting the fact. But that MT is still rudimentary, even if adequate for constrained bureaucratic purposes. So, where will more advanced MT come from? I take it for granted that advance in MT will come from "phenomena of scale": the use of very large dictionaries in particular, and the extraction from them, and from large text samples, of collocational, semantic and pragmatic information, as well as new techniques for combining these sources in differing circumstances. It will also require, as it has with historical MT, an understanding of, as well as techniques for, maintaining and adapting very large programs whose original structure has become obscure. I doubt very much that what still passes for syntactic research on English will ever yield the robustness that real MT requires.

I am also one who accepts the negative side of the connectionist movement, in that its criticisms of NLP would be almost exactly those above, even though I have no real faith in its remedies. To say this is not to be a cynic about the notion of theory or formal system, on the contrary, but rather that the history of MT shows, to me at least, the truth of two (barely compatible) principles which we cited in an earlier chapter and which could be put crudely as:

> Virtually any theory, no matter how silly, can be the basis of some effective MT
> and
> Successful MT systems rarely work with the theory they claim to.

SYSTRAN is a fine example of both: its real techniques owe a great deal to good software engineering, good software support, and bizarre atheoretic devices that are closer to certain artificial intelligence programs than linguistics. It could be fun assessing existing MT systems against those principles: with commercial systems it is easier to see they obey the first than the second, since they rarely make theoretical claims. The last refuge of the empiricist is that "Time will tell", though it is harder to know just when it will tell us and (given the second principle above) what conclusions we will be able to draw from substantial, unquestionable, large-scale success in high-quality MT when it comes. But one substantial ground for empirical optimism, however, is that the evaluation of MT systems is almost certainly more developed than MT itself, and if that were not so, claims and counter-claims would be untestable, and so the scepticism mentioned above (of one who still does not really accept that MT exists) would become a defensible position. XXXBLEU HERE??

"Why does MT work even when it shouldn't?" seems to be a nagging question that will not go away. It has always been asked of SYSTRAN, of many less successful and less determined companies, and it was the instant reaction of many to Jelinek's initial 50% success rate with CANDIDE in 1990. But if we turn at last from the past to the future, I suggest the following as a set of hints as to where the future MT research should be directed, above and beyond the slow improvement of quality that seems to come from sheer persistence with existing systems and with the new statistical systems coming into being:

- There is not a single High-Quality MT problem; to suggest there is encourages the "snake oil salesmen" – those with permanent research methods and no evaluated results. It used to be conventional to say: "Of course MT cannot do poetry". I am no longer sure this is true; at the end of this chapter I report on putting a famous German poem through two web page translators and I think they are, taken together, pretty impressive, almost poetical.
- The modular disintegration of MT – as just one among a range of language-related office techniques – parallels the modular disintegration of empirical linguistics into sub-tasks (for evaluation). In the latter case, it may well be time for re-integration and a review of fundamentals, and that trend, if it happens, will affect MT radically in time.
- However, few would now argue that any reinvestment in HQMT should be anything like, say, EUROTRA, which is to say, a large new theoretically-motivated MT system. That adventure only proved the inability of public systems to compete with private ones; and specifically to relate user needs to available technology.
- In the US also, there have been new attempts at general, flexible, Government-funded MT systems for new/unknown languages related usually to current military needs: systems with rapid flexible development, such as EXPEDITION. These have turned, under pressure of delivery, into very simple workbench techniques allied to rapid provision of resources in remote languages, like Pashto. That may be a benefit, but is not what was hoped for; certainly, in the EU the

needs are not defence/strategy driven but internal/civil and will therefore be different.

- In a sense, SYSTRAN already had a well-established commercial methodology for extending to new languages at the same, usable, level of MT; and there is no need to use research funds to establish that. Nor is there any pressing need to find corpora to reproduce SYSTRAN's level of success on "close" European languages, like French and Russian in relation to English, by statistical methods. Although it is hard to know commercial details, it seems clear that some of the free web page translators use established SYSTRAN-like technology for closer languages and newly created statistical systems for ones not available or adequately treated by SYSTRAN. This is an interesting and novel form of hybridisation of system types.
- One major problem is that of starting point: so much work is needed to reach the frontier of MT delivery, where SYSTRAN, Siemens et al. (using the old US METAL system) already got to by symbolic methods. Yet those companies find it hard or impossible to reconfigure the basics of their legacy systems. Statistical methods (usually Example-based MT (EBMT) or Statistically-based MT (SBMT)) are now the only way available for starting a new language pair from scratch.
- Donald Michie argued long ago that a major future role of AI should be the reuse/continuing use of legacy software; we should perhaps investigate if that could be applied to MT. Could wrappers be put round old MT systems – treated as black boxes – to improve their output?
- I think this deserves exploration at least as much as "hybrid" systems to combine statistical and symbolic methodologies. Most researchers are unsure what that means or could mean. Perhaps the main achievement of statistical-MT at IBM was good output: plausible, smooth, generated English and French that was much better than from rule systems. Could that be applied, as a smoothing final wrapper, to existing large MT systems, no matter what method they worked with internally?
- I have a hunch that intelligent, multilingual generation is a more interesting (and potentially rewarding) place right now than another attack on content analysis; new content analysis may come, perhaps from successful technologies like Information Extraction and Information Retrieval. Intelligent, multilingual, generation (e.g. Donia Scott's DRAFTER (Paris and Van der Linden, 1996) can serve immediate needs in an office setting but is not directly MT, but could bear on MT, as IE/IR also can.
- The EC should be using its considerable influence, if possible to ensure that the current international XML design protocols reflect later NLP needs that cannot now be fully predicted e.g. that there should be the possibility of mark up at semantic levels, (i.e. semantic tagging at text generation time) so that not all meaning tags are at the level of "Japanese Company Annual Turnover".

The XML mark-up-at-generation issue (and it will involve the Microsoft Office juggernaut that none of us in research may be able to influence) is going to change the analysis vs. generation balance in NLP and MT: IE as an analysis technology will be largely bypassed by automatic generation time XML tagging unseen by the author, and IE, as an analysis technique, as it now is, will be replaced by the same IE skills being needed for that authoring markup. This change is in fact coming about, and is one of the intellectual inputs to the Semantic Web movement (q.v.)

The Crucial Issue of Automation in Future MT R&D

A sceptic might infer from the IBM statistical MT program, and its now well-understood limitations, that that alone showed the limits of automation in MT in a dramatic manner. On that view, IBM's methodology was to do MT only from automated data and the fact the system seemed to "top out" somewhere around 50% of sentences correctly translated showed that was all automated resources could achieve, and that this was confirmed by the fact that the IBM team then turned to gathering more conventional linguistic resources such as lexicons and grammars.

But that account, not one any researcher has argued in print of course, is far too simplistic: the later move was not away from automated resources but directed towards the gathering of a different sort or level of automated resources, namely grammars and lexicons which we discussed at length in Chapters 10 and 13. This point, if I am right, confirms that automation is not, as some would assume, connected in any way with any particular level or type of linguistic resources but is simply an acquisition methodology. If there is only very little (and there is some) data on human pragmatics acquired automatically, that is perhaps only because few people have looked for it, not because it is inherently absurd to look e.g. in Web chatrooms. This point may be obvious to many but it is not yet uniformly accepted.

What also muddles discussion of this issue is that automatic acquisition is often from resources that are, in whole or part, much more than normal human language production: some, like MRDs, are explicitly *intended* as resources. This fact does not shift the practical issue of resource acquisition for NLP – one should get what one can, wherever one can – but it does shift the issue if, anywhere in the back of one's mind is a Chomsky-style analogy between acquisition for NLP and for first language learning. First language learners do not have access to MRDs or bilingual parallel text, so acquisition from them cannot be in any way related to arguments about how humans acquire a first language and what existing apparatus, if any, that acquisition requires.

One useful side effect of the use of the web to obtain corpora is that it has reached scales where the whole issue of "what exposure to language a human needs to learn X" is relegated to psychology proper and shown of no relevance at all to our tasks. Roger Moore (2003) has shown that if babies learned to speak in the any way analogous to ASR (Automatic Speech Recognition) systems work, it would take over 100 years of constant exposure to learn to talk. All this shows is that even the best ASR systems have nothing to do with human learning. Similarly, NLP experiments with billions of words of text are now commonplace but gain unrelated to human capacities.

Jelinek always said that the main barrier to further success with CANDIDE was "data sparsity" the fact that language events are generally rare and his training corpora allowed only a low probability that any required trigram for MT would already have been seen in a language. In some recent work at Sheffield, Louise Guthrie and her colleagues (Guthrie et al., 2006), including this author, have shown (a) that the current size of web in English is such that, by extrapolation, a full model of English could be constructed from it, one where it was almost certain that any given trigram would have been seen and (b) by using a technique called skipgrams (i.e. trigram with up to 4 "holes" or gaps in them) a full model could be computed from a fraction (probably a quarter) of that corpus, without any loss of quality. These might be quite important results for the future of statistical models, for they represent a real amelioration of what Jelinek saw as the major barrier to further success.

This is, for me, the nub of the practical matter, and why I remain pro-automation as far as it can go but do not believe full automation, unsupervised, and from raw unprimed text or dialogue, can provide all we need, no matter what the outcome of outstanding issues in learnability theory or the advance to the "full language model" in the sense above. So, I take the most pressing research question, as do many others, to be: how do we tune a lexicon to a new corpus, automatically if possible (see Wilks and Catizone, 2002). But note that that formulation assumes we already have a human-created resource, i.e. the lexicon we started with. It is thus (to return to the distinction of Chapter 13) situation I not II:

I: structure1 + corpus → structure2

which indicates that an earlier state of the structure itself plays a role in the acquisition, of which structure2 is then a proper extension (capturing new concepts, senses etc). This is a different model from the wholly automatic model of lexicon acquisition often used in, say, Information Extraction schemes like TIPSTER (Marsh, 1998), which can be written:

II: corpus → structure

This latter situation is one which does not update or "tune" an existing lexicon but derives one directly and automatically from a corpus, in an unsupervised manner I am arguing the essential role of a representational structure in this process, and hence *for* the first process where possible, which we may also take to involve some essential human intervention as well.

The assumption here is that we cannot understand the nature of the representation of meaning in lexicons, or elsewhere, unless and until we can see how to extend lexicons in the presence of incoming data that does not fit the lexicon we start with. Extension of representation is thus part of an adequate theory of representation. Notice, of course, that this presentation of the issue assumes the acceptance of the position that some (albeit statistically-derived) structures are necessary for MT. If one thinks only in terms of a "pure" unannotated, corpus as input to MT, then no talk of word-sense has any meaning, let alone "new sense" or "metaphorical sense" has any meaning. It is useful to remember that that position – that there are only words and no structures are necessary to get what we want – remains the basic orthodoxy in

Information Retrieval (IR), and that position was stated elegantly time and gain by the late Karen Sparck Jones (2003). IR is not MT of course, and they need not keep in step, though it is interesting to note that man of the NLP techniques that followed Jelinek's work are now imported into IR under the rubric : "MT methods in IR" (Berger and Lafferty, 1999, see also Wilks 2004). There are, it must be added, those in IR who do not share this view, such as Van Rijsbergen (2006) and Stzalkowski (with Strzalkowski and Perez-Carballo, 2000)

However, what are we to do in the pressing practical situation of wholly unknown languages, ones perhaps with electronic texts available, but no lexicons: in that case, only mode II is possible initially. But, almost certainly, on the above assumptions, human informants will also be necessary to move from mode I to mode II, so as to have a lexicon to tune. It is, at the moment just a hope that processes like II, with human assistance, will provide lexicons for tuning processes like I.

Even so, I still believe we ought to act as if all possible automation should be used wherever possible, and that our encyclopaedist/lexicographic tendencies should be repressed, as leading to vast resource creation that is never properly made usc of because the purpose and the real task ahead cannot not be fully foreseen. Automation cuts down the drudgery and keeps us sane and focussed, so let us limit human intervention as far as we can within the current paradigm, which is currently highly active and producing new results. It will time after that fades, or goes into real commercial systems, to revive the blue-sky needs to which much of this book has been devoted.

By that I mean the current two-headed approach sometimes known as Statistically based MT (SBMT) but also as Example-Based MT (EBMT) which derived from ideas of Nagao (1990) and was not initially seen as a purely statistical task, more a pattern matching task based on very large amounts of real data from translators. Both paradigms have now evolved to a point where it is hard to distinguish them clearly (see Somers and Fernandez Diaz, 2004). There are many hybrids about and the fine point of difference is concerned with how translated sentence parts are reassembled in real time for output. Somers has argued that this represents a return of straightforwardly linguistic considerations to an MT that had been gripped by the statistical paradigm for a decade, and hence the long awaited hybridness of approach. There is currently a renaissance in these forms of MT on both sides of the Atlantic, under Koehn at Edinburgh (Schwenk and Koehn, 2008), Yarowsky at Johns Hopkins (Yarowsky et al., 2001), Knight at ISI-USC (May and Knight, 2007) and Ney at Aachen (Och and Ney, 2004) among many others.

Their wave is currently high and we must all wish them well; the old questions in this book will return when the wave breaks, hopefully with commercial fall out. I wrote earlier that one should not casually dismiss current free web MT, nor always repeat the mantra "Of course MT cannot do poetry". Indeed the web has given MT a new lease of life, in that it has shown a large population that, contrary to rumour, it is far from dead. Just for fun, I have put chunks of Rilke's poetry through various web translators, choosing him not only because (according to T.S. Eliot) he was the greatest 20C poet, but because he used a simple German both in vocabulary and grammar, so he seemed a good bet. The output below for Rilke's Herbst

(Autumn – from The Book of Photos) – for which I do not give the German so a reader can judge whether or not they get any poetic feeling from it. It has been edited only in that Babelfish and Google each left some words untranslated, but different ones, so I have simply conflated the two translation outputs, but in a simple way an automaton could do; I personally get rather an interesting feeling from it!

The leaves fall, fall as from far,
as if gardens withered in the skies far;
they fall with negative gesture.
And in the nights the heavy earth from all stars falls into solitude.
We all fall. This hand falls there.
And look at others: it is in all.
And nevertheless it is one which this fallen infinitely gently holds in his hand

References

ALPAC. (1966) Language and Machines: Computers in Translation and Linguistics. A report by the Automatic Language Processing Advisory Committee (ALPAC). Division of Behavioral Sciences, National Academy of Sciences, National Research Council Publication 1416. Washington: NAS/NRC.

Amsler R.A, (1980) The Structure of the Merriam-Webster Pocket Dictionary Technical Report TR-164. Austin: University of Texas.

Amsler R and White J (1979) Development of a Computational Methodology for Deriving Natural Language Semantic Structures via Analysis of Machine Readable Dictionaries. NSF Technical Report MCS77-01315.

Antal L (1963) Questions of Meaning, Mouton: The Hague.

Appelt D, (1989). Bidirectional grammars and the design of natural language generation systems. In Wilks Y (ed.) Theoretical Issues in Natural Language Processing. Hillsdale, NJ: Erlbaum.

Arnold D Balkan, L Humphries R.L, Meijer S, Sadler L (1994) Machine Translation: an Introductory Guide. Oxford: NCC Blackwell.

Atkins B (1990) The Dynamic Database, a Collaborative Methodology for Developing a Large-Scale Electronic Dictionary. In Proceedings of the International Workshop on Electronic Dictionaries. Oiso, Japan: Japan Electronic Dictionary Research Institute, Ltd.

Ballim A (1988) A Language for Representing and Reasoning with Nested Beliefs. In 1st Annual Conference on Artificial Intelligence and Cognitive Science, Dublin, Ireland.

Ballim A, Wilks Y, Barnden J (1988) Belief Ascription, Metaphor, and Intensional Identification. CRL Memoranda in Computer and Cognitive Science, MCCS-88-138. New Mexico: CRL, NMSU, Cognitive Science.

Ballim A and Wilks Y (1990) Stereotypical Belief and Dynamic Agent Modeling. In Proceedings of the Second International Workshop on User Modeling. Honolulu, Hawaii, USA: University of Hawaii at Manoa, March.

Bar-Hillel Y (1960) The Present Status of Automatic Translation of Languages. In F. Alt (ed.) Advances in Computers (Vol 1). New York: Academic Press.

Bar-Hillel Y (1962) The Future of Machine Translation. Times Literary Supplement. London: Times Newspapers. April 20th.

Bar-Hillel Y (1970) Some Reflections on the Present Outlook for High-Quality Machine Translation. Austin: Mimeo, University of Texas.

Bar-Hillel Y (1971) Some Reflections on the Present Outlook for High-quality Machine Translation. In feasibility study on fully automated high quality translation, W Lehmann and R. Stachowitz (eds.), 73–76. Rome AFB, Rome, NY: Rome Air Development Center.

Barnden J A (2001). Application of the ATT-Meta Metaphor-Understanding Approach to Various Examples in the ATT-Meta Project Databank. Technical Report CSRP–01–02, School of Computer Science. U.K.: The University of Birmingham.

Barnden J A, Glasbey S R, Lee M G & Wallington A M (2002). Reasoning in Metaphor Understanding: The ATT-Meta Approach and System. In Proc 19th International Conference on Computational Linguistics. San Francisco: Morgan Kaufman. 1188–1193.

Berger A and Lafferty J (1999) Information Retrieval as Statistical Translation Proceedings of the ACM SIGIR Conference on Research and Development in Information Retrieval (SIGIR'99).

Berners-Lee T, Hendler J, and Lassila O (2001). Scientific American.

Bierwisch M. (1970) Semantics, in New Horizons in Linguistics, Lyons, J. (ed.), London, Pelican Books.

Bobrow D and Winograd T (1977) KRL—An Overview of a Knowledge Representation Language. Cognitive Science. 1, 3–46.

Boguraev B, Briscoe T, Carroll J, Carter D and Grover C (1987) The Derivation of a Grammatically Indexed Lexicon from the Longman Dictionary of Contemporary English.In Proceedings of the 25th Annual Meeting of the Association for Computational Linguistics. 193–200.

Briscoe T and Copestake A (1996). Controlling the Application of Lexical rules. In Proceedings of the ACL SIGLEX Workshop on Breadth and Depth of Semantic Lexicons, Santa Cru. 7–19.

Brown, et al (1989) A Statistical Approach to Machine Translation. IBM Research Division Technical Report in Computer Science RC 14773 (#66226), Yorktown Heights, NY: T J Watson Research Center.

Brown P F, Cocke J, Della Pietra S A, Della Pietra V J, Jelinek F, Lafferty J D, Mercer L, and Roossin P S (1990) A Statistical Approach to Machine Translation. Computational Linguistics. 16, 79–85, June.

Brown P F, Della Pietra S A, Della Pietra V J, Lafferty J D and Mercer R L (1992) Analysis, Statistical Transfer, and Synthesis in Machine Translation. In Proceedings of the Fourth International Conference on Theoretical and Methodological Issues in Machine Translation, Montreal, Canada. 83–100.

Brown P F, Lai J C, and Mercer R L (1991) Aligning Sentences in Parallel Corpora. in Proceedings 29th Annual Meeting of the Association for Computational Linguistics, Berkeley, CA. 169–176, June.

Bruce B, Guthrie L and Wilks Y A (1993) Automatic Lexical Extraction: Theories and Applications. In F. Beckmann & G. Heyer, Theorie und Praxis des Lexicons: A Festschrift for Helmut Schnelle Berlin: De Gruyter.

Bruce R and Wiebe J (1994) Word-sense disambiguation using decomposable models. In Proceedings of ACL94, Las Cruces, NM.

Bruderer H (1977) Handbook of Machine Translation and Machine-Aided Translation. Amsterdam: North Holland.

Buitelaar P, Cimiano P and Magnini B (eds.) (2005) Ontology Learning from Text: Methods, Evaluation and Applications, vol. 123 of Frontiers in Artificial Intelligence and Applications. Amsterdam, The Netherlands: IOS Press.

Callison-Burch C, Osborne M and Koehn P (2006) Re-evaluating the Role of BLEU in Machine Translation Research. In 11th Conference of the European Chapter of the Association for Computational Linguistics. Trento, Italy: EACL 2006. 249–256.

Carroll J B (1966) An Experiment in Evaluating the Quality of Translations. Mechanical Translation and Computational Linguistics, 9(3 & 4), 55–66.

Chandioux J (1976) METEO, In Hays and Mathias (eds.). F.B.I.S. Seminar on Machine Translation. American Journal of Computational Linguistics. 2, microfiche 46.

Charniak E. (1973) Jack and Jane in Search of a Theory of Knowledge. In: Proceedings of the Third International Joint Conference on Artificial Intelligence. Menlo Park, California: Stanford Research Institute. 115–124.

Charniak E (1975) Organization and Inference. In: Proceedings of the Theoretical Issues in Natural Language Processing. Cambridge, Mass: M.I.T. 105–114.

Charniak E (2001) Immediate-Head Parsing for Language Models Proceedings of the 39th Annual Meeting of the Association for Computational Linguistics.

Chodorow M S, Byrd R J and Heidorn G E (1985) Extracting Semantic Hierarchies from a Large On-Line Dictionary Proceedings of the 23rd Annual Meeting of the ACL, Chicago, Illinois, USA. 299–304.

Chomsky N (1957) Syntactic Structures. Mouton: The Hague.

Chomsky N (1966) Aspects of the theory of syntax. Cambridge, MA: MIT Press.

Church K et al (1989) Parsing, Word-Association and Typical Predicate Argument Relations. In Tomita, M. (ed.) Proceedings of the International Workshop on Parsing Technologies. Carnegie Mellon University.

Copestake A and Briscoe T (1991) Lexical operations in a unification-based framework. In Proceedings of ACL SIGLEX Workshop Berkeley.

Cowie J, Guthrie G and Guthrie J (1992) Lexical disambiguation using simulated annealing. In Proceedings of COLING92, Nantes, France.

Dagon I and Itai A (1994) Word-sense disambiguation using a second language monolingual corpus. Computational Linguistics, 20.

Dennett D (1991) Consciousness Explained. Cambridge, MA: Bradford Books.

Dennett D (1978) Brainstorms. Montgomery, VT: Bradford Books.

Dymetman M. and Isabelle P (1990) Reversible Unification Based Machine Translation. In Proc International Conference On Computational, Helsinki, Finland.

Edmonds P and Kilgarriff A (eds.) (2003). Journal of Natural Language Engineering (special issue based on Senseval-2). 9(1).

EDR (1989) An Overview of the EDR Electronic Dictionaries. Japan Electronic Dictionary Research Inst TR-024, Tokyo.

Evans R and Gazdar G (1990) The DATR Papers. Technical Memorandum, The University of Sussex. School of Cognitive Science. Sussex, UK: Falmer.

Farwell D and Wilks Y (1989) ULTRA a Multilingual Machine Translation System. CRL-NMSU.

Farwell D and Wilks Y (1990) ULTRA: A Multilingual Machine Translator. Memoranda in Computer and Cognitive Science, MCCS-90-202. Las Cruces, NM: Computing Research Laboratory.

Farwell D, Guthrie L and Wilks Y (1993) Automatically Creating Lexical Entries for ULTRA, a Multi-lingual MT System, Journal of Machine Translation, 8(3).

Fass D (1987) Collative Semantics: Lexical Ambiguity Resolution and Semantic Relations (with Particular Reference to Metonymy). CRL Memoranda in Computer and Cognitive Science, MCCS-86-59, New Mexico CRL, NMSU.

Fass D C (1988) Collative Semantics: A Semantics for Natural Language Processing. Memorandum in Computer and Cognitive Science, MCCS-88-118. New Mexico: Computing Research Laboratory, New Mexico State University.

Fauconnier G (1985) Mental Spaces: Aspects of Meaning Construction in Natural Language. Cambridge, MA: MIT Press.

Fodor J (1976) The Language of Thought. New York: Thomas Y Crowell.

Gale W and Church K (1990) Poor Estimates of Context are Worse than none. Proceedings of the June 1990 DARPA Speech and Language Meeting. Hidden Valley, PA.

Gale W, Church K and Yarowsky D (1992) One Sense per Discourse. In Proceedings of DARPA Speech and Language Workshop, Harriman NY, 233–237.

Gazdar G, Klein E, Pullum G and Sag I (1985) Generalized Phrase Structure Grammar. Oxford: Basil Blackwell.

Givon T (1967) The structure of ellipsis. Mimeo. Santa Monica, California: Systems Development Corp.

Grice P (1989) Studies in the Way of Words, Harvard University Press: Cambridge, MA.

Grishman R and Sterling J (1989) Preference Semantics for Message Understanding. In Proceedings DARPA Speech and Natural Language Workshop. New York University.

Guha R V and Lenat D B (1990) Cyc: A midterm report. AI Magazine, 11(3).

Guo C M (ed.) (1992) Machine Tractable Dictionaries: Design and Construction. Norwood N J: Ablex.

Guthrie D, Allison B, Liu W, Guthrie, and Wilks Y (2006) A Closer Look at Skip-gram Modelling. Proceedings of the Fifth International Conference on Language Resources and Evaluation (LREC-2006), Genoa, Italy.

Guthrie L, Slator B, Wilks Y, and Bruce R (1990) Is there Content in Empty Heads? Proceedings of the 15th International Conference on Computational Linguistics (COLING90), Helsinki, Finland. 138–143.

Hanks P (1991) The Role of Dictionaries in Language Engineering, an Oxford View, Pre-Print. Huang, XM: 1988, Semantic Analysis in XTRA, an English-Chinese Machine Translation System. Computers and Translation 3, 101–120.

Hanks P (1994) personal communication.

Hovy E and Nirenburg S (1992) Approximating an Interlingua in a Principled Way In Proceedings of the June DARPA Speech and Language Workshop, Harriman, N.Y.

Huang X (1988) XTRA: The Design and Implementation of A Fully Automatic Machine Translation System. CRL Memoranda in Computer and Cognitive Science, MCCS-88-121. New Mexico: CRL, NMSU.

Huang X-M. (1988) Semantic Analysis in XTRA, an English-Chinese Machine Translation System. Computers and Translation 3, 101–120.

Ide N and Veronis J (1994) Have we wasted our time? In Proceedings of International Workshop on the Future of the Dictionary, Grenoble.

Jacobs P (1988) Achieving Bidirectionality In Proceedings COLING-88. Budapest.

Jacobs P (1990) Why Text Planning isn't Planning. In Proceedings NATO Advanced Workshop on Computational Theories of Communication. Trentino, Italy.

Jacobs P, Krupka G and Rau L (1991) Lexico-Semantic Pattern Matching as a Companion to Parsing in Text Understanding, In Proceedings of the DARPA Speech and Natural Language Workshop, Monterey, CA.

JEIDA report (1989) A Japanese View of Machine Translation In Light of the Considerations and Recommendations. Reported by ALPAC, Japan Electronic Industry Development Association. Tokyo.

Jelinek F and Mercer R L (1980) Interpolated Estimation of Markov Source Parameters from Sparse Data. In Proceedings of the Workshop on Pattern Recognition in Practice, Amsterdam, The Netherlands, North-Holland, May.

Jelinek F (2004) Some of my Best Friends are Linguists, Antonio Zampolli Prize Talk, LREC '04, Lisbon, Portugal.

Jin W and Simmons R (1986) Symmetric Rules for Translation of English and Chinese. Computers and Translation 1, 153–167.

Johnson R, King M, and des Tombe L (1985) EUROTRA: A Multilingual System under Development. In Computational Linguistics 11(2–3), 155–169.

Joos M (1972) Semantic Axiom Number One. Language, 48, (1972): 257–265.

Jorgensen J (1990) The Psychological Reality of Word-Senses, Journal of Psycholinguistic Research, 19.

Karlsson F (1990) Constraint Grammar as a Framework for Parsing Running Text. In Proceedings of the COLING90, Helsinki.

Katz J and Fodor J (1963) The Structure of a Semantic Theory. Language 11.

Kay M (1984) Functional Unification Grammar. In Proceedings COLING-84. Palo Alto, CA.

Kay M (1989) The Concrete Lexicon and the Abstract Dictionary. In Proceedings of the 5th Annual Conference of the UW Centre for the New Oxford English Dictionary, Oxford, England. 35–41.

Kay M (1997) The Proper Place of Men and Machines in Language Translation. Machine Translation 12, 3–23.

Kenji I and Eiichiro S (2002) Bilingual Corpus Cleaning Focusing on Translation Literality. ICSLP 2002 (7th International Conference on Spoken Language Processing), 3, 1713–1716.

Kilgarriff A (1993) Dictionary Word-Sense Distinctions: an Enquiry into their Nature. Computers and the Humanities.

Kilgarriff A (1998) SENSEVAL, a exercise in evaluating word-sense disambiguation programs. In Proceedings of First LREC Conference, Granada, Spain.

King G (1956) Stochastic Methods of Mechanical Translation, Mechanical Translation 3.

King H and Wilks Y (1977) Semantics, Preference and Inference. Geneva: Institute for Semantic and Cognitive Studies.

King M (1982) EUROTRA: An Attempt to Achieve Multilingual MT. In: V. Lawson (ed.). Practical Experience in Machine Translation. Amsterdam: North Holland. 139–148.

Klein S, et al (1968) The Autoling System, Tech. Report. #43, Computer Science Department, University of Wisconsin, 1968.

Krotov A, Hepple M, Gaizauskas R, and Wilks Y (1998) Compacting the Penn Treebank grammar, Proceedings of the 17th International Conference on Computational linguistics, August 10–14, Montreal, Quebec, Canada

Lakoff G (1970) Linguistics and Natural Logic, Studies in Generative Semantics #1. Ann Arbor: University of Michigan.

Lakoff G and Johnson M (1980) Metaphors We Live. Chicago, IL: University of Chicago Press.

Landsbergen J (1987): Isomorphic Grammars and their Use in the Rosetta translation system. In: King M (ed.) Machine Translation Today: The State of the art. Proceedings of the Third Lugano Tutorial April 1984. Edinburgh: Edinburgh Univ Press.

Langendoen D, Terence and Paul M Postal (1984). The Vastness of Natural Languages. Oxford: Basil Blackwell.

Lehmann W and Stachowitz R, (eds.) (1971) Feasibility Study on Fully Automatic High-Quality Translation, Report RADC-TR-71-295. Rome, NY: Rome A F Development Center.

Lehnert W and Sundheim B (1991) A Performance Evaluation of Text Analysis Technologies. AI magazine, Vol 12.

Levin J and Moore J (1976) Dialogue Games. In Proc A.I.S.B. Conference, Edinburgh: Department of Artificial Intelligence.

Mahesh K and Nirenburg S (1995) A Situated Ontology for Practical NLP. In Proceedings Workshop on Ontological Issues in Knowledge Sharing, International Joint Conference on Artificial Intelligence (IJCAI-95), August 19–20, Montreal, Canada.

Mandelbrot B (1962) Word Frequencies and Markovian Models of Discourse. In Symposia in Applied Mathematics, Vol XII, American Mathematical Society.

Marsh E (ed.) (1998) TIPSTER Information Extraction Evaluation: Proceedings of the MUC-7 workshop, Baltimore, MD.

May J and Knight K (2007) Syntactic Re-Alignment Models for Machine Translation, Proceedings EMNLP-CoNLL.

McCarthy J and Hayes P (1969) Some Philosophical Problems from the Standpoint of Artificial Intelligence. In Machine Intelligence 4, Edinburgh.

McCord M (1989) A New Version of the Machine Translation System LMT. Literary & Linguistic Computing 4.

McNaught J (1990) Reusability of lexical and Terminological Resources: Steps Towards Independence. In Proceedings of the International Workshop on Electronic Dictionaries, Japan Electronic Dictionary Research Institute, Ltd., Oiso, Japan.

Michie D (1971) On Not Seeing Things, Experimental Programming Reports #22, University of Edinburgh.

Miike S (1990) How to Define Concepts for Electronic Dictionaries. In Proceedings of the International Workshop on Electronic Dictionaries. Japan Electronic Dictionary Research Institute, Ltd Oiso, Japan.

Miller G A (1985) WordNet: A Dictionary Browser. In: Proceedings of the First International Conference on Information in Data, University of Waterloo, Waterloo, 1985.

Minsky M (ed.) (1968) Semantic Information Processing. Cambridge, Mass: MIT Press.

Minsky M (1975) A Framework for Representing Knowledge. In Winston (ed.) The Psychology of Computer Vision. New York: McGraw Hill. 211–277.

Montague R (1970) English as a Formal Language. In Linguaggi nella Societa e nella Tecnica, Milan.

Moore R K (2003). A Comparison of Data Requirements for ASR Systems and Human Listeners, In Proceedings EUROSPEECH 2003.

Nagao M (1989) Machine Translation: How Far can It go? Oxford University Press: Oxford.

Nagao M (1990) Towards Memory-Based Translation. In Proceedings of COLING-90. Helsinki.
Nagao M, Tsujii J C, and Nakamura J C (1985) The Japanese Government Project for Machine Translation. Computational Linguistics 11, 91–110.
Neff M and McCord M (1990) Acquiring Lexical Data from Machine-Readable Dictionary Resources for Machine Translation, In Proceedings of the Third International.
Neumann G and van Noord G (1993) Reversibility and Self-Monitoring in Natural Language Generation. In: Strzalkowski (ed.) Reversible Grammars in NLP. Dordrecht: Kluwer Academic Publishers, 1994.
Nida E and Taber C (1969) The Theory and Practice of Translation. E. J. Brill: Leiden.
Nirenburg S (ed.) (1987) Machine Translation: Theoretical and Methodological Issues. Cambridge: Cambridge University Press. xv + 350. 30 pounds and 12.50 (paper).
Nirenburg S (1989) Lexicons for Computer Programs and Lexicons for People. Proceedings of the 5th Annual Conference of the UW Centre for the New Oxford English Dictionary. 43–66. St. Catherine's College, Oxford, England.
Nirenburg S, Beale S, Mahesh K, Onyshkevych B, Raskin V, Viegas E, Wilks Y and Zajac R (1996) Lexicons in the Mikrokosmos Project. In Proceedings of the Society for Artificial Intelligence and Simulated Behavior Workshop on Multilinguality in the Lexicon, Brighton, UK.
Och F J and Ney H (2004) The Alignment Template Approach to Statistical Machine Translation. Computational Linguistics. v30 i4. 417–449.
Ogden C K (1942) The General Basic English Dictionary W. W. Norton: New York.
Onyshkevych B and Nirenburg S (1991) Lexicon, Ontology, and Text Meaning. SIGLEX Workshop, 289–303.
Papieni K, Roukos S, Ward T and Zhu W-J (2002) BLEU: A Method for Automatic Evaluation of Machine Translation. In Proceedings of the 40th Annual Meeting of the Association for the Computational Linguistics (ACL), Philadelphia, USA, 311–318.
Paris C and Vander Linden K (1996) Building Knowledge Bases for the Generation of Software Documentation. COLING, 734–739
Pereira F and Warren D (1980) Parsing as Deduction. In Proceedings of the 21st Annual Meeting on Association for Computational Linguistics, Cambridge, MA.
Perrault R and Allen J (1980) A Plan-Based Analysis of Indirect Speech acts. J American Journal of Computational Linguistics 6, 167–182.
Phillips J D (2001) The Bible as a Basis for Machine Translation. In Proceedings of Pacling 2001. Pacific Association for Computational Linguistics.
Procter P, Ilson R.F, Ayto J, et al (1978) Longman Dictionary of Contemporary English. Harlow, Essex, England: Longman Group Limited.
Pustejovsky J (1990) On the Nature of Lexical Knowledge. Machine Translation, 5(1), 1–4
Pustejovsky J (1993) The Generative Lexicon, Cambridge, MA: MIT Press.
Pustejovsky J (1995) The Generative Lexicon, MIT Press: Cambridge, MA.
Quillian R (1969) The Teachable Language Comprehender. CACM.
Russell G, Carroll J and Warwick-Armstrong S (1991) Multiple Default Inheritance in a Unification-Based Lexicon. ACL, 216–221
Russell G, Warwick S, and Carroll J (1990) Asymmetry in Parsing and Generating with Unification Grammars. In Proceedings Conference of the Assn for Computational Linguistics, Pittsburgh.
Sandewall E (1971) Representing Natural Language Information in Predicate Calculus, Machine Intelligence 6. Edinburgh: Edinburgh University Press.
Schank R. (1971) Finding the Conceptual Content and Intention of an Utterance in Natural Language Conversation. In Proceedings of the 2nd Joint International Conference on Artificial Intelligence, London.
Schank R. (1975a) Using knowledge to Understand. In Proc Theoretical issues in Natural Language Processing. Cambridge, Mass: M.I.T. Press. 67–77.
Schank R. (ed.) (1975b) Conceptual Information Processing. Amsterdam: North-Holland Press.
Schank R.C. (1973) Identification of Conceptualizations Underlying Natural Language In Roger C Schank and Kenneth M Colby (eds.) Computer Models of Thought and Language San Francisco: W H. Freeman.

Schetze H and Pederson J (1995) Information retrieval based on word-sense. In Proceedings of 4th Symposium on Document Analysis and Information Retrieval, 161–175.

Schwenk H and Koehn P (2008) Large and Diverse Language Models for Statistical Machine Translation, Proceedings of the IJCNLP, 2008.

Searle J (1980) Minds, Brains and Programs, Behavioral and Brain Sciences, 3(3): 417–457

Sharman R., Jelinek F. and Mercer R. (1988) Generating a Grammar for Statistical Training, Proceedings of the IBM Conference on Natural Language Processing, Thornwood, N.Y.

Simmons R. (1970) Some Semantic Structures for Representing English Meanings, Tech. Report #NL-l. Austin: University of Texas.

Simmons R., and Yu Y-H. (l990) Training a Neural Network to be a Context-Sensitive Grammar. In Proceedings of the Fifth Rocky Mountain Conference on AI, Las Cruces, NM.

Simon H. (l969) The Architecture of Complexity. In The Sciences of the Artificial. Cambridge, MA: MIT Press.

Slator B.M. (1988) Constructing Contextually Organized Lexical Semantic Knowledge-Bases. Proceedings of the Third Annual Rocky Mountain Conference on Artificial Intelligence, Denver, CO, (June 13–15). 142–148.

Small S, Cottrell G and Tannenhaus M (1988) Lexical Ambiguity Resolution, Morgan Kaufman: San Mateo CA.

Somers H L (1993) Current research in Machine Translation. Machine Translation, 7, 231–246.

Somers H and Fernandez Diaz G (2004) Translation Memory vs. Example-based MT: What is the difference? International Journal of Translation 16(2), 5–33.

Sparck Jones K (2003). Document Retrieval: Shallow Data, Deep Theories, Historical Reflections and Future Directions. Proc 25th European IR Conference (ECIR03). Lecture Notes in Computer Science, Berlin: Springer. 1–11.

Speer A (1970) Inside the Third Reich. Macmillan: New York and Toronto. [Translated from the German by Richard and Clara Winston].

Steiner G (1975) After Babel: Aspects of Language and Translation. London: Oxford University Press.

Stevenson M and Wilks Y (2001) The Interaction of Knowledge Sources in Word Sense Disambiguation. Computational Linguistics.

Strzalkowski T and Perez-Carballo J (2000) Natural Language Information Retrieval: Progrcss Report, Information Processing & Management 36(1), 155–178.

Sumita E and Imamura K (2002) Bilingual Corpus Cleaning Focusing on Translation Literality. ICSLP 2002 (7th International Conference on Spoken Language Processing), Vol. 3, pp. 1713–1716.

SYSTRAN (1991) Company handout.

Tennant H (1981) Natural Language Processing. New York: Petrocelli.

Toma P (1976) An Operational Machine Translation System. In: Brislin, R W (ed.) Translation: applications and research. New York: Gardner P. 247–259.

Toma P (1977) SYSTRAN as a Multi-Lingual Machine Translation System. In Commission of European Communities: Overcoming the Language Barrier. Munich: Dokumentation Verlag. 129–160.

Uszkoreit H (1986) Categorial Unification Grammars. COLING 187–194

Utsuro T, Ikeda H, Yamanae M, Matsumoto Y and Nagao M (1994) Bilingual Text Matching Using Bilingual Dictionary and Statistics. In Proceedings of the COLING94, Kyoto.

Van Rijsbergen C J (2006) Geometry and Meaning, Computational Linguistics.

Van Slype (1976) Etat des activites multilinques en matiere d'information scientifique et technique: Vol l, Rapport Final. Bureau Van Dijk, Brussels.

Vossen P (ed.) (1998) EuroWordNet. Kluwer: Dordrecht, Holland.

Wahlster W (ed.) (2000) Speech to Speech Translation. Berlin: Springer.

Walker D E and Amsler R A (1986) The Use of Machine-Readable Dictionaries in Sublanguage Analysis. In Grishman R and Kittredge R (eds.). Analyzing Language in Restricted Domains, Lawrence Erlbaum: Hillsdale, NJ.

Webb N, Hepple M and Wilks Y (2005) Dialog Act Classification Based on Intra-Utterance Features. In Proceedings of the AAAI Workshop on Spoken Language Understanding.

White J and O'Connell T (1996) Adaptation of the DARPA machine translation evaluation paradigm to end-to-end systems. Proceedings of AMTA-96.
Whitelock P (1992) Shake and Bake Translation. In Proceedings of the 14th conference on Computational linguistics – Vol. 2, Association for Computational Linguistics.
Wierzbicka A (1989) Semantics, Culture and Cognition, Oxford University Press: Oxford.
Wilks Y (1967) Computable Semantic Derivations. S P 2758. Santa Monica: Systems Development Corporation.
Wilks Y (1968) On-Line Semantic Analysis of English Texts, Machine Translation and Comp Linguistics.
Wilks Y (1971) Decidability and Natural Language, Mind 80, 497–516.
Wilks Y (1972) Grammar, Meaning and the Machine Analysis of Natural Language. London: Routledge.
Wilks Y (1973a) An Artificial Intelligence Approach to Machine Translation. Artificial Intelligence Laboratory Report No AIM-161, February 1972, and in R Schank and K Colby (eds.), Computer Models of Thought and Language. San Francisco: Freeman. 114–151.
Wilks Y (1973b) The Stanford Machine Translation and Understanding Project. Proceedings Conference on Natural Language Processing, Courant Institute of Mathematics, New York, December 1971, and in R. Rustin (ed.) Natural Language Processing. New York: Academic Press.
Wilks Y (1973c) Preference Semantics. In Keenan, (ed.) The Formal Semantics of Natural Language. Cambridge University Press: Cambridge
Wilks Y (1975) An Intelligent Analyser and Understander for English. Communications of the ACM 18, 264–274.
Wilks Y (1976a) De Minimis: The Archaeology of Frames. In Proceedings of the AISB Conference. Dept of A I, Edinburgh. 133–142.
Wilks Y (1976b) Processing Case. American Journal of Computing Language. 56.
Wilks Y (1977a) Frames, Scripts, Stories and Fantasies. Pragmatics Microfiche. 3.
Wilks Y (1977b) Making Preferences More Active. Mimeo Edinburgh: Department of A I, memo No 32.
Wilks Y (1978) A Preferential Pattern-Matching Semantics for Natural Language Understanding. Artificial Intelligence Vol II.
Wilks Y (1979) Machine Translation and Artificial Intelligence. In B Snell (ed.), Translation and the Computer. North Holland: Amsterdam.
Wilks Y (1983) Deep and Superficial Parsing. In M. King (ed.), Parsing Natural Language. New York: Academic Press. Reprinted in Woods and Fallside (ed.) Computer Speech Processing. New York: Prentice Hall.
Wilks Y (1989) More Advanced Machine Translation? International Forum for Translation Technology IFTT '89, Harmonizing Human Beings and Computers in Translation, Oiso, Japan: Manuscripts and Program. 59.
Wilks Y (1990a) Form and Content in Semantics. In Synthese 82, 329–351.
Wilks Y (1990b) Combining Weak Methods in Large-Scale Text Processing. In P Jacobs (ed.) Text-Based Intelligent Systems. General Electric R and D Center, Technical Information Series, Number 90-CRD-198.
Wilks Y (1991) SYSTRAN: It Obviously Works, but how much can it be Improved? Memorandum in Computer and Cognitive Science, MCCS-91-215. Las Cruces, NM: New Mexico State University.
Wilks Y (1997) Senses and Texts. In N Ide (ed.) special issue of Computers and the Humanities.
Wilks Y (2004) The MT and IR Paradigms: Some New Developments. In Proceedings of Theoretical Machine Translation Conference (TIMIT'04), Baltimore.
Wilks Y (2008) The Semantic Web: Apotheosis of Annotation? But what are its Semantics? IEEE Transactions on Information Systems.
Wilks Y and Ballim A (1988) Belief Systems and the Heuristic Ascription of Belief. In Christaller (ed.) Kuenstliche Intelligenz. Cologne: Springer Verlag.

Wilks Y and Ballim A (1989) Shifting the Belief Engine into Higher Gear. Proceedings of the International Conference on AI Methodology Systems Applications, (AIMSA'88), T O'Shea and V Sgurev (eds.), Amsterdam: Elsevier.

Wilks Y and Ballim A (1993) Artificial Believers. Norwood, NJ: Lawrence Erlbaum Associates.

Wilks Y and Bien J (1979) Speech Acts and Multiple Environments. Proceedings of the 6th International Joint Conference on Artificial Intelligence (IJCAI-79 Tokyo). 968–970.

Wilks Y and Bien J (1983) Beliefs, Points of View and Multiple Environments. In Cognitive Science 8:120–146, 1983; Essex Cognitive Studies Centre, Memo No 5, June 1981. A different version is in Elithorn and Bannerji (eds.), Artificial and Human Intelligence, Elsevier, 1984.

Wilks Y, Carbonell J, Farwell D, Hovy E. and Nirenburg S (1990) Machine Translation Again? In Proceedings of the DARPA Speech and Natural Language Workshop.

Wilks Y A, Fass D C, Guo C-M, McDonald J E, Plate T and Slator B M (1987) A Tractable Machine Dictionary as a Resource for Computational Semantics. Memorandum in Computer and Cognitive Science, MCCS-86-105, Computing Research Laboratory, New Mexico State University, New Mexico. Also in Bran Boguraev and Ted Briscoe (eds.), 1989, Computational Lexicography for Natural Language Processing, pp 193–228. Harlow, Essex, England: Longman.

Wilks Y, Slator B and Guthrie L (1995) Electronic Words: Dictionaries, Computers and Meanings. Cambridge, MA: MIT Press.

Wilks Y, Slator B, and Guthrie L (1996) Electric Works: Computers, Dictionaries and Meanings. Cambridge, MA: MIT Press.

Winograd T (1972) Understanding Natural Language. Edinburgh: Edinburgh University Press.

Wittgenstein L (1956) Remarks on the Foundations of Mathematics. Oxford: Blackwell.

Yarowsky D (1992) Word-sense discrimination using statistical models of Roget's categories. In COLING92 Nantes, France.

Yarowsky D (1993) One sense per collocation. In Proceedings of DARPA Human Language Technology Workshop, 266–271.

Yarowsky D (1995) Unsupervised word sense discrimination rivaling supervised methods, In Proc. ACL95, 189–196.

Index